ROMANTICISM'S OTHER MINDS

COGNITIVE APPROACHES TO CULTURE
Frederick Luis Aldama, Patrick Colm Hogan,
Lalita Pandit Hogan, and Sue J. Kim, Series Editors

ROMANTICISM'S OTHER MINDS

Poetry, Cognition, and the Science of Sociability

∾

JOHN SAVARESE

THE OHIO STATE UNIVERSITY PRESS
COLUMBUS

Copyright © 2020 by The Ohio State University.
All rights reserved.

Library of Congress Cataloging-in-Publication Data
Names: Savarese, John, author.
Title: Romanticism's other minds : poetry, cognition, and the science of sociability / John Savarese.
Other titles: Cognitive approaches to culture.
Description: Columbus : The Ohio State University Press, [2020] | Series: Cognitive approaches to culture | Includes bibliographical references and index. | Summary: "Reassesses early negotiations between poetry and the sciences of the mind to offer a prehistory of cognitive approaches to literature. Engages with the works of James Macpherson, Anna Letitia Barbauld, William Wordsworth, and Walter Scott"— Provided by publisher.
Identifiers: LCCN 2020018276 | ISBN 9780814214503 (cloth) | ISBN 0814214509 (cloth) | ISBN 9780814278475 (ebook) | ISBN 0814278477 (ebook)
Subjects: LCSH: English poetry—18th century—History and criticism. | English poetry—19th century—History and criticism. | Romanticism—Great Britain. | Cognition in literature.
Classification: LCC PE1404 .S327 2020 | DDC 821/.509336—dc23
LC record available at https://lccn.loc.gov/2020018276

Other identifiers: ISBN 9780814256053 (paper) | ISBN 0814256058 (paper)

Cover design by Jordan Wannemacher
Text design by Juliet Williams
Type set in Adobe Minion Pro

CONTENTS

Acknowledgments		*vii*
Introduction		*1*
CHAPTER 1	Poetry, Conjecture, and Experiment	17
CHAPTER 2	Ossian's Folk Psychology	41
CHAPTER 3	Barbauld and the Growth of the Poet's Mind	71
CHAPTER 4	Wordsworth's Scattered Minds	103
CHAPTER 5	"Incoherent Song": Scott and the Margins of Sociability	135
AFTERWORD	Reading One's Own Mind	165
Bibliography		*171*
Index		*185*

ACKNOWLEDGMENTS

I COULD NOT have written this book without the early and continuing support of the Rutgers University community. Colin Jager, William Galperin, and Jonathan Kramnick have been early readers of many of its pages and models of the kind of scholarship I hope those pages offer. While at I was at Rutgers, the Center for Cultural Analysis laid some of the earliest seeds of this project and indeed for just about everything I have done since. I owe particular thanks to its two-year program titled "Mind and Culture" and to a rewarding fellowship year in its seminar "The Everyday and the Ordinary." Many friends left their mark on this book, including Joshua Fesi, Joshua Gang, Devin Griffiths, Lizzie Oldfather, Debapriya Sarkar and—over the long haul—Sean Barry and Greg Ellerman, who continue to be the best of readers and writing group partners.

The book took shape in a number of places, departments, and transitional years. I cannot overstate how much I owe to the colleagues who kept me afloat during that time and who read, discussed, and pushed back on various parts of the book as it came together in Austin and Berkeley. Thanks especially to Sam Baker, Ian Thomas-Bignami, Liz Cullingford, Ian Duncan, Anne-Lise François, Steve Goldsmith, Kevis Goodman, Bo Jacks, Celeste Langan, Grace Lavery, Lisa Moore, and Janet Sorensen. At Waterloo, where the majority of the book was written, I found an incredibly supportive place to bring the project to completion. Thanks to all of my colleagues here for making that possible. Special thanks to Tristanne Connolly, Fraser Easton, Alice Kuzniar, Andrea Speltz, and Rebecca Tierney-Hynes, who read and responded to portions of the book at various stages. Double thanks to Alice for her intrepid leadership of the working group "Poetics and Nature," with the support of the Waterloo Centre for German Studies behind it, and to the network of southern Ontario researchers who took part in it its gatherings over the years—especially Angela Borchert, Elizabeth Effinger, Christine Lehleiter, Paola Mayer, and Jean Wilson. I am also grateful to the University of Toronto's Work in Nineteenth-Century Studies Group and the Guelph Centre for Scottish Studies for their generous reading of chapters 4 and 5, respectively. In the broader community of Romantic studies, I have been lucky to benefit from support, feedback, and pointers of various kinds: thanks in particular to James Brooke-Smith, Andrew Burkett, Noah Heringman, Noel Jackson, Maureen McLane, Adela Pinch, Alan Richardson, Lisa Ann Robertson, Terry Robinson, Jonathan Sachs, and Richard Sha.

This book received crucial financial support at many steps along the way, notably from the Rutgers Center for Cultural Analysis; the Daniel Francis Howard Travel Award; the University of Texas at Austin, the University of California, Berkeley, and the American Council of Learned Societies New Faculty Fellows program; a University of Waterloo/SSHRC 4A Award; and most recently the David L. Kalstone Memorial Fund at Rutgers University. Two portions of the book have appeared elsewhere: An earlier version of chapter 2 appeared in *English Literary History,* and part of chapter 5 was originally published electronically on the University of Colorado's Romantic Circles website. Thanks to both venues for allowing the publication of that material in its new form here.

I would also like to take this opportunity to thank some earlier, formative teachers and mentors—especially Stephen Balletta, Friedrich Ulfers, and Laurence Lockridge; and (in memoriam) George Zehnle, Paul Magnuson, and Marilyn Gaull. My most important thanks go to my whole family for their support over the years. To Liz and James, in particular: You have shared your time with this book for too long. Thanks for your patience, and making it all worthwhile.

INTRODUCTION

~

THIS BOOK argues that a familiar Romantic claim about poetry—namely, that it has a special relationship to the mind's inner workings—has not always been what it seems. To be sure, some well-known Romantic pronouncements align poetry with inward, private, or solitary acts of mind. Yet that very turn to the cognitive also motivated a different set of Romantic arguments, which just as often highlighted the mind's social abilities and interpersonal entanglements. As a result, even when they fastened poetic form to the underlying structures of human cognition, Romantic poets and poetic theorists wound up making poetry a staging ground for debates about the mind's outward-directed, social powers.

As the chapters that follow will show, arguments about the social mind run through many of the major eighteenth- and early nineteenth-century discourses about poetry, including those that did the most to forge that close relationship between poetry and the mind's inward materials. For example, in the turn to the popular ballad, in conjectural histories of the origin of language, and in natural histories of art and culture—to name some of the earlier conversations this book will track through Romantic writing—poetry became positioned as a type of language that arose early in human history and retained special ties to the most foundational, innermost forms of thought and feeling. That affiliation of poetry with an inward or underlying domain of sensation and passion has long been central to accounts of Romanticism's aesthetic ideologies and to the caricature of Romantic poetry as an affair of involuted or solipsistic consciousness. Lately, though, that very commitment to inwardness has become the basis for a different, revisionary account of Romanticism and its ties to the material sciences. In *British Romanticism and the Sciences of the Mind* (2001), Alan Richardson has shown that Romantic explorations of interiority were thoroughly enmeshed in the emerging language of physiological psychology and an embodied mind. If it was a turn inward, in other words, it looked inward toward the embodiment of the brain and nerves rather than strictly toward a disembodied or transcendental inner subject. Subsequently, in *Science and Sensation in Romantic Poetry* (2008), Noel Jackson has shown that this close relationship between poetry and the science of sensation had clear social and political stakes, too, and opened out onto a broader interpersonal terrain. For Jackson, in fact, poetry could become most politically potent when it was most committed to the near-solipsism of "radical inwardness" (124).

Studies like Richardson's and Jackson's have moved the conversation about poetic inwardness in a new direction, one that is more embodied and socially situated. From a different angle, though—especially given the wealth of work on poetry and social and collective life—the turn to the Romantic sciences of mind might seem to intensify that era's commitment to inwardness, or to what Richard Sha has recently and compellingly termed the period's broad, cross-disciplinary "turn to phenomenality."[1] Recovering Romantic poetry's ties to the sciences, in other words, has the potential to reinforce the Romantic idea that poetry was most at home in the inward domain of thought and feeling. This book takes that turn to phenomenality as a generative moment, but emphasizes that its turn inward helped produce many different arguments about how the mind and its social powers worked, in keeping with what Sha has called a concomitant turn to "relationality" (6). One of the premises from which I begin is that Romanticism produces an approach to poetry we might now call *cognitivist*.[2] If we join Richardson in naming the Romantic era as an early moment in the prehistory of the cognitive sciences, it follows that the period's literary theory would also stand in the prehistory of more recent cognitive approaches to literature and culture. Like those newer interdisciplinary

---

1. Sha, *Imagination* 1. On poetry's entanglements with social attitudes, social contact, and interpersonal or collective experience see especially Thomas Pfau, *Romantic Moods*; Kevis Goodman, *Georgic Modernity*; Adela Pinch, *Thinking about Other People*; and Nancy Yousef, *Romantic Intimacy*.

2. In keeping with current usage in philosophy and cognitive science, I will use the term *cognitive* in this book to refer not just to rational or computational processes but to the full range of the mind's activities, including the emotions.

ventures, in the eighteenth and early nineteenth centuries poets and critics labored to define poetry as a type of writing that could illuminate the mind's inner structures and its mechanisms for processing the world around it. In this very broad sense early cognitive approaches to poetry would include, among other things, Joseph Addison's claim that popular ballads tell us about timeless, universal principles of taste; Edmund Burke's physiological account of the sublime and beautiful; and Samuel Taylor Coleridge's conviction that poetry reflected the inner motions of the "free spirit." In the long run, their afterlife would come to encompass post-Romantic ideas about the lyric's capacity to capture an especially weighty kind of thinking or to bear a particularly high cognitive load.[3]

Yet—to reiterate this book's central claim—this early cognitive approach to poetry was more diverse than its post-Romantic inheritors remembered it to be. For example, an important eighteenth-century debate in moral philosophy concerned whether the mind was originally solitary and self-interested or, instead, whether it had "natural" or at least early developing mechanisms for social engagement. As Nancy Yousef (one of the most important influences on the current study) has shown, the idea of an originally autonomous, asocial mind eventually became one of the Enlightenment's most potent and contentious claims; yet it remained one argument among many, and its proponents needed to reassert it repeatedly in a field of intellectual debate that was considerably more varied.[4] Making cognitive claims about poetry fed into those debates. At its most internalist and essentialist, Romanticism's cognitive poetics toyed with the idea that the mind had built-in or natural social powers. At its most experimental, cognitive approaches to poetry gave poets and antiquarians license to advance counterintuitive or exploratory claims about mental functioning.

Those are the two senses built into this book's title, *Romanticism's Other Minds*. It is, in the first place, about Romanticism's commitment to thinking about other people. In that capacity it hopes to contribute to a long-standing conversation about the Romantic response to skepticism, and specifically to the question of knowing other minds.[5] Yet, in a second sense, that philosophical challenge led writers to seek other, alternative accounts of what it

---

3. For an overview of this array of approaches to literature and cognition see Lisa Zunshine, ed., *Introduction to Cognitive Cultural Studies*. On Coleridge see Kevis Goodman, "Reading Motion." On Burke's aesthetics as protocognitive see Vanessa Ryan, "The Physiological Sublime," and Alan Richardson, *The Neural Sublime* 17–37. On the post-Romantic concept of lyric see especially Virginia Jackson and Jonathan Culler, discussed below.

4. Nancy Yousef, *Isolated Cases*.

5. See especially Stanley Cavell, *In Quest of the Ordinary*.

meant to have a mind in the first place: to develop other models of mind and to picture them differently. So, again in the context of poetic antiquarianism, the very fact that poetry seemed to offer a window into the mind's inner workings meant that ancient or popular poems became pieces of evidence in unsettled interdisciplinary debates. Scholars, antiquarians, and literary forgers alike scoured the poetic archive for evidence about the early mind's original sociability; they wrote poetic thought experiments that imagined material, embodied modes of inter-mental contact; and they entertained the notion that the mind spreads across bodies and linguistic technologies—including the technologies of poetry—in a social environment made up of other minds.

For an important countertradition in Romantic poetics, in other words, poetic form arose not just from the basic structures of private consciousness, but from a set of social powers built into a naturally sociable mind, and from the social context in which minds remained entangled. In Romantic-era writing, those mental powers can seem quite familiar, like the drive toward fellow-feeling defended by Anna Letitia Barbauld, Joseph Priestley, and other theorists of benevolence. They can also be deeply strange, like the innate faculties of mind detection defended by some students of philosopher Thomas Reid, or like the theories of external mental content advanced in their own ways by Barbauld, William Wordsworth, and Walter Scott. The chapters that follow explore how these poets and theorists mined traditional literatures and recent scientific conjectures to produce alternate histories of cognition, histories that variously emphasized the impersonal, the intersubjective, and the collective.

Finally, by reassessing these early negotiations between poetry and the sciences of the mind, this book hopes to offer a prehistory of cognitive approaches to literature that might feed back into our understanding of that newer field. In recent decades, endeavors such as cognitive poetics and cognitive aesthetics have echoed some of Romanticism's own arguments about poetry's fidelity to the mind's core sensory and linguistic processes. Such endeavors might seem to reinforce the Romantic association of poetry with the most foundational types of inner cognitive processing. Meanwhile, though, a different set of cognitive literary theories focused on narrative have framed literature's fundamental task as the exercise of a specifically *social* intelligence. Understood this way—as an exercise of the basic strategies of social recognition, agent tracking, and perspective-taking—literature seems to depend on a set of cognitive abilities very different from those of the poetry of introspection or affective intensity. To be sure, these latter, cognitive-narratological approaches are usually focused on fiction, often specifically on the realist novel. That division in focus can reinforce the sense of a divide between poetry and narrative, or between literature's inwardness and its sociability. And yet that conversation about literature and "theory of mind," which the next section of this introduction will discuss in more detail, has been an interesting reminder that cognitive approaches to literature can just as easily foreground the social mind—and that in the Romantic era, such theories often did.

POETRY'S DIVIDED FACULTIES

Within poetic theory, Romantic poetics has been credited—or, just as often, blamed—for the production of "the lyric" as we now know it.[6] On Virginia Jackson's account, the late eighteenth century saw the beginnings of a turn away from poetry's social occasions and the materiality of the print market, toward an ideal of immediacy that readers still tend to associate with reading lyric poems. Even as the turn to oral culture and antiquarian documents produced a heightened awareness of poetry's *mediacy*, it also marked, in turn, the beginning of a long process Jackson calls *lyricization*: the gradual trend by which a broad range of "poetic subgenres collapsed into the expressive romantic lyric of the nineteenth century."[7] While only fully developed in the twentieth century, the foundations of this lyricized concept of the poem were well entrenched by the publication of John Stuart Mill's "What Is Poetry?" (1833). Mill's well-known definition of poetry as "feeling confessing itself to itself in moments of solitude" has long served as a benchmark for the post-Romantic alignment of poetry with the inwardness and immediacy of mental operations.[8] By 1833, the story goes, poetry was the mode of writing that seemed to have the closest relationship to the mind itself.

---

6. So, for Jonathan Culler, the Romantic era's "more vigorous and highly developed conception of the individual subject" finally made it possible to elevate the lyric to one of literature's major genres, though the result was an unfortunately narrowed definition of the lyric that modern readers inevitably approach either as dramatic monologues or as individual "personal expression" (1, 5).

7. Jackson, *Dickinson's Misery* 7. To the degree that this book enters at all into debates about the nature of poetry, or theory of the lyric, my commitments are closest to Jackson's: I do not presume "the lyric" (or, really, "poetry") to be a single, coherent category in the first place, but consider them loaded terms that need to be historicized. My contribution would rather be that even when Romantic poets *do* explicitly seek to make poems represent cognitive processes, the models of poetry, and associated models of mind, are just as diverse and varied; moreover, they often serve to defamiliarize ideas about cognition rather than render it more intuitive and naturalistic.

8. John Stuart Mill, *Collected Works* 1.348. As Yopie Prins and Virginia Jackson point out, Mill's definition is aspirational: He cannot offer an example of a poet who meets its conditions, but poetry aspires to be an unmediated, internal affair of self-reflective feeling (*Lyric Theory Reader* 3.)

However, it is worth noting that Mill does just as much in that essay to make *narrative*, too, a fundamentally human trait. For Mill, interest in narrative "incident" and in the doings of other people is also an early feature of ordinary thinking and of historically early literary practice. However, it is one that Mill wants to frame as rudimentary, trifling, or distracted, as opposed to poetry's more focused or refined attention to basic thoughts and sentiments (344). Mill goes so far as to write that poetry and narrative represent "two sources of interest" and that these literary interests "correspond to two distinct, and (as respects their greatest development) mutually exclusive, characters of mind" (345). Both are part of human nature's basic foundations, but one type of foundational ability is lauded as difficult and refined, while the other is denigrated as rudimentary or primitive. Mill writes, for example, that the "passion for a story, for almost any kind of story, merely as a story," is "most intense [...] in childhood," while "the feelings with which it [poetry] is especially conversant are yet undeveloped" (345). Narrative might come first chronologically in a primitive society, but poetry—even if its development takes longer—taps into more deeply rooted aspects of mental experience. In other words, Mill naturalizes both lyrical sentiment and narrative interest, but he naturalizes them in different ways. One of them is a primitive hunger (or perhaps, with Wordsworth, a degrading thirst) for incident; it is natural to children and to early societies, but the mature mind should set it aside.[9] The other is a foundational, internal capacity, but one the mature mind only gradually becomes capable of appreciating. For Mill, narrative interest is a feature of human nature we should at least partly grow out of. Lyric feeling is also a feature of human nature, but it is one we are meant to grow into. As a result, while Mill thinks everyone is basically capable of interest in both poetic sentiment and narrative incident, he suggests that some people remain naively absorbed in that "passion for a story," while others cultivate an appreciation for poetry along with other features of mature, autonomous subjecthood.

Post-Romantic poetic theory thus inherits two different, overlapping accounts of human origins: In one version of the story of humanity, the primitive mind is solitary, depends on first-person sensation, and only gradually develops strategies for sympathizing with other people and cultivating society. In another version of the story, the primitive mind was actually sociable from the start, and society's progress through its developmental stages was in large part a matter of individuation: a gradual process of development by which people, and their cultural and literary products, went from being more dependent and collectivist to being more autonomous. Mill's politics required

---

9. William Wordsworth, *Lyrical Ballads* 747.

that both of those things be true. More broadly, those two accounts overlapped throughout the Romantic era, in histories of society and of literature that alternately emphasized the early mind's solitude and its sociability.

In short, I suggest that Mill's essay does not just mark the arrival of an internalized, post-Romantic concept of poetry: It also marks the increasing compartmentalization of two different human dispositions or abilities. That separation of solitary and sociable acts of mind already had a long history, notably in Edmund Burke's *Philosophical Enquiry into the Origin of Our Ideas of the Sublime and Beautiful* (1757), where Burke attributes the feeling of the beautiful and sublime to two distinct drives: a solitary drive toward self-preservation and a sociable drive aimed at procreation (35–36). In the later eighteenth and early nineteenth centuries, theorists increasingly framed the mind as a still more diverse set of specialized organs, in ways that have invited comparison to more recent accounts of the "modular" mind.[10] Mill's essay is one influential example of how those separate powers came to be mapped onto literary genres. In his case, poetry became a vehicle of private sensuous experience, while narrative was the domain of social intelligence.

More recent cognitive approaches to literature have participated in a similar parceling out of literary "characters of mind."[11] Since the 1980s, the "cognitive turn" in literary studies has generated a large, methodologically diverse field that reads literary practices in light of the evolved abilities and constraints of brain and body. Lisa Zunshine has proposed the umbrella term "cognitive cultural studies" for this cluster of interpretive methods. The emphasis on the term *cultural* underscores that this turn to the innate or universal is meant to complement, rather than oppose or contradict, the study of the culturally constructed, contingent, and variable.[12] As an example of that blending of the universal with the variable, Patrick Colm Hogan has argued that while poetic line length varies widely across cultures, poetic lines overwhelmingly favor a length of five to nine words.[13] For Rueven Tsur, a "cognitive poetics" would enable us to formalize our description of readerly experience in all its varieties, using the tools of cognitive linguistics and cognitive psychology. And for G. Gabrielle Starr, neuroscience offers us a new basis for making claims about the experience of beauty and aesthetic judgment.[14]

---

10. See Richardson, *British Romanticism* 3.
11. Mill, *Collected Works* 1.345.
12. For Zunshine's relation of this field to cultural studies, by way of Raymond Williams see her *Introduction* 5ff. A founding text in this project—to make cognitive theory reinforce rather than oppose the insights of cultural studies—was Ellen Spolsky's *Gaps in Nature*.
13. See Patrick Colm Hogan, "Literary Universals," in Zunshine, *Introduction*.
14. Rueven Tsur, *Toward a Theory of Cognitive Poetics*; G. Gabrielle Starr, *Feeling Beauty*.

On the other hand, a different set of "cognitive approaches" to literature turned from the basic operations of sensory and linguistic processing to the more functionally specific domain of social intelligence.[15] Narrative had always been important to the field, as in Mark Turner's *The Literary Mind*, which positions stories as one of the fundamental ways the mind processes any kind of information about the world. David Herman, Alan Palmer, and others subsequently blended approaches from cognitive linguistics with an attention to the range of specific cognitive tasks that social intelligence involves: identifying intentional agents, attributing beliefs and desires to characters, and keeping track of the complex range of opinions, attitudes, and relationships that populate a story's social networks.[16] By 2010, a cluster of studies had explored some more specific theories of social intelligence. William Flesch's *Comeuppance* (2007) and Blakey Vermeule's *Why Do We Care about Literary Characters?* (2010) turned to evolutionary psychology and framed readers' lively interest in fictional characters—whether manifested as sympathy, *schadenfreude*, or suspicion—as evolved strategies for navigating social situations. In some of its applications, evolutionary psychology has generated the starkest opposition between social intelligence (as manifested in narrative) and more basic forms of verbal and sonic play (as found in poetry). Some, like "literary Darwinist" Brian Boyd, go so far as to align these literary modes with distinct evolutionary adaptations. That extreme separation is underscored by the titles of Boyd's two books on the subject, *On the Origin of Stories* (2009) and *Why Lyrics Last* (2012). For Boyd, telling fictional stories is an adaptation of a species that needed to remain attuned to "rich patterns of social information," whereas the pleasures of lyric poetry derive from a more basic, foundational "passion for nonnarrative pattern" that "reaches its most concentrated form in lyrics—in poems without stories."[17]

---

15. Studies of social cognition, in this sense, deal with the mind's strategies for processing information about the social world and hew close to the individualist, internalist, and representationalist commitments of the first cognitive revolution. The term ought to be understood differently from similar terms such as *social psychology* (the sociologically influenced psychology of group dynamics) or theories of *socially extended* or *group* mind that I will discuss later. On social cognition's basic individualism see the introduction to Augoustinos, Walker, and Donaghue, eds., *Social Cognition*.

16. Herman frames narrative both as a general cognitive tool for processing information and as deploying protocols for engaging with fictional minds ("Narrative Theory," in Zunshine, *Introduction*). Alan Palmer draws on a long tradition of narratological work—notably Dorrit Cohn's *Transparent Minds*; Ann Banfield's *Unspeakable Sentences*; and Monika Fludernik's *Towards a Natural Narratology*—to show how narratology has come to place the fictional mind at the center of narrative theory. See Palmer, *Fictional Minds* and *Social Minds in the Novel*.

17. Brian Boyd, *On the Origin of Stories* 192; *Why Lyrics Last* 4.

There are good reasons to be skeptical about such claims: Beyond many humanists' basic misgivings about the program of evolutionary psychology in general, Jonathan Kramnick, in "Against Literary Darwinism," has argued that there are conceptual limits to what literary works could possibly tell us about evolutionary adaptations and what features of such works "could be threaded back to the environment in which minds supposedly adapted" (329). There have been interesting provocations, though, from scholars who have taken cognitive approaches as an opportunity to foreground literature's basic formal investments in social intelligence. Lisa Zunshine's *Why We Read Fiction* (2006), for example, examines how novelistic form manipulates everyday strategies for attributing intentions to social agents. For Zunshine, there seems to be a natural fit between novelistic technique and the basic ability cognitive psychologists call a "theory of mind"—or, more playfully, the skill of "mindreading." That term, *mindreading*, is often used in cognitive psychology in order to emphasize that, although we might take it for granted, it is actually remarkable that we can infer mental states from other people's actions at all.[18] On such theories, it is important to note, ordinary mindreading is not infallible. It is prone to error and miscommunication. As a foundational study by Fritz Heider and Marianne Simmel showed, people tend to project elaborate motivations, emotions, and relationships even onto simple geometric figures. In fact, for some philosophers of mind, the assumption that there are mental states at all may not even be a good account of human action in the first place: It could be a very *bad* theory, based on a commonsense "folk psychology" that turns out to be wildly mistaken about what actually goes on inside people's heads.[19] Yet, by even the most skeptical accounts, this folk psychology is reliable enough to serve as an everyday strategy for navigating the social world. More to the point, it seems to match the kinds of assumptions novelists make about how readers keep track of characters and become invested in their stories.[20]

---

18. On the utility of *mindreading* as a term see Zunshine, *Why We Read Fiction* 6.

19. The idea that social cognition is based on a "folk psychology" is usually sourced to Wilfred Sellars, "Empiricism and the Philosophy of the Mind." Paul Churchland and Patricia Churchland have argued that people do use such a theory of behavior, but that it is a mistaken theory, since (on their eliminative materialist argument) inner propositional states do not actually exist. See Paul Churchland, "Eliminative Materialism," and Patricia Smith Churchland, *Neurophilosophy*.

20. This is Daniel Dennett's argument in *The Intentional Stance*, which argues that while we may never know what goes on in another person's head or resolve debates such as the nature of mental representations or the nature of volition, we nevertheless adopt an "intentional stance" toward the world because it affords "an extraordinarily powerful tool in prediction" (24).

This book is not specifically invested in "theory of mind" theory, on its own terms. It is more interested in the way that its sudden emergence in literary criticism has made it possible to imagine a scientific account of literature squarely focused on the mind's social powers. Moreover, the ongoing debate about just how mindreading works offers a useful point of comparison with earlier, Romantic-era debates about social intelligence. The current scientific conversation about theory of mind is, after all, controversial in its own right and fraught with its own internal tensions. From one side, "rationality theorists" like Alison Gopnik have argued that mindreading actually is (as the term "theory of mind" implies) an explicitly held theory—that is, it describes a type of rational theorizing about other people's actions.[21] Alternatively, Robert Gordon and Alvin Goldman have advanced the position that the term *theory* is altogether a misnomer: We do not actually need to theorize about other minds at all, they argue, because we have a simpler option. As Adam Smith described in his eighteenth-century theory of sympathy, Gordon and Goldman argue that we run "simulations" of other people's mental states on our own cognitive hardware and simply imagine ourselves in their shoes.[22] These simulationist approaches emphasize how natural, effortless, or fundamentally human these abilities can be. That focus on effortlessness and naturalness is even stronger, though, in the theorists that feature most prominently in Lisa Zunshine's *Why We Read Fiction*. Modular nativists, such as Simon Baron-Cohen, Alan Leslie, and Uta Frith, argue that mindreading is powered by a dedicated, evolved "theory of mind mechanism," which is localized to particular regions of the brain.[23] Proponents of this modular-nativist view cite as evidence the emergence of a theory of mind very early in childhood; the surprising regularity with which it emerges in the third and fourth years of

---

21. See, for example, Alison Gopnik and Henry M. Wellman, "Why the Child's Theory of Mind Really Is a Theory," which defends the "theory theory" against the simulation routine Gordon and Goldman had recently proposed as an alternative. See Robert M. Gordon, "Folk Psychology as Simulation," and Alvin Goldman, *Simulating Minds*.

22. See Gordon, "Folk Psychology," and Goldman, *Simulating Minds*. Goldman explicitly mentions Adam Smith's *Theory of Moral Sentiments* as a precursor to simulation theory, and specifically as anticipating more recent accounts of "motor mimicry" and "affective simulation" (17).

23. "Modularity" in cognitive science refers to lower-level processes performed quickly and automatically by a dedicated, domain-specific system, running independently from and not interacting with other processes or domains. For a foundational version of the argument that the mind's computational systems are modular in this sense see Jerry Fodor, *The Modularity of Mind*. For the argument that "theory of mind" is driven by a specific module see Baron-Cohen, Leslie, and Frith, "Does the Autistic Child Have a 'Theory of Mind?'"

life; and an observed correlation between damage to particular brain regions and a reduction in those abilities.[24]

It is interesting that Zunshine's argument—in its boldest form, that theory of mind "makes literature as we know it possible"—deploys this latter, modular-nativist view (198). As my quick survey has shown, that theory represents one position within a much wider field. Yet modular nativism is worth dwelling on for a moment because it captures in a particularly strong form some of the desires of the broader field of cognitive approaches to literature. It captures that field's desire to talk about biological universals, in the first place; an even longer-standing desire to make literature the expression of something fundamentally and specially human; and, as the language of innate, modular processes makes particularly pointed, the desire to frame literary activities as surprising abilities we use every day but should not take for granted.[25] That last aspect of cognitive narratology—its rediscovery of the ordinary—gives it particular echoes with eighteenth- and nineteenth-century defenses of novels, which needed to fend off accusations that the novel was an unsophisticated, commonplace, or vulgar form. So, for example, Blakey Vermeule's defense of "gossip" as a model for literary narrative can be read as one more attempt to celebrate and revalue what John Stuart Mill had derided as a vulgar or rudimentary interest in stories, and in other people, as opposed to a more refined literary mode of overheard soliloquy and inner speech.[26] That same privileging of refined feeling over vulgar story was also, in ways that will be even more central to this book's concerns, a liability that eighteenth-century ballad scholars had needed to build into their theories of oral poetry: Ballads were, after all, a body of historical literature with an outsized investment in narrative. The

---

24. In terms of the treatment of "impairments" to theory of mind, it should be noted that not only does this body of work use traditional studies of brain lesions through traumatic injury; it also depends on a controversial set of claims about Autism Spectrum Disorder, framed as a "deficit" in social intelligence or empathy. The very title of Baron-Cohen, Leslie, and Frith's paper announces the focus on Autism Spectrum Disorder with a callous echo of one of the founding studies in theory of mind theory it builds on: David Premack and Guy Woodruff's "Does the Chimpanzee Have a Theory of Mind?" Moreover, Baron-Cohen controversially framed Autism Spectrum Disorder as a form of "mindblindness," and subsequently as a type of "extreme male brain." See Simon Baron-Cohen, *Mindblindness* and "The Extreme Male Brain Theory of Autism." For critiques of theory of mind theory's approach to disability, made from within the field of disability studies, see, for example, Jordynn Jack, "'The Extreme Male Brain?'"; and, explicitly in dialogue with cognitive literary studies, Ralph James Savarese and Lisa Zunshine, "The Critic as Neurocosmopolite."

25. Ellen Spolsky's early recruitment of the modularity hypothesis is very much in this spirit: She frames the modular mind and cultural construction as "co-legislator[s]" of human life, not as antagonists; she emphasizes the ways that innate, modular processes are generative too, and the ways they enable the mind's creative engagement with the world (*Gaps* 3).

26. See Vermeule, *Why Do We Care?* 150–70.

idea of an ordinary yet remarkable social drive was an important part of how the ballad revival reframed popular literature's cultural value.

Methodologically speaking, this is what I find to be most interesting and generative about cognitive literary studies: how it replays, with a new vocabulary, arguments that might sound strangely familiar to readers of eighteenth- and nineteenth-century literature. In that respect, my method in this book owes a good deal to the way Alan Richardson uses neuroscience in *British Romanticism and the Science of the Mind*. As he explains there, "The lens of contemporary neuroscience, which has returned (in its own way) to one after another concern of Romantic psychology," can help the historian of science and literature locate previously overlooked aspects of Romanticism's own scientific concerns (xv). For my purposes, that logic carries over to the way a Romanticist might make heuristic use of cognitive literary studies, which has returned to some of the concerns and tensions Romantic-era writers themselves encountered when they used science to make arguments about literature or used literature to make arguments about the science of the mind. For that reason, I would compare this book's methods to what Richardson has elsewhere termed *cognitive historicism*—a method that looks to contemporary cognitive science as a way to strengthen the historicist project rather than to challenge it. Richardson's initial definition of cognitive historicism—as a method that "recruits and selectively adapts theories, methods, and findings from the sciences of mind and brain, partly in the hope that these will provide suggestive (although, it is understood, necessarily imperfect) analogies with past models"—is a fair enough description of how this book takes more recent cognitive approaches to literature as a prod to further historical study.[27] I would, however, qualify this book's relation to the second half of Richardson's formulation: that if cognitive historicism lets "historical differences [...] emerge *more clearly*," it does so by setting them "against what appear to be stable and invariant aspects of human cognition and behavior" (68). To be sure, some of my questions—for example, in chapter 4, how theories of distributed cognition might reframe Wordsworth's account of collaborations between mind and world—are willing to entertain the idea that Wordsworth, like more recent philosophers of mind, is trying to describe something "true" about cognitive systems, something that might hold continuing appeal in the present. However, the book's primary commitment is to the historical discourse, not really to any claim about how the mind actually, in fact, works. Moreover, one of the book's central claims is that Romantic writers made physiological

---

27. Alan Richardson, "Facial Expression Theory" 67.

approaches to the mind the basis for an array of contingent, culturally embedded accounts of cognition, as well as (and alongside) their approaches to its apparently "stable and invariant" features. That is why, in addition to the theories of social intelligence briefly sketched above, the chapters that follow also incorporate a different set of theories about "distributed cognition"—a cluster of approaches linked by their commitment that cognition does not just happen in brains but that it also involves the non-neural body and the physical, artifactual, and social environment.[28] Stated a different way: For Romantic writers, the pursuit of a social mind often served as a hinge between internalist, innatist views about natural sociability and more socially contingent views of a mind structured or scaffolded by social environments. The chapters of this book follow that tension—between a naturally sociable mind and a contingent, socially embedded mind—from the eighteenth-century ballad revival to the early decades of the nineteenth century.

CHAPTER SUMMARIES: OTHER MINDS, ALTERNATE HISTORIES

The book's first chapter, "Poetry, Conjecture, and Experiment," offers a broad survey of eighteenth-century poetic antiquarianism and the ways that theorizing ancient and popular poetry became central to conjectures about human mental development. Theorists such as Joseph Addison and Thomas Blackwell made poems into evidence about the mind's universal properties as well as its historical contingencies, and into records of its inward feelings as well as its social impulses. By the middle of the eighteenth century, writers such as Robert Lowth, Johann Gottfried Herder, and Hugh Blair had positioned poetic form as a vestige of an early, foundational moment in cognitive development, a moment they alternately defined by its fidelity to private sensation, its penchant for metaphorical figuration, or its dependence upon social perspective-taking. The conflict between the solitary mind and the social mind comes to a peak in the heated argument between ballad collectors Thomas Percy and Joseph Ritson, whose well-known scholarly disagreement, I suggest, hinged on their rival views about social intelligence, specifically about whether cognition itself should be pictured as individual or as socially distributed.

---

28. For an overview of the diverse theories operating under the umbrella of distributed cognition see Miranda Anderson, George Rousseau, and Michael Wheeler, eds., *Distributed Cognition in Enlightenment and Romantic Culture*.

Chapter 2, "Ossian's Folk Psychology," examines that antiquarian debate more concretely by turning to one of its most influential works, James Macpherson's 1760 *Fragments of Ancient Poetry*. Although Macpherson presented his poems as genuine evidence from primitive Scotland, the poems were by most accounts his own forged or reimagined works. As a result, the "Ossian" poems can be read as what Scottish Enlightenment philosopher Dugald Stewart called "conjectural histories"—thought experiments that imagine an early moment in the history of cognition and that, in Macpherson's hands, license the exploration of surprising, sometimes anachronistic, ideas such as ancient materialism and primitive animism. Macpherson studied at King's College, Aberdeen, during Thomas Reid's tenure as Regent, and I argue that despite his interest in the strangeness of the past, Macpherson's return to concepts from ancient, popular poetry nevertheless echoes Reid's own turn to "common sense" in two significant ways: in its gamble that ordinary, "folk" concepts from the past might ultimately serve as a reliable guide for the modern reader; and, more specifically, in the Ossian poems' Reidian faith about the possibility of real, embodied mental contact between minds.

Chapter 3, "Barbauld and the Growth of the Poet's Mind," considers Anna Letitia Barbauld as a transitional figure who, in her writings of the 1770s and 1780s, blended Macpherson's brand of poetic primitivism with Enlightenment theories of scaffolded mental development. Barbauld's poetics grew out of a commitment she shared with scientist and theologian Joseph Priestley and with her brother the physician John Aikin: that thinking depends upon the mind's physical substrates, both in the body and in the social, cultural, and technological environment. Barbauld's poetry engages with theories of the mind's physiological origins and its historical development. Moreover, it brings arguments for natural sociability into contact with the concepts of a socially distributed mind that circulated in her Dissenting intellectual networks. In her poetic imitation of Ossian and in her *Hymns in Prose for Children*, Barbauld uses the tension between primitivist and civilizing poetics to negotiate between private and socially embedded accounts of cognition.

Chapter 4, "Wordsworth's Scattered Minds," looks at how that commitment to a socially "scaffolded" mind shaped Wordsworth's career-long attempt to describe the mind's entanglements with its natural and social environments. While usually framed as a reciprocity between mind and nature, or in terms of the collaborative nature of perception, many moments in Wordsworth's poetry make a bolder and stranger claim that nature does some of his thinking for him. In order to find a language for this sometimes cryptic Wordsworthian argument, I recruit more recent approaches to distributed cognition, including philosopher Andy Clark's notion of cognition as an "extended" process that takes place partly outside the brain and body altogether. In the *Lyrical Ballads*' depictions of social encounter, and in the mingling of mind and landscape in poems like the sonnet "To Toussaint L'Ouverture," the faculties that drive sociability are the same ones that the individual mind relies upon to perform the basic, situated work of thinking and feeling. In his major work, the 1805 *Prelude*, Wordsworth experiments with a number of different ways to make that faith in inter-mental relationships into an account of nature's active cognitive agency.

Chapter 5, "'Incoherent Song': Scott and the Margins of Sociability," shows how Walter Scott's engagement with Wordsworthian poetics—above all in his response to Wordsworth's poem "The Idiot Boy"—led him to frame poetry as a window into cognitive difference rather than cognitive universality. His first novel, *Waverley*, casts the intellectually disabled minstrel Davie Gellatley as a character who reduces lyric expressivity to the brute elements of memorization and counting. Scott seems to use Davie's disability, which the novel aligns with his lyrical practice, in order to render visible the clunky, quasimechanical operations—the rote memorization and the play with potentially unmeaning sound—found at the core of cognition. Yet, like many of Scott's other disabled, mad, or otherwise marginalized poet figures, Davie's disruptive, satirical, and critical modes of social engagement also offer a challenge to antiquarian theories that aligned traditional poetry with social cohesion or uniformity. Romantic-era materialist scientists, like more recent cognitive accounts of social intelligence, were interested in studying disabled minds to illuminate "normal" social functioning. Scott, in contrast, remains sensitive to a range of mental dispositions and modes of relating to other minds, and *Waverley* ultimately correlates the triumph of one genre—the realist novel—with the decreased tolerance for individuals like Davie in modernizing Britain.

The book's concluding thought, "Reading One's Own Mind," suggests an alternate legacy of this strain of Romantic poetics. Against John Stuart Mill's description of poetry as the overhearing of solitary expression, I suggest that this alternate strain of Romantic theory is better elucidated by the more heavily mediated, socialized picture of private thought on offer in Letitia Elizabeth Landon's *The Improvisatrice* (1824). By replacing lyric introspection with ballad storytelling, Landon helps point the way to a different afterlife for Romantic poetics, one that—in keeping with theories of mediated self-knowledge on offer in William Hazlitt and John Keats—places narrative strategies, fictional characters, and social intelligence at the center of even an individual's most private, introspective moments.

From the 1760s to the 1820s, the idea that poetry was a window into the mind's component parts wound up bringing together a wide variety of distinct, overlapping, and sometimes contradictory concepts, from innate "mindreading" abilities to a socially distributed view of cognition itself. Moreover, Romantic writers regularly recruited those concepts to a number of competing intellectual and ideological aims. Before turning to my first major case study, Macpherson's Ossian in chapter 2, I will lay out in chapter 1 how those ideas came together in the eighteenth century to form the contentious field of debate that conditioned Romantic poetics.

CHAPTER 1

Poetry, Conjecture, and Experiment

> The social sympathies, or those laws from which, as from
> its elements, society results, begin to develop themselves
> from the moment that two human beings coexist. [...]
> It [poetry] is the faculty which contains within itself the
> seeds at once of its own and of social renovation.[1]

WHEN PERCY BYSSHE SHELLEY wrote that poetry is a "social" power, he meant a few different things. The goal of his "Defence of Poetry" (1821) was, first and foremost, to return poetry to the realm of society and its material institutions. His jarringly casual list of poetry's elements—"language, colour, form, and religious and civil habits of action"—implies a picture of poetics that ties it to the basic materials of sensation but that also takes its place among the elements of the built, social environment (513). Yet Shelley's remarks can also be taken in a spirit less sociological than psychological: Poetry pertains to the "social sympathies" that exist among people and that seem, for him at least, to have a natural basis in human nature. His assertion that those sympathies "begin to develop themselves from the moment that two human beings coexist" builds an account of natural social feeling into the "laws" of society itself. For that reason, the "Defence" treats poetry at once as an external technology for administering society and as an internal, foundational capability to take an interest in other people in the first place. When Shelley relates poetry to the "vitally metaphorical" origins of language, for example, he invokes a long, diverse tradition that ties poetry to the mind's basic, constitutional abilities and to the powers that underlie language (512). Shelley's focus on metaphor and resemblance joins a long tradition within Enlightenment histories of language and literature. It gestures toward the Romantic primitivist idea

---

1. Percy Bysshe Shelley, *Shelley's Poetry and Prose* 511, 522.

that poetry represents a special, foundational kind of language, one that is closer to the mind's basic core processes of thinking and feeling. Yet the generally sociopolitical orientation of his essay led him to weave that foundational power more intimately into a picture of a sympathetic and collaborative mind, one that works in the socially embedded medium of language and that remains, itself, subject to continual "renovation."

In 1821, Shelley could frame this argument as itself a renovation of existing theories of poetry and the poet's role in society. But, as this chapter will show, there was a long history to the idea that poetry spoke to the mind's fundamental social powers. That history spread across the various "predisciplinary" conversations to be found in natural history, moral philosophy, antiquarianism, and belletristic writing.[2] Writers on those different subjects grappled with some of the same ongoing and hotly debated questions about human nature: Were people originally self-interested or benevolent? Is the mind originally focused only narrowly on objects of sensation, or are more complex attitudes like social recognition and fellow-feeling fundamental "dispositions" too? Were poetic artifacts more like windows into the inner life of the early or "primitive" mind, or were they more like external technologies that regulated social life and assisted its development?

Many answers to those questions emphasized the mind's fundamental or natural sociability. This chapter offers a broad overview of those theories as they developed in eighteenth-century poetry and poetics, and as they set the terms for the debates that subsequent chapters will examine in particular case studies. Specifically, the chapter argues that in the eighteenth century, "natural sociability" arguments about poetry fall into two broad categories, one of which was more internalist and one of which was more externalist. Some accounts of the poetic mind saw ancient poetry as offering evidence about the mind's inner, original, and natural social abilities. Like more recent theories of "theory of mind" or "mindreading," these eighteenth-century theories run the gamut from explicitly innatist theories of social powers or faculties; to sentimentalist accounts of social feeling; to accounts of rational or imaginative strategies the mind has for navigating the social world.[3] Meanwhile, a different set of arguments emphasized poetry as a linguistic and social artifact and as

---

2. I borrow the useful term *predisciplinary*, and its insight about the transitional moments in the history of disciplinary formation, from Luisa Calè and Adriana Craciun, "The Disorder of Things," and Noah Heringman, *Sciences of Antiquity*. For a compelling account of the overlap between material science, spiritual philosophy, and literary theory in this period under the rubric of "pneumatology," see Sara Landreth, "Breaking the Laws of Motion."

3. For an overview of the analogues for these positions in more recent cognitive science see the introduction's summary of the "modular-nativist," "simulationist," and "rationality" theories of mindreading.

part of the cultural environment that supported and scaffolded the individual mind from the outside in. These approaches, which were especially plentiful in celebratory accounts of society's civilizing progress, often have less in common with theories of social intelligence and more with theories of socially "distributed" cognition.[4] For these theorists of mind and culture, poetic artifacts, like language itself, were part of a broader zone of inter-mental contact. These two approaches diverge, overlap, and contend with one another in the diverse field this chapter will now survey.

CONJECTURAL HISTORY AND EXPERIMENTAL POETRY

Some early Romantic arguments about poetry as cognition are well known: arguments, for example, that poetry takes us back to the origins of language and thought; or, as scholars of literature and science have shown, that poetry's purchase on inwardness seemed to grant it a special relationship to the mind's underlying, physiological mechanisms.[5] In her study of the formation of the intellectual disciplines, Robin Valenza has argued that as poets sought to distance themselves from the increasingly specialized domain of the modern disciplines, they wound up articulating poetry's starkly different goals as a disciplinary specialization of its own—one that, paradoxically, laid specialized claim to the whole domain of human experience.[6] Affiliating poetry with the apparently unscientific domain of "experience" could, to be sure, be a way of distancing it from the sciences altogether. Yet it was also, as Richard Sha has recently put it, part of literature and science's shared "turn to phenomenality."[7] Especially when it came to inward experience, the two modes of writing aimed to describe the same thing. In the same context, Noel Jackson has argued that

---

4. On distributed cognition in this period, see especially Miranda Anderson, George Rousseau, and Michael Wheeler, eds., *Distributed Cognition in Enlightenment and Romantic Culture*.

5. On poetry's ties to the physiology of sensation and cognition see Richardson, *British Romanticism*, and Noel Jackson, *Science and Sensation in Romantic Poetry*. On theories of poetic language as a historical or "original" form of language see Alan Bewell, *Wordsworth and the Enlightenment* 51–70; Robert N. Essick, *William Blake and the Language of Adam*; and Anna Weirda Rowland, *Romanticism and Childhood*.

6. Robin Valenza, *Literature, Language, and the Rise of the Intellectual Discipline*. The dynamic Valenza describes here bears some resemblance to literature's interdisciplinary situation in Philippe Lacoue-Labarthe and Jean-Luc Nancy's *The Literary Absolute*. Romanticism, on their account, forges a concept of literature as uniquely able to provide "its own theory, positing itself as a totalizing auto-presentation of the subject that ultimately completes the work of philosophy" (xiii).

7. Sha, *Imagination* 1.

the lyric poem offered a type of "self-experiment" and stood for a mode of introspection that yielded otherwise-inaccessible evidence about first-person experience. As the Romantic essayist William Hazlitt writes in one of his most pointed critiques of materialist sciences of the mind, we delude ourselves if we "think of looking into the bottom of our own minds by means of any other instrument than a sharpened intellect."[8] Yet by trying to retreat from the sciences in this way, poetry wound up claiming that it could offer a particularly important kind of evidence—evidence that could itself be construed as a supplement to the sciences.

Something similar can be said about poetry's association with antiquity and early cognition, which sometimes reinforced a separation of poetry's supposedly timeless characteristics from the domain of progressive, instrumental scientific knowledge. As Jon Klancher has argued, the uneasy differentiation of the arts and sciences throughout the eighteenth and nineteenth centuries was informed by the older "Quarrel of the Ancients and the Moderns," a debate about the relative value of classical and modern modes of knowledge. What did the progressive logic of the new sciences mean in the literary domain, where the standard of value was typically set early in antiquity, by a "human nature" that seems never to have changed? As Klancher notes, the quarrel ultimately issued in a new categorical distinction between two different types of knowledge production. In the eighteenth century's compromise, the defenders of the "moderns" were right when it came to the sciences, since the experimental program implied continual progress and growth. The "ancients," for their part, were right when it came to the arts.[9]

Yet art's affiliation with the ancient was not always a means of separating it from the sciences in this way. It was also one of the reasons that antiquarians could claim poetry's *relevance to* the human sciences, whether construed in terms of the evidence antiquities provided about humanity's ostensibly precultural origins or in terms of human nature's progression through earlier, historically remote developmental stages.[10] Hazlitt's own well-known entry in the quarrel, his short essay "Why the Arts Are Not Progressive" (1814), shows how the alignment of art with the ancient came to look beyond classical aesthetics and to aim, instead, for underlying or "original" features of the human

---

8. This remark comes from Hazlitt's "Essay on the Principles of Human Action" in *Selected Writings* 1.56.

9. See Jon Klancher, *Transfiguring Arts and Sciences* 13. Klancher's argument is that the distinction between "arts" and "sciences" was messier and less clearly demarcated than this neat separation would imply.

10. For a detailed study of the reciprocal relationship between the scientific disciplines and the project of antiquarianism see Heringman, *Sciences of Antiquity*.

mind.[11] Hazlitt distinguishes the progressive sciences, which are "mechanical, reducible to rule, or capable of demonstration," from artwork, which is "not mechanical or definite, but depends on genius, taste, and feeling."[12] "Genius, taste, and feeling" are framed here as constitutional features of the human mind. Poetry's domain, for Hazlitt, is that of the senses and the passions, which are most clearly and authentically expressed in the earliest ages, before they are overwritten by custom and poetic convention. For Hazlitt, it was not merely that the arts eventually reach their peak while the sciences keep progressing. Rather, art is pointedly aligned with an originating moment: the arts "have always leaped at once from infancy to manhood [. . .] and have in general declined ever after" (2.159). Hazlitt's argument presumes that the arts, and painting and poetry in particular, are inward, private, and individual: They often depict social life but derive from (and tell us most directly about) the inner life of individual genius. Poetry, he says, remains "conversant with the world of thought within us, and with the world of sense without us—with what we know, and see, and feel intimately" (2.159). In his 1818 lecture "On Poetry in General," Hazlitt goes further and equates poetry with an inner, prelinguistic medium of thought and feeling: "Poetry," he asserts, "is the universal language which the heart holds with nature and itself."[13] In other words, the logic of the Quarrel enables universalist arguments like Hazlitt's to frame poetry as a window into humanity's diachronic origins and to provide evidence about the precultural mind. Since human nature has not changed, he argues, these early artifacts tell modern readers about their own underlying, synchronic mental architecture too. Instead of actually divorcing poems from the sciences, then, Hazlitt's rhetorical move can be seen as further aligning poetry (and increasingly lyric poetry in particular) with the earliest stages of cognitive life—with a moment represented alternately by Homeric Greek, biblical Hebrew, or Ossianic Gaelic poetry.

---

11. Klancher reads Hazlitt's essay as a symptom of a continual need "to reassert the Quarrel's key principle" that the arts operated outside the logic of progressive modernization, against intervening efforts such as those of the Royal Academy "to make the fine arts a modernizing domain of practices and knowledge" (*Transfiguring* 13).

12. Hazlitt, *Selected Writings* 2.158.

13. Ibid. 2.165. This defense of inward, poetic introspection was one of Hazlitt's major intellectual convictions, though it came into conflict with his strongest conviction: the possibility of an altruistic or disinterested motivation. His attempt to integrate the two into a coherent philosophy of mind was the bracingly depersonalizing theory of volition he lays out in his *Essay on the Principles of Human Action* (*Selected Works*, Vol. 1). On Hazlitt's consideration of the essay on human action as his major contribution to letters see Uttara Natarajan's "Introduction" to *Metaphysical Hazlitt*. For a discussion of Hazlitt's theory of 'anonymous' or prepersonal mental life see Jacques Khalip, *Anonymous Life*. For my own reading of Hazlitt in light of social intelligence theories, see John Savarese, "Reading One's Own Mind."

In *Sciences of Antiquity* (2013), Noah Heringman describes a shift around 1760 toward an increasingly professionalized approach to "antiquity" and "prehistory," which brought together the methods of antiquarians and natural historians (2–3). It is in roughly that same period that we see poetic artifacts, as documents from the deep human past, becoming more emphatically and polemically framed as evidence about "original" cognition.[14] This was especially true of theories that rooted language in the passions. Étienne Bonnot de Condillac's *Essay on the Origin of Human Knowledge* (1746) had aligned the rudimentary, emotional origins of language with the "prosody, inversions, and figures" that also characterized early poetry.[15] Jean-Jacques Rousseau's "Essay on the Origin of Languages" (written by the early 1760s and published posthumously in 1781) linked both poetic and musical form to a shared, originating phase of impassioned and figurative expression, at a prehistorical moment in which "only poetry was spoken."[16] For Johann Gottfried Herder, poetry originates not as a discursive structure, but as the foundational activity that gives rise to discourse in the first place. His fragmentary "Treatise on the Ode" (1764) makes this equation eloquently: "Affect, which at the outset silently, encapsulated within, benumbed the entire body and surged as a dark feeling, gradually pervades all slight stirrings, until it finds expression in recognizable signs" (36). Here, poetry reflects the mind's original, founding movements, and its key features, such as figuration and rhythm, mirror the developmental form of cognition itself.[17] This philosophical conversation tends to place language's origins in a fundamentally social and relational scene of exchange, but, as Nancy Yousef has shown, writers like Rousseau often repress that social dimension to reinforce, instead, a vision of an originally autonomous, self-contained mind.[18] Imagining the origins of poetry was therefore part of a bigger debate about whether human origins ought to be imagined as solitary or social—autonomous and independent or relational and dependent. This entailed a further debate about whether the state before society was a scene

---

14. For a discussion of the "origins of art" conversation as it bore upon artifact-focused antiquarianism see "The Natural History of Art" in Heringman, *Sciences of Antiquity* 155–218. For an early study of the foundations of English primitivism see Lois Whitney, "English Primitivistic Theories of Epic Origins," and, more recently, Maureen N. McLane and Laura Slatkin, "British Romantic Homer."

15. Christopher Coski, "Emotion and Poetry in Condillac's Theory of Language and Mind" 160.

16. Jean-Jacques Rousseau, *Essay on the Origin of Languages* 294.

17. On the German context for such theories of rhythmic recapitulation see Janina Wellman, *The Form of Becoming*.

18. See Nancy Yousef, *Isolated Cases*.

of self-interested contest or, with Pope and Burns, marked by the plenitude of "nature's social union."[19]

On some theories, humanity's social origins were the result of specifically social powers built into the mind itself—like the Earl of Shaftesbury's concept of a "moral sense," which Francis Hutcheson developed further as an array of aesthetic and social abilities.[20] For others, notably David Hume, humanity was naturally sociable *in spite of* its lack of any such powers.[21] Hume's philosophical project was, in large part, to explain how an "egoistically" conceived mind—one limited to the basic materials of the senses and the passions—generated the social strategies that enabled life among others and held society together. Hume called this project "an attempt to introduce the experimental method into moral subjects"—or, in other words, an attempt to base the study of human nature and society on naturalistic principles and observed evidence.[22]

By the end of the eighteenth century, the Humean project of writing society's "natural history" had become aligned with a particular, narrative genre known as "conjectural history."[23] The term's emphasis on "conjecture" came about because telling a natural history of human origins could happen only if the theorist made an inferential leap beyond the bounds of available documentary evidence. The term *conjectural history* itself was coined by Dugald Stewart in his discussion of Adam Smith's conjectures on the origin of language. There, Stewart suggests that Smith's curiosity about the origin of language was a type of curiosity most people have: "It cannot fail to occur to us as an interesting question," he writes, "by what gradual steps the transition has been made from the first simple efforts of uncultivated nature, to a

---

19. Yousef links Enlightenment philosophy's interest in "conceiv[ing] the mind's autonomous workings and the individual's autonomous survival in a state outside of and prior to society" with a need to justify society rather than taking it for granted (*Isolated Cases* 1). On Burns's "To a Mouse" (*The Works of Robert Burns*), and its invocation of "nature's social union" in allusion to Pope's *Essay on Man* see Nigel Leask, *Robert Burns and Pastoral* 161–62.

20. See Francis Hutcheson, *Logic, Metaphysics, and the Natural Sociability of Mankind*. On Shaftesbury's founding role in "moral sense" theory see Robert B. Voitle, "Shaftesbury's Moral Sense."

21. On this divide in Hume's thinking see D. F. Norton, *David Hume: Common-Sense Moralist, Sceptical Metaphysician*.

22. This latter phrase, in fact, is the subtitle of Hume's *Treatise of Human Nature*. For an account of how Hume and other theorists of sociability focus on the strategies that hold societies together see Blakey Vermeule, *The Party of Humanity*. On Hume as one of the "eighteenth-century theorists of natural sociability," who had to negotiate between theories of solitary and social origins, see Yousef, *Isolated Cases* 18.

23. For an overview see Alexander Broadie, "Introduction: What Was the Scottish Enlightenment?" 24–25. On the role of conjectural history's fictions in Hume's experimental project see Mary Poovey, *A History of the Modern Fact* 214ff.

state of things so wonderfully artificial and complicated."[24] Stewart offers to name such storytelling "*Theoretic* or *Conjectural History*," a term which he notes "coincides pretty nearly in its meaning with that of *Natural History*, as employed by Mr Hume" (293). In Stewart's words, "If we can shew, from the known principles of human nature, how all its various parts might gradually have arisen, the mind is not only to a certain degree satisfied, but a check is given to that indolent philosophy, which refers to a miracle, whatever appearances, both in the natural and moral worlds, it is unable to explain" (293). The point is not just that we can get from a presocial state to a social one by way of incremental steps but that human origins are broadly continuous with the present, differing only in degree.

For Adam Ferguson, who by the time of Stewart's summary would have been one of the names most readily attached to this view, such incrementalism specifically meant that there had never been such a mythical, presocial time in human history. Ferguson devotes the opening pages of his *Essay on the History of Civil Society* to dismissing the idea of a state of nature as mere speculative fiction. Instead, he asserts that "the character of man, as he now exists" ought to serve as a reliable guide to what human origins were like (4). Specifically, he argues both that humanity is fundamentally enmeshed in technology, as "the latest efforts of human invention are but a continuation of certain devices which were practiced in the earliest ages of the world" (13); and that human nature is fundamentally social, which means that "mankind are to be taken in groupes [*sic*], as they have always subsisted" (6). Ferguson's assertion of the always already social nature of human society was not merely a strategy for connecting past and present. It was a real commitment to the idea that sociability was a fundamental "disposition" of human nature.[25] For Ferguson, human dispositions included both those "which tend to [. . .] animal preservation" and those "which lead to society" (17). Because he saw sociability as fundamental to human nature, Ferguson even refused to acknowledge the coherence of any distinction between "natural" and "unnatural" and denied that humanity had truly left its state of nature at all (13, 16). Ferguson's *Essay* thus speaks to the Scottish Enlightenment's "culturalist" approach to human nature, in which society, technology, and economy were just as important as the bodily. Nevertheless, it would still not be completely accurate to see Ferguson as a cultural constructivist. Indeed, by relating everything people do to their underlying nature, and even positing that art itself was foundational to human nature, some elements of his thinking are actually closer in spirit

---

24. Dugald Stewart, "Account of the Life and Writings of Adam Smith" 292, 263–35.

25. For a reading of Ferguson's commitments to the "benevolist" tradition of Francis Hutcheson see Gordon Graham, "Francis Hutcheson and Adam Ferguson on Sociability."

to more recent evolutionary approaches to a language or art instinct. Social institutions, technologies, and even "art itself," Ferguson writes, are "natural to man" (10). As a result, the history of art offers to tell us not just about the broad arc of historical development but also about the underlying embodied drivers of culture—which were, for Ferguson, foundational and universal.

SOLITARY AND SOCIAL POETIC ORIGINS: ADDISON, BLACKWELL, BLAIR

A similar approach to the history of poetry, which looked alternately to social being and to an underlying, universal human nature, was already on offer in an earlier eighteenth-century turn to oral literature. That turn was signaled as early as Joseph Addison's 1711 *Spectator* papers on "The Ballad of Chevy Chase."[26] Describing that ballad's continuing popularity over the centuries, Addison asserts, "It is impossible that anything should be universally tasted and approved by the multitude, though they are only the rabble of a nation, which hath not in it some peculiar aptness to gratify the mind of man."[27] Addison's approach to the popular ballad anticipates the way that conjectural histories would come to look to earlier cultural moments in order to locate original or foundational elements of human nature. As they later were for Adam Ferguson, literary artifacts were here seen as good evidence that human nature has not changed over time and still produces similar artifacts as it has for centuries. For Addison, this is because the type of art that lasts and continues to please people over that duration—that is, simple, narrative poetry—speaks to those features of human nature that have not changed since the beginning. As it would be for Hazlitt a century later, the "mind of man" here is not progressive but remains constant despite the various twists and turns of cultural development. Addison often phrases his turn to simplicity as a turn to "nature," as in his assertion that highly wrought verse "would never have become the delight of the common people [. . .] it is only nature that can have that effect" (383). Addison finds the mind's underlying nature not in exemplars of literary refinement but in the simplest productions that have always shown a "peculiar aptness" to please the vulgar.

In keeping with that focus on common humanity, Addison makes ballad poetry a vehicle for natural social sentiment and an instrument of social cohesion. This is clear when he articulates the purposes poetry served for

---

26. On the eighteenth-century appeal of "popular" literature see Albert B. Friedman, *The Ballad Revival*, and, more recently, Steve Newman, *Ballad Collecting, Lyric, and the Canon*.

27. *Selections from Addison's Papers* 378.

early societies: Ballads, as much as epics, he writes, are calculated to "establish among them an union which was so necessary for their safety" and "to celebrate persons and actions which do honour to their country" (379–80). For Addison, early poetry speaks to the mind's basic, inner dispositions of taste. It would have been common sense for Addison that language was also crucially a feature of the social environment and a means of establishing connections with other people.[28] But the specific way he makes poetry into a social institution is in broad keeping with what would soon become the project of Enlightenment natural historians of society, such as David Hume or Adam Ferguson. Early poetry is rooted in basic, socially oriented elements of the human mind and provides a natural mechanism by which we can plausibly explain what holds people together in social unions.

That does not mean, though, that Addison views these shared judgments of taste as collective or communal acts. Such judgments are still individual and private. Addison's theory of taste was distinctive at the time because he granted the imagination a central role in furnishing the materials of aesthetic judgment. This was in contrast to "inner sense" theorists, like Shaftesbury and Hutcheson, who refer judgments of taste to their own specific senses within the mind. Addison, on the other hand, was developing an aesthetics rooted firmly in the mind's basic materials as furnished by sensation and passion.[29] For Addison, aesthetic consensus arises because we all (he argues) share the same powers of judgment, and often like the same things.[30] Specifically, according to Addison we all like seeing simple, true representations of human thought in action. For example, he often writes of the ballad's "simplicity of thought," or "the thoughts of this poem, which naturally arise from [its] subject" and "are always simple" (378, 387). That type of inter-mental recognition—readers' comparison of a poet's mind with the same basic propensities in their own minds—was one basis for theorizing poetry's communal functions. Another basis was the way that poetry seemed to Addison, from

---

28. See John Locke's *An Essay Concerning Human Understanding*; or, later, Jean-Jacques Rousseau's *Essay on the Origin of Languages*.

29. On Addison's basic commitment to "sensational psychology" see Clarence DeWitt Thorpe, "Addison and Hutcheson on the Imagination" 225. On Addison's broader compatibility with Francis Hutcheson—and Hutcheson's eventual adoption of Addison's term "pleasures of the imagination" within his internal sense theory of aesthetics—see Thorpe 219–20.

30. The idea that poetry's commitment to inwardness is compatible with (even crucial to) its social and collective functions has broad purchase in poetic theory, more recently by way of Theodore Adorno's "Lyric Poetry and Society." Adorno argues that even the most intensely private lyric sensation presents its readers with a picture of a shared, common humanity and can point the way toward a progressive, collectivist politics. Noel Jackson has shown how that logic kept Romantic-era appeals to poetic "sensation" oriented toward a social horizon (*Science and Sensation*).

the earliest known examples, to have hinged on "some important precept of morality" and had sought to "celebrate persons and actions" that ought to be approved by the multitude (379). Rather than solely emphasize the richness of sensation and feeling, or the inventiveness of metaphor, for Addison it is also social approbation, the celebration of heroism, and the exercise of moral judgment that form early narrative poetry's most basic elements.

In the long run, the turn to poetic sensation tended to produce a starker account of human origins. Thomas Blackwell's *Enquiry into the Life and Writings of Homer* (1735) proceeds from the same premise as Addison's—the identity of poetry with the powers of sensation.[31] As Maureen McLane and Laura Slatkin note, Blackwell was "part of a broader sociological-cultural turn [. . .] conceiving *poiesis* (poetic making in the broadest sense) as a mode of cultural production" (691). Yet Blackwell's emphasis on Homer as a well-attuned reporter of his particular landscape and social milieu also pushed toward the naturalist poetics of sensation. Homer tells us about life in his particular cultural moment, but that moment is closer to the common origins that stadial theory presumed all societies had (McLane and Slatkin 692–93). Moreover, Blackwell, in *An Enquiry*, sees the mind as originally tied to its own private sensations: "It is certain, that the *primitive Parts* of the Languages reputed *Original*, are many of them rough, undeclined, impersonal Monosyllables; expressive commonly of the highest *Passions*, and most *striking Objects* that present themselves in *solitary savage Life*" (40). The original mind is a solitary mind, focused merely on sensation and on its own passions. Moreover, unlike others' celebration of metaphor as a foundational cognitive ability—a proposition this chapter has affiliated with Shelley's eventual celebration of "vitally metaphorical" early language—Blackwell and those who shared his line of thinking described metaphor in negative terms, as a result of early language's rudimentary vocabulary. He writes:

> From this Deduction, it is plain that any Language, formed as above described, must be full of Metaphor; and that Metaphor of the boldest, daring, and most natural kind: For Words taken wholly from Nature, and invented under some Passion [. . .] would be expressive of that Fanaticism and Dread, which is incident to Creatures living wild and defenceless. (41–42)

Early language—aligned specifically here with a privative, terrifying state of nature—had very few words, and so those words had to be used in a less

---

31. Thomas Blackwell, *An Enquiry into the Life and Writings of Homer.*

discriminating manner. Metaphor was not the outcome of the mind's remarkable powers of comparison and synthesis (as, we will see, it was for other poetic primitivists like Herder), but the happy accident of a struggling, early moment in language use. Accordingly, Blackwell could celebrate the vibrant, figural nature of Homer's poetry as a feature of its proximity to language's origins—"its *Original, amazing, metaphorick Tincture*" (46)—even as Homer's society had advanced far enough that the solitary mind had been to some degree socialized. The Greek language, he writes, had been "brought to express all the best and bravest of the human Feelings," including what Blackwell calls "the social Passions, and noblest Affections" which "must prevail in an *Epic Poem*" (46). As for Addison, early poetry emphasized the social (and socially approvable) passions. But for Blackwell, the primitive mind that dealt only with simple sensations and passions had *less* ability to recognize or describe interpersonal judgments like "bravery." Per Blackwell's history, society—and, with it, poetry—passed from the primitive "terror" of "*solitary savage* Life" (40–41) to a more developed state in which new emotions of "*Admiration* and *Wonder* will succeed" (42). It moved from solitude to sociability.

Blackwell's focus on the presocial nature of early poetry takes an extreme form in Hugh Blair's later "Critical Dissertation on the Poems of Ossian" (1763). James Macpherson's *Fragments of Ancient Poetry* (1760), which in the next chapter will serve as this book's first major case study, performs its own conjectural thought experiments about the history of poetry and sociability, as it reconstructs and reimagines the poetry of a prehistoric Scottish bard.[32] In fact, as the next chapter will argue, "Ossianism" is centrally engaged with theories of natural sociability and inter-mental contact. Blair, however, takes Ossian as an exemplar of the early, primitive mind. For Blair, Ossian seems even more rudimentary or developmentally early than Homer and represents an original, universal stage of poetic development, to be found in the precultural or early productions of all nations. In his words, Ossian's poetry "is characteristical of an age rather than a country, and belongs, in some measure, to all nations at a certain period" (347). For Blair, that age is closer to a presocial origin point: "The ideas of men at first" are not capable of abstraction, or of processing social information; thus, he bizarrely writes of Ossian, "A publick, a community, the universe, were conceptions beyond his sphere" (354).

It is worth noting again that the time of Blair's writing, in 1763, also saw the sharpening of poetry's affiliation with the origins of language by Rousseau, Herder, and others. A few years later, Adam Ferguson published his revisionary conjectural history, *An Essay on the History of Civil Society*, to reassert

---

32. In Macpherson, *The Poems of Ossian* 1–31.

humanity's social foundations and the social origins of literature. When it comes to early language, Ferguson agrees with both Blackwell and Blair that "the language of early ages is, in one respect, simple and confined" (289). Like Herder and other primitivists, he acknowledges that this simplicity and restriction lead to "liberties, which, to the poet of after-times, are denied" (289). The strength of poetic language is in part its rudimentary quality, which makes up for its imprecision with freedom and variety. For Ferguson, though, that picture of a sparse vocabulary did not imply anything like a presocial state. When it comes to metaphor, Ferguson equivocates: While it may be the case, he grants, that the poet is "at first obliged by the mere defects of his tongue, and the scantiness of proper expressions," it may just as easily be that early poets are "seduced by a pleasure of fancy in stating the analogy of its objects" (286). That propensity for analogical thinking would be rooted in the mind's positive powers, not its early deficiencies. The implication, for Ferguson, is that "man is a poet by nature" (286). Whether it simply follows from the general nature of things, or from something particular to the human constitution, poetic features like metaphor speak to "natural" abilities.

POETIC FIGURE AND SOCIAL INTELLIGENCE: LOWTH, HERDER

For one tradition, one particularly aligned with the study of Hebrew poetry, there was a still closer connection between the mind's figurative powers and its social powers. Turning to two of those writers—Robert Lowth and Johann Gottfried Herder—will help show how the association of metaphor with a "deficiency" in early language linked up to some related ways of theorizing social intelligence.

Robert Lowth's *Lectures on the Sacred Poetry of the Hebrews,* originally published in Latin in 1754 and translated into English in 1787, was influential for later historicist interpretations of the Bible.[33] Lowth explicitly frames his historicism as a form of historical conjecture. His assertion that we must "endeavour as much as possible to read Hebrew as the Hebrews would have read it," for example, required the textual historian to become intimate with another age's thoughts and feelings: "We must even investigate their inmost sentiments, the manner and connexion of their thoughts" (113). He compares this type of historicism to a different kind of scientific conjecture, which he

---

33. Lowth has an important place in histories of biblical criticism. See, for example, Stephen Prickett, *Words and the Word* 95–122; Maurice Olender, *The Languages of Paradise* 21–36; and Jonathan Sheehan, *The Enlightenment Bible* 148–81.

takes from the domain of astronomy: "We must act as the astronomers," he suggests, "who [. . .] conceive themselves as passing through, and surveying the whole universe, migrating from one planet to another, and becoming for a short time the inhabitants of each" (113–14). It is a historicism, in other words, with a decidedly speculative cast.

Accordingly, Lowth's discussion of the "origin and first use" of poetry makes substantial conjectures about the early poet's cognitive abilities and about how feeling is generally structured in the mind,. Lowth writes:

> The origin and first use of poetical language are undoubtedly to be traced into the vehement affections of the mind. For what is meant by that singular frenzy of poets, which the Greeks, ascribing to divine inspiration, distinguished by the appellation of *enthusiasm,* but a style and expression directly prompted by nature itself, and exhibiting the true and express image of a mind violently agitated? When, as it were, the secret avenues, the interior recesses of the soul are thrown open; when the inmost conceptions are displayed, rushing together in one turbid stream, without order or connexion. (79)

For Lowth, biblical poetic form is not the result of divine inspiration but a type of language rooted in the passions and "prompted by nature itself" (79). An impassioned, poetic manner of speaking—including the kind of connective imagery of metaphorical expression—is related to the way "conceptions" are organized in the mind and are liable to run together or become crosswired, so to speak, when agitated by passion.[34]

This focus on the sensorium and its structural organization was one reason that Lowth's biblical historicism soon found favor with an audience more radical than he himself was. The first English translation of his lectures was published by Joseph Johnson; in Johnson's catalog it joined recent scientific publications, including the "physiological psychology" of David Hartley, Erasmus Darwin, and Joseph Priestley.[35] Moreover, the translation and its editorial apparatus were the work of George Gregory, whom Helen Brathwaite styles as "an Anglican clergyman with strong dissenting sympathies."[36] Besides translating Lowth's work, Gregory also added an extensive set of notes that

---

34. For an account of Lowth's "reli[ance] on a specific understanding of the workings of the mind," see Anna Cullhed, "Original Poetry" 39.

35. Johnson has a well-deserved reputation as a publisher of controversial and radical ideas, including the major works of Mary Wollstonecraft, William Godwin, Joseph Priestley, and Erasmus Darwin. On the question of Johnson's politics see John Bugg, "How Radical Was Joseph Johnson?" On the eighteenth-century rise of "physiological psychology" see Alan Richardson, *British Romanticism* 9.

36. Helen Brathwaite, *Romanticism, Publishing, and Dissent* 76.

situated Lowth's speculations within more recent Dissenting biblical scholarship and radical philosophy of mind. For example, Gregory routinely glosses Lowth's comments on sensation, feeling, or figuration in terms of a tradition he aligns with the physiological, "associationist" psychology of David Hartley and Joseph Priestley. Where Lowth sources metaphorical diction to the basic principle of "resemblance," Gregory appends a footnote on the foundational role of Hartleyan association in the primitive mind: In the same way that "we naturally apply the associating principle to furnish an illustration," he writes, so too "when a savage experienced a sensation, for which he had as yet no name, he applied that of the idea which most resembled it" (106).[37] In other words, Lowth's theory of Hebrew poetry tied the poetic to the cognitive in ways that someone like Gregory found generative in the context of physiological psychology.

Importantly, for Lowth himself, the same principle of "agitation" that motivated loose, suggestive poetic language also structured some foundational acts of social intelligence, including mental state attribution. Lowth frames "agitation" as a form of cognitive deficit—a passion-clouded inability to keep track of sensations—and, on Lowth's account, it generated poetic expressions in a manner similar to Thomas Blackwell's logic of metaphor. Lowth describes early poetry's social propensities in a similar way. He explains the frequency of apostrophe and personification in ancient poetry by relating those figures to the way that, "to those who are violently agitated themselves, the universal nature of things seems under a necessity of being affected with similar emotions" (79). To use the vocabulary of Alvin Goldman, a more recent theorist of mental state ascription, these figures result from a failure to "quarantine" one's own mental states, and to avoid letting them color one's perception of other things, and other minds.[38] Rather than seeing personification as an early inclination toward society, what Lowth offers is a theory of an early mind (or a more modern mind, if clouded by passion) that does not know where it ends and the world begins. Moreover, Lowth adheres to a profoundly internal, egoistic account of any social intelligence. He writes that "from what he feels and perceives in himself, he conjectures concerning others; and apprehends and describes the manners, affections, conceptions of others from his own" (117). This is firmly in the "projectivist" tradition of social intelligence theory that, in the eighteenth century, runs from David Hume to Adam Smith. Just like

---

37. Gregory also slips in approving references to Joseph Priestley and David Hartley to elaborate on the basis for tropes (metonymy and prosopopoeia) and, more pointedly, as a gloss on Lowth's use of the term "moral sense" (109, 280, 371). On the adapting of Hutchesonian moral sense theory to the more radical context of later eighteenth-century Dissent see chapter 3.

38. See Goldman, *Simulating Minds* 164.

the historicist's approach to Hebrew poetry, thinking about any other person requires "conjectures concerning others" and inferences about them which we make on the basis of what we know of ourselves. In his discussion of prosopopoeia, Lowth relates this projectivist type of social inference to the more general "principle of resemblance" that underlies metaphor, too: He suggests that attributing personhood to a lifeless thing is really just a "bolder species of metaphor" (106–8). Overall, Lowth's poetics point to metaphor as a foundational cognitive power. Yet he remains firmly locked within an epistemology in which, as David Bromwich puts it, "all sympathy begins at home."[39]

Johann Gottfried Herder is frequently linked to Lowth in discussions of biblical hermeneutics. However, their approach to the poetic mind, "original" language, and social intelligence are in many ways worlds apart.[40] They share some basic, core principles of historical interpretation, such as using philological research to place oneself in the shoes of a historical subject. They also share some core beliefs about the mind's structure. For Herder as for Lowth, cognition is to be identified with a unified, indivisible sensorium. Early language is more rudimentary, more passionate, and more irregular; and poetic language retains vestiges of earlier habits of mind.[41] His theory of social intelligence, however, is far less dependent upon self-projection or the sympathetic imagination. In his *Treatise on the Origin of Language* (1772), he theorizes a natural language, rooted in the expressions of the face and the gestures of the body, and in the fact that "Nature [. . .] bonded together the human being" with other beings "through necessity and a caring parental drive."[42] In "On the Cognition and Sensation of the Human Soul" (1778), he imagines a natural correspondence between minds and writes both of the "harmonious dispositions" that connect people and of an "obscure effect" by which social passions like "sympathy and love, pleasure and ambition, envy and jealousy solve,

---

39. See Bromwich, *Hazlitt: The Mind of a Critic* 142.
40. On Herder (and Lowth's influence on Herder) see Stephen Prickett, *Modernity and the Reinvention of Tradition* 107ff.
41. On the "indivisible work of the formation of ideas," see Herder, *Outlines of a Philosophy of the History of Man* 1.136. On the liberty of early, oral poetics as opposed to the "dead letter," see Herder, "Extract from a Correspondence on Ossian" 156. On the ode as the "firstborn child of sensibility," see Herder, "Fragment of a Treatise" 36.
42. In Herder, *Philosophical Writings* 141. On Herder's natural language as a Romantic-era "embodied universalism," see Alan Richardson, *British Romanticism* 177ff. Richardson notes that Herder's affinities with the Romantic era's "embodied universalism" come with significant liabilities—namely, "how readily it could give way to a science of human differences marked upon racialized bodies" (177). For a more extensive discussion of Romantic theories of facial expression and natural language see Richardson, "Facial Expression Theory." In Zunshine, *Introduction* 65–83.

through looks, through secret hints, the riddle of what lies so well hidden beneath the breast."[43]

These social capabilities can sound like internal senses or special powers, but across his writings Herder more consistently depicts them as features of people's embeddedness in external, social systems. To begin with, cognition itself, for Herder, was embedded in and dependent upon language, which he framed as an extended, material technology of thought. "Language, the principal instrument of our thought," as he calls it, is not just a means of expression or communication but is the physical location in which cognition happens.[44] Amanda Jo Goldstein has offered a reminder that this was a reciprocal formulation for Herder: It applied to mental representation, too, at the physiological level of the nerves. For Herder, Goldstein has shown, "bodily nerves and fibers enact forms of nonverbal figuration [. . .] such that sensory experience might be consciously borne."[45] Figuration is not a kind of inner thought, as it was for Lowth, but a lower-order process that structured experience from the outside in.

In his *Outlines of a Philosophy of the History of Man* (1800), Herder extends that line of thinking and discusses at length how linguistic artifacts become constitutive to the mind's functioning. He asserts, for example, that "Nature has evidently calculated our whole mechanism, with the condition and duration of each period of our lives, for this foreign aid" (406). The mind's dependency on its environment is a matter of physiology, since, to begin with, the "brain of infants" is "soft" and only gradually takes shape and "hardens" through experience and since, moreover, this physiological plasticity remains dependent on the work of culture, or what Herder calls a "chain of socialness and plastic tradition" (406–7). Like Adam Ferguson, Herder erases the boundary between the natural and the artificial. But where for Ferguson this meant that all artifice, and all the apparatuses of society, were part of human nature, Herder reverses that formula and declares "man an artificial machine" (406).[46] Ferguson, we might say, builds art and artifice into humanity's cognitive foundations. Herder spreads those cognitive foundations out into artwork.

---

43. *Herder: Philosophical Writings* 199.

44. Herder, *Outlines of a Philosophy* 406. On Herder's "constitutive" theory of language, which holds that "reflective consciousness only comes to exist in its expression," see Charles Taylor, *Human Agency and Philosophy* 229.

45. See Amanda Jo Goldstein, *Sweet Science* 8. For a detailed discussion of Herder on the figurative nature of sensation see Amanda Jo Goldstein, "Irritable Figures: Herder's Poetic Empiricism," in *The Relevance of Romanticism*, edited by Dalia Nassar 273–95.

46. Herder is likely alluding, with a culturalist twist, to Julien Offray de la Mettrie's scandalous 1748 work *L'Homme Machine* [*Machine Man*].

This intimacy of thought with art and artifice is a clear point of connection between Herder's philosophy of mind and his approach to traditional literature. It is also broadly in keeping with the links that Maureen McLane, Paula McDowell, and others have drawn between eighteenth-century ballad studies and theories of mediation.[47] Herder had a theory of natural sociability, communication, and innate "mindreading" abilities that keep people in contact. But those features of social life were structured, supported, and underpinned by the shared medium of language and the externally distributed realm of culture. The boundary was not a firm one. If Herder has long been seen as central to the story of cultural nationalism and theories of the "folk," his accounts of the social and collective dimension of mental life also provided an inventive answer to a key question of the eighteenth-century science of poetry: Does poetry tell us about the mind's foundational, social powers, or about the culture that surrounds them?[48] Herder makes a connection between those two options that can be found in the Anglophone tradition too, though usually in a more implicit manner. He makes a connection between the drive to make the mind itself capable of social recognition, and a different, more external mode of connection between minds, one based in the socially embedded or socially distributed nature of mental processing.

TWO THEORIES OF THE SOCIALLY DISTRIBUTED MIND: PERCY, RITSON

To conclude this chapter, I want to suggest that what was at stake in Herder's account of popular literature and ballad poetry—a model of cognition as socially distributed and of poetry as a means of socializing the mind—was also at stake in the British antiquarian conversation after 1760. Specifically, it structured the heated argument between rival ballad scholars Thomas Percy and Joseph Ritson. Percy and Ritson's well-documented disagreement had to

---

47. It is also compatible with a number of more recent approaches to mind and technology, such as Andy Clark, *Natural Born Cyborgs*, and N. Katherine Hayles, *How We Became Posthuman*. For an explicit connection between "extended mind" theory and media theory see Hayles, *How We Think* 93ff.

48. For a foundational reading see Royal J. Schmidt, "Cultural Nationalism in Herder." For a more recent view of Herder's collectivism as radical and anti-imperialist see John K. Noyes, *Herder: Aesthetics against Imperialism*. For an overview of how such collectivism is being reformulated by theorists of "distributed cognition," see Deborah Perron Tollefsen, *Groups as Agents*. I owe the connection between Herder and recent philosophical approaches to "group minds" to a lecture Tollefsen delivered for the University of Edinburgh's History of Distributed Cognition project in 2015.

do with the nature of the ancient English minstrel: Was he a bardic culture hero or a common musical entertainer?[49] In light of the broader history this chapter has laid out, I would propose that their exchange can also be read as a dispute about the relation between popular literature and the social mind, and the competing ideological purposes distributed cognition could be made to serve.

In his writings on the ancient English minstrel, Percy's main agenda was to reframe the minstrel not just as a musician or an entertainer but as a bardic figure who united the arts of poetry and music and who played a crucial, authoritative role in his culture. In Kathryn Sutherland's words, Percy's minstrel was "a revered historian of the deeds of the great" (416).[50] Percy's ulterior motive, by most accounts, was to accrue special value to native British literary traditions.[51] While the first edition of his *Reliques of Ancient English Poetry* (1765) did not yet contain his lengthy "Essay on the Ancient English Minstrels," which he would add to the second edition, it does open with a set of systematic claims about the ancient minstrel and his role in society's collective mental development.[52] The dedicatory epistle to the Countess of Northumberland declares that the following poems "are presented [. . .] not as labours of art, but as effusions of nature, shewing the first efforts of ancient genius, and exhibiting the customs and opinions of remote ages" (vi). "By such Bards," he goes on, "was the infancy of genius nurtured and advanced, by such were the minds of unlettered warriors softened and enlarged," and "by such was the memory of illustrious actions preserved and propagated" (vii). Minstrels (here styled as *bards*) act as court historians, but they also serve an educational or civilizing function for the "minds of unlettered warriors." When Percy writes of "genius," he is writing not only about the exemplary or special character of mind possessed by the ancient bardic minstrels themselves, but also about a broader, collective character of mind to be found in the culture at large and imbibed vicariously through poetry. For that reason, the poems show us the

---

49. For Devin Griffiths, the main contest was about the scholarly approach to history. Ritson's main victory over Percy was on the basis of scholarly precision and "forensic inquiry" and was for that reason related to the way that eighteenth-century antiquarianism "laid the foundations of nineteenth-century historicism" (Griffiths, *The Age of Analogy* 99). On their debate as an important moment in the serious consideration of oral cultures as civilized see Paula McDowell, *The Invention of the Oral* 258.

50. Sutherland, "The Native Poet" 416.

51. Ibid. 420.

52. For a comprehensive study of Percy in the context of eighteenth-century ballad antiquarianism see Nick Groom, *The Making of Percy's Reliques*. For a reading of Percy's relationship to conjectural history see John Regan, "Ambiguous Progress and Its Poetic Correlatives."

"first efforts of ancient genius" in a collective sense, as the individual minstrel tutors the "genius" of the age as a whole.

Percy's general account here matches the idea of poetry as collective social scaffolding that Adam Ferguson was also formulating around the same time. For Ferguson, poetry "served to diffuse those improvements of reason, imagination, and sentiment" among the population at large, until "the passions of the poet pervaded the minds of the people, and the conceptions of men of genius being communicated to the vulgar, became the incentives of a national spirit."[53] The implication is that people who are held together in society naturally experience a mixture or "diffusion" of ideas and sentiments among their social body. Minds are made to mingle. But in Percy's version of that claim, poetry's tutelage becomes a more hierarchical type of divided cognitive labor, whereby men of genius communicate refined ideas and sentiments to the population at large. While in general the ballad poetry that Percy helped bring into the mainstream reinforced a dispersed or decentralized model of poetic authorship, Percy himself seems to have had a different picture of the mediated mind.[54] In fact, Percy's major piece of antiquarian commentary on ballad poetry—his 1767 "Essay on the Ancient English Minstrels"—reinforces the idea of single authorship. It opens with the specific claim that the minstrels wrote their own songs and enacted all aspects of their performance themselves, serving as figures who "united the arts of poetry and music, and sung verses to the harp of their own composing."[55] The creative process is the autonomous labor of a strong, unified individual mind, and Percy's minstrels look for all practical purposes like centers of cultural authority. Percy's theory of balladry was, to be sure, a theory both of individuals' embeddedness in broader cognitive systems and of the national "genius" depending on the scaffolding and assistance of poetry. But it is a centralized, hierarchical picture of shared cognitive labor in which "civilization" looks less like a wide social "diffusion" of sentiment than a top-down education, in which "ignorant people" of lesser abilities are supported and guided by those who "excell them in intellectual accomplishments" (xv).

This is the reason Percy's main antagonist, the antiquarian Joseph Ritson, reacted so strongly against him. Jon Mee has described Ritson's ballad studies as a paradigmatic case of the Revolutionary era's "radical antiquarian-

---

53. Ferguson, *Essay* 117.

54. Percy's focus on the individual, authoritative poet is worth keeping in mind because of the way that ballad aesthetics are increasingly being seen as a challenge or alternative to the individualist aesthetics of high Romanticism. See Newman, *Ballad Collecting*; Maureen N. McLane, *Balladeering, Minstrelsy, and the Making of British Romantic Poetry*; and Erik Simpson, *Literary Minstrelsy, 1770–1830*.

55. Thomas Percy, *Four Essays, as Improved and Enlarged in the Second Edition* 3.

ism," which found new and urgent political applications of the distant past.[56] On my argument, Ritson saw Percy as appropriating ballad literature's model of a social or relational self and bending it to his own elitist agenda. Rather than view popular poetry as a set of dispersed practices generated by and sustaining a naturally "social union," Percy was instituting a more Hobbesian, top-down view of social regulation. In place of Addisonian consensus and common humanity, Percy's history of minstrelsy implied a trickle-down theory of genius.

Most explicitly, Ritson took issue with Percy's claim that the minstrel was a particularly talented cultural authority who united music and poetry, performance and original composition in a single person. For Ritson, the medium of popular poetry—and the mental "cultivation" it scaffolded—was more distributed than that. In terms of its invention as well as its circulation, ballad poetry was distributed among its different component parts: lyrical composition, musical composition, singing, and instrumentalism. The prefatory essay to Ritson's own collection of ballads, *Ancient Songs* (1790), embedded this relation among the different components of musical production in its title, "Ancient Songs and Music." In that essay, Ritson denies that minstrels were both singers and musicians—or, in Percy's original words, which Ritson repeatedly quotes with thick irony, people "who united the arts of poetry and music and sung verses to the harp of their own composing."[57] He even suggests that one of his antiquarian source texts shows that this supposed "respectable order of men, 'who united the arts of poetry and music, and sung verses to the harp of their own composing,' were," in fact, merely fiddlers "most miserably twanging and scraping in the booths of Chester fair" (vi–vii).[58] Ritson's main point is that the term *minstrel* never referred to a bardlike creative genius in the first place, but only "ever implied an instrumental performer, and generally a fidler, or such like base musician" (xii). Ritson's broader, egalitarian point is that one does not need to be a cultural authority, or a particularly gifted person, to contribute to popular culture. As he puts it, "Men equally ignorant, have in all ages and in all countries, been possessed of the same talent" (xvi). Read against Percy's account of men of particular "intellectual accomplishments," Ritson's alternative view is a picture of poetry as a divided, distributed process that circulates across society's divisions in a radically decentered way.

---

56. Jon Mee, *Dangerous Enthusiasm* 120. For Mee's discussion of Ritson's radical antiquarianism and its likely influence on William Blake see 113–20.

57. Ritson's first of many quotations of this phrase from Percy occurs in Ritson, *Ancient Songs* vi.

58. The text in dispute was a document in which the fifth Earl of Chester granted the use of his minstrels to his steward Dutton. See Ritson, *Ancient Songs* v–vii.

One implication of Ritson's argument would be a different view of poetry's relation to cognitive origins. Whereas Percy is committed to a brand of poetic primitivism that made the bardic poet the strongest exemplar of native genius, for Ritson, poetry was never the expression of an authentic, individual, self-contained mind in the first place. In fact, as his engagement with Enlightenment language theory suggests, there was nothing natural about such abilities at all, and the types of thinking language supported needed to be considered artificial and external to anyone's native abilities. In Ritson's words, "No man, left to himself from the moment of his birth, would ever be able to utter an articulate sound; language or speech must be taught [. . .] and is the effect of education, not of nature" (16–17).[59] Human nature is the same as animal nature, and the vast majority of our higher cognitive functions are mediated and enabled by linguistic artifice. In fact, this remark on language comes not from Ritson's ballad studies but from his 1802 defense of a vegetarian diet, titled *An Essay on Abstinence from Animal Food, as a Moral Duty* (1802). That essay offers a vision of cross-species sympathy that draws on a wide range of evidence, from classical mythology to philosophical writings on the mind's natural sympathies, comparative anatomy, and physiological treatises on diet and digestion. In that context, the point of Ritson's argument about language's artificiality is that what we usually think of as human intelligence actually has very little to do with humanity's innate or embodied mental structure. He does leave ample room for a physiology of the senses and social passions, but, as for Herder, higher cognitive functions have a more external and socially distributed origin, in the medium of language.

Ritson's writings on vegetarianism also reinforce his allegiances to theories of natural sociability. His leveling of human and nonhuman animals is clearly proto-evolutionary, especially in the way he narrows the gap between humans and other great apes. However, his worldview is closer to Erasmus Darwin's than to Charles Darwin's, and his theory is based on a vision of nature as social plenitude rather than Malthusian competition.[60] The original state of nature, and the original propensities of *human* nature, were for Ritson naturally benevolent, nonpredatory, and vegetarian. He is even interested in physiological accounts of the mind, drawn from medical writing, that might speak to this idea of a naturally benevolent disposition toward all animals.

---

59. Joseph Ritson, *An Essay on Abstinence from Animal Food*. Ritson's argument hinges on the non-uniqueness of human language, including the propositions that "'articulation is not natural to man,' and that language was the invention of society, and rose from natural inarticulate crys [cries]" (16n).

60. On the context of Charles Darwin's Malthusian turn around 1838 see Adrian Desmond and James Moore, *Darwin's Sacred Cause* 146ff.

For example, he approvingly cites George Cheyne's *Essay of Health and Long Life,* which asserts that humans not only lack "strong and fit organs for digesting" meat but also constitutionally lack "those cruel and hard hearts, or those diabolical passions, which could easeyly [*sic*] suffer them to tear and destroy their fellow creatures; at least not in the first and early ageës [*sic*]" (49–50).[61] Though he comments a bit more skeptically that Cheyne "must refer to a state of nature, as no beast of prey is so wantonly and malignantly cruel as man in society," he is happy enough to recruit to his cause basic, physiological features of the human frame as well as conjectures on a natural or original propensity toward sympathy or benevolence (50n).

Ritson's conviction in the continuity between human and animal life is consistent with his views on ballad poetry. He saw *poiesis,* like cognition itself, as dispersed among many parts, socially distributed, and materially contingent.[62] That material and even atomistic approach to language can even be detected in his proposed system of reformed spelling, on display in the passages from the *Essay on Abstinence* quoted above.[63] His principle of retaining every graphic unit, even when phonetically redundant, matches his theory of language as a material, aggregate system that cumulatively forms the material basis of thought. Moreover, his *Essay on Abstinence* makes more explicit his commitments to a benevolist view of human nature and to the foundational role of the social passions. As for Adam Ferguson, traditional literature provided evidence that humanity's social propensities were not a feature of late growth, but were there from the start.

To return, by way of conclusion, to Ritson's essay *Ancient Songs,* it is an important detail that his picture of early poetry was not focused on sensation and passion, as Percy's was, but was oriented toward a perennial popular interest in stories. Ritson aligns his scraping fiddlers and ordinary singers with a natural interest in other people, whether historical heroes or fictional characters. He notes that "all the minstrel songs which have found their way

---

61. For the original text in question see George Cheyne, *An Essay of Health and Long Life.* While Cheyne is best known for *The English Malady* (1733), which includes ample discussion of diet, his broader dietary writings have also received attention in histories of medicine. See, for example, Bryan S. Turner, *Regulating Bodies,* and Lucy Yardley, *Material Discourses of Health and Illness.*

62. See Amanda Jo Goldstein, *Sweet Science,* for an account of how this same cultural moment produced a Lucretian-influenced view of material contingency of life and mind that was formative for Blake, Goethe, and Percy Shelley. Additionally, Timothy Morton has argued that Ritson was a likely influence for Percy Shelley, who recruited Lucretian materialism to his own defense of the vegetable diet ("Joseph Ritson, Percy Shelley, and the Making of Romantic Vegetarianism").

63. On Ritson's proposed system of spelling reform and his use of it in his publications after 1800 see Henry Alfred Burd, *Joseph Ritson* 132–36.

to us, are merely narrative; nothing of passion, sentiment, or even description, being to be discovered among them" (xvi). These are not the songs of Percy's feeling bards, who will elevate and refine the lowly minds around them. They are, as Ritson puts it, in an echo of Addison, the "amusement of the common people" (xvii). What the common folk have always liked, in all ages of society, has been to hear about other people.

Discussions of poetry's intimacy with cognition would before long become tethered to a different sort of argument, one that favored the deep mining of sentiment and edification represented by Percy's bardic minstrels. Ritson offers an alternate history of poetic sentiment, one that had little patience for high-minded defenses of inward feeling and was concerned instead with the foundational nature of social interest. He also offers a good reminder that for much of the eighteenth century, cognitivist approaches to poetry did just as much to link poetic form and tradition to the mind's social powers, its social origins, and its social embeddedness. Even the furthest-reaching conjectural histories, which looked back to the mind's precultural or native dispositions, could at least conceivably find poetry to be already motivated by social impulses. In the chapters that follow, this book will trace those accounts of the social mind from the 1760s scene of poetic antiquarianism through some of its main Romantic proponents: Barbauld, Wordsworth, and Scott. Most immediately though, the next chapter will turn to James Macpherson's *Fragments of Ancient Poetry* (1760), which Macpherson presented as the recently discovered relics of an ancient Scottish bard and as a window into an early—but already thoroughly social—moment in human history. Macpherson's poems were a motivating force for both Percy's turn to England's own "reliques," and for Ritson's and others' experiments with radical antiquarianism.

For his part—and with good reason—Ritson was skeptical about Ossian's authenticity. He seems to have treated what he calls "Oisiniana" as a faddish or overly exuberant scholarly attitude of the 1760s and 1770s, marked by an unscholarly overconfidence about the historian's ability to know the past.[64] But, as the next chapter will show, it is precisely for that reason—Macpherson's willingness to take liberties with antiquarian evidence and to experiment with the materials ancient poetry afforded—that the Ossianic project turned up new ways of thinking about the social mind.

---

64. On Ritson's less-than-enthusiastic response to Ossian and Ossianism see Henry Alfred Burd, *Joseph Ritson* 239–40.

CHAPTER 2

Ossian's Folk Psychology

And take care that I do not shortly afflict you with a psychology
based on Ossian's Poems! The ideas for one, at least, are stirring
alive and deep in my heart, and would make very strange reading![1]

HERDER WAS ONTO SOMETHING when he suggested that a psychology from Ossian's poems would be strange reading—but, nevertheless, developing a psychology from the poems seemed precisely what Ossian, the ancient Scottish bard, was asking readers to do. The strangeness of an Ossianic psychology has a lot to do with the peculiar way that the poems of Ossian treat minds, spirits, and bodies, that is, by making them at once highly material presences and ghostly voices that seem barely there. From its first publication in the controversial volume *Fragments of Ancient Poetry* (1760), the reconstructed Ossianic corpus fostered a critical vocabulary of apparition and spectrality, not least with regard to the spectral nature of the poems themselves.[2] James Macpherson, who styled himself as the translator of newly discovered poems by Ossian, offered these fragments as brief glimpses of ancient Scotland and the hazy domain of oral tradition. Soon, heated debates regarding the poems' authenticity subsequently cast Ossian himself in ghostly shades.[3] William

---

1. Johann Gottfried Herder, "Extract from a Correspondence on Ossian" 156.
2. James Macpherson, *The Poems of Ossian* 1-31.
3. The controversy regarding Macpherson's status as forger endures, for example, in Thomas M. Curley's *Samuel Johnson, the Ossian Fraud, and the Celtic Revival in Great Britain and Ireland*. As Curley acknowledges, though, the past decades have seen a resurgence of interest in Macpherson's original achievement, early signaled by Fiona J. Stafford's *The Sublime Savage*.

Hazlitt, alluding to the forgery debates but defending Ossianism nonetheless, writes, "If it were indeed possible to shew that this writer was nothing, it would only be another instance of mutability, another blank made, another void left in the heart."[4] As an author function, and as the poetic voice that offers itself in the printed fragments, "Ossian" communicated to his audience a ghostliness still more thorough than that of ancient Scotland.

Criticism of Macpherson has likewise subscribed rather readily to a decorporealizing poetics. For Katie Trumpener and Murray Pittock, Ossianic poetry offers shades of a Gaelic past in the face of Scotland's increasingly circumscribed political future within the British Empire.[5] For scholars of orality, Ossian represents the lure of a past conceived nostalgically as an oral culture, which was thereby removed from the gritty materiality of the eighteenth century's rapidly expanding print market.[6] Maureen McLane, for instance, describes how a Romantic writer like Wordsworth could idealize the "spirit of Ossian" while still reviling that spirit's dubious modern history in print. Not only Macpherson's reputation as forger but also the status of print itself helps explain why Wordsworth is happy to reclaim the ancient bard "in soul [. . .] but not in textual body."[7] Extending this argument, James Mulholland finds in Macpherson's Ossian a poetics of voice, one that deftly negotiates the trappings of print even as it becomes "unmoored from the constraints of human corporeality."[8] Both figuratively and literally, then, the poems become artifacts of a particular kind of "spirit."

It is not too surprising to see Ossian marked as intangible and spectral in this way. When McLane refers to Ossian's "textual body," she implicitly invokes the biblical language of "letter" and "spirit" which for Herder offered an insight into the nature of poetry in general. In his "Extract from a Correspondence on Ossian" (1773), Herder writes, "The more remote a people is from an artificial, scientific manner of thinking, speaking, and writing, the less its songs are made for paper and print, the less its verses are written for the dead letter" (156). Ancient poetry (as Herder would more famously write of Hebrew biblical poetry) was a poetics of the spirit. This poetic theory was intimately

---

4. William Hazlitt, *Selected Writings* 2.180.

5. Katie Trumpener, *Bardic Nationalism*; Murray Pittock, *Poetry and Jacobite Politics in Eighteenth-Century Literature and Thought*. For a different take on the theoretical and political stakes of the phantasmal see Orrin N. C. Wang, "Ghost Theory."

6. For an account of antiquarians' use of orality to simulate presence and immediacy see Susan Stewart, *Crimes of Writing*.

7. Maureen N. McLane, *Balladeering* 239.

8. James Mulholland, "James Macpherson's Ossian Poems, Oral Traditions, and the Invention of Voice" 402. On the Ossianic voice in relation to empire see James Mulholland, *Sounding Imperial*.

connected to his theory of *national* spirit and to his interpretive method of reading the "spirit" of a text. Within the Romantic period, of course, that equation of poetry with the spirit became a common way of defining *poiesis* as a special kind of activity, rooted in the intuition of a certain kind of feeling but frequently raised to the level of rarefied or transcendent faculties of mind.

Scholars of the culture of Sensibility, on the other hand, offer some alternatives to this decorporealizing poetics. Studies by Jerome McGann and Adela Pinch have portrayed Sensibility as a literary movement that was strongly motivated to find continuities between mental states and the social environment in which they subsist.[9] McGann, in his *Poetics of Sensibility*, finds in Macpherson's Ossian, in particular, a nostalgia for an earlier age of pagan materialism and a poetic practice that "erodes the sharp divisions of matter and spirit, body and soul, at every textual level" (37). This chapter follows McGann in seeing Macpherson's project as an exploration of the mind's corporeality. Of course, one need look no further than the corpses strewn about Ossian's Highland settings to see that these are poems about *particular* bodies. This chapter's argument, though, is that Macpherson also offers a general theory of an embodied mind, one drawn from the way he repurposes his ancient sources. The Ossian poems may encourage a language that sets poetic "spirit" against its textual and bodily medium, but Macpherson's experimentation with refashioning ancient poetry consistently pushes toward new models of an embodied and socially embedded mind.

Returning to ancient ideas about mind and body formed a well-known pattern in Romantic-era radical philosophy, from what Jeffrey Cox has termed "cockney classicism" to the neo-Lucretian materialism Amanda Jo Goldstein has located in Blake, Goethe, and Percy Shelley.[10] I suggest that Macpherson's earlier project already radically repurposes the past and finds in it the potential for radically different visions of human nature.[11] However, rather than turn strictly to ancient philosophy, Macpherson also turns to folk concepts—or, to use a more recent term, to a *folk psychology*. In its contemporary philosophical usage, "folk psychology" has become a name for people's everyday understanding of how other minds work. For example, ordinary nonphilosophers generally think that other people's behavior is best explained by referring to

---

9. See Adela Pinch, *Strange Fits of Passion*, and Jerome J. McGann, *The Poetics of Sensibility*. For a more recent approach to the vitality of objects see Jane Bennett, *Vibrant Matter*.

10. See Jeffrey N. Cox, *Poetry and Politics in the Cockney School*, and Goldstein, *Sweet Science*.

11. On the ways that women writers, in particular, took Ossianism as an invitation to write alternate histories of society and gender construction see JoEllen DeLucia, *A Feminine Enlightenment*.

mental states, which can be described using terms like *beliefs, desires,* and *intentions*: He raises the glass because he *wants* to take a sip; Elizabeth refuses Mr. Darcy's proposal because she *believes* he is an unjust and ungenerous man, and she *wants* nothing to do with him.[12] Most philosophers who identify a prereflective folk psychology of this kind grant that it is a dependable strategy for explaining human behavior—even if they think that the language of mental states is a vulgar illusion, which will ultimately evaporate into the more nuanced language of a mature science.

When Macpherson turns to popular literature, he finds in it something like a folk psychology: a primitive theory of mind that offers a new way into contested questions about what minds are and how we recognize them. While the content of such theories is often strange, surprising, or heterodox, Macpherson works to grant them the weight of common sense. Thus the first section of this chapter frames the Ossianic project as an intervention in then-current theories of ancient poetry, which made the ancient text the site of information about the primitive mind. These poems offered a repository of "philosophically impoverished" models of mental life; yet, because that tied them to humanity's mental origins, they also became a source of information about even contemporary people's most basic mental architecture. Macpherson's ostensibly ancient poems, that is, offer a prephilosophical or naive theory about mental states and their relationship to the body.

For a cognate project, I turn to the philosophy of Thomas Reid, who was the towering figure in Aberdeen's university system in the 1750s, when Macpherson was matriculated there. While it struck some as baroque, Reid presented his philosophy as a vindication of "common sense"—that is, of what the common folk have always, in all ages, believed. Macpherson, too, turns to the ideas of the common people and their commonsense notions about other people's minds. Yet that vernacular packaging ultimately delivers a philosophy closer to the more starkly counterintuitive models of mindedness then in circulation: primitive animism, radical materialism, and innate powers of mind-recognition. I turn finally to one of the stranger moments in the 1760 *Fragments*—the death of the character Morna in fragment fifteen—as Macpherson's attempt to make "common sense" answerable to these more experimental models of embodied mentality. In the process, Macpherson not only asserts ancient literature's usefulness for ongoing debates about materialism; but, more broadly, he also seeks a materialism that might inform literary methodology and that could situate the literary artifact within a broader, interdisciplinary terrain.

---

12. For an account of Restoration and eighteenth-century debates around mental state terms see Jonathan Kramnick, *Actions and Objects from Hobbes to Richardson*.

MENTAL INVESTIGATIONS IN ABERDEEN

In 1759 Macpherson met the poet and dramatist John Home. Home was acutely interested in Scottish tradition and had already instigated William Collins's *Ode on the Popular Superstitions of the Highlands of Scotland*. When Macpherson claimed to have collected a body of traditional literature in the original Gaelic, Home asked to see a sample. Macpherson reluctantly produced an English "translation" of one of these poems, which Home immediately brought to the attention of Hugh Blair. With Blair's encouragement, Macpherson published *Fragments of Ancient Poetry, Collected in the Highlands of Scotland, and Translated from the GALIC or ERSE Language* in June 1760.[13] The volume offers brief glimpses of life in the militarized Scottish Highlands during and after the wars of Fingal (the traditional figure Fionn mac Cumhaill, who appears here as a Scottish king). Its final three fragments offer glimpses of a larger epic on these wars, which Blair hints might yet be found and reconstructed. That epic poem, *Fingal,* appeared in December 1761 and was followed by another, *Temora,* in March 1763. These latter, epic productions made Ossian world-famous and obtained the admiration of a public that included Goethe and Napoleon. *Fingal* recounts Danish aggression against the Irish tribes led by Cuchullin and the defeat of those invading forces with Fingal's help. The earlier *Fragments,* by contrast, had explored the public and private damage that resulted from those wars. Ossian, the son of Fingal, survives his contemporaries and his own son to become a melancholy and nostalgic bard, whose poetry alternates between descriptions of military exploits and private affective exchange. Everything about the *Fragments* culminates in trauma and loss and voices a third-century Highland society already lamenting its own demise.

Despite their broad success and the emphatic support of Scots like Blair and David Hume, doubts about the authenticity of the poems arose from their first publication. Macpherson was reluctant to produce his translations, and he repeatedly refused to show his Gaelic originals. Thomas Gray was one of the first to voice his suspicions, and scholars of Welsh and Irish literature soon became skeptical about Macpherson's scholarly and editorial methods. While these doubts were briefly put to rest by Blair's "Critical Dissertation" and the appendix to the 1765 *Poems of Ossian,* the next decade renewed the controversy. In 1775, Hume reluctantly confessed his doubt at the poems' authenticity. In the same year, Samuel Johnson published his *Journey to the Western Isles,* which boasted firsthand investigations that proved the Ossian poems to

---

13. *The Poems of Ossian* 5–31.

be total fabrications. After Macpherson's death, the "Report of the Committee of the Highland Society of Scotland" officially concluded that he had not, in fact, translated particular poems but had creatively reimagined a body of traditional motifs and characters.[14] Like the "Report," the poems' reception down to the present day has remained curiously divided between aesthetic appreciation of the poems—which remain crucially important to the development of British nationalism and what used to be called the transition "from Sensibility to Romanticism"—and an ambivalent stance toward Macpherson himself as a literary opportunist riding the coattails of his country's famed philosophers. The poems' *philosophical* impact has thus been seen as largely indirect, mediated by figures like Blair in Britain and Herder in Germany.[15]

It is usually not emphasized, however, that Macpherson's poetry was actively engaged with the ideas of that broader philosophical environment. This environment consisted of the network of Scottish learning centered in the major university towns, especially the "ancient universities" at St. Andrews, Glasgow, Aberdeen, and Edinburgh. Macpherson spent time at the latter two of those universities. He began his studies at King's College, Aberdeen, in 1752, when the university was freshly reformed on Enlightenment principles and invigorated by a philosophical society that included curriculum reformer Alexander Gerard, land reformer William Ogilvie, and philosopher Thomas Reid.[16] Macpherson matriculated at King's in the first year of the new curriculum: Students now began with concrete, empirical subjects like history and geography and then worked their way up to the more abstract sciences. The next year—when Macpherson began the second-year course in philosophy—Thomas Reid became Regent.[17] There Reid conceived, presented, and worked out with students what became his *Inquiry into the Human Mind on the Principles of Common Sense*.

On the received account, Macpherson was a disaffected student: Little inclined to strict study, he preferred the pleasures of imaginative poetry. Thus Thomas Bailey Saunders, writing in 1895 and evincing his own nostalgia for the age of Reid, suggests that while at King's Macpherson "showed no inclination to philosophy" and so "neglected the special opportunities of the

---

14. Curley, *Samuel Johnson* 8.

15. On Ossian's mediation see Howard Gaskill, ed., *The Reception of Ossian in Europe*.

16. Macpherson transferred to Aberdeen's Marischal College in 1755. That same year he likely also studied in Edinburgh, without matriculating, before returning home to rural Ruthven. See Stafford, *Sublime Savage* 24ff.

17. On Aberdeen's curricular reform see Paul B. Wood, *The Aberdeen Enlightenment*, and Stafford, *Sublime Savage* 26–28.

place."[18] Fiona Stafford concurs: Reid's philosophical scrupulousness would have repelled Macpherson, and so his "creative talents" received "no formal encouragement" (27). Nevertheless, as nearly all his critics have acknowledged, Macpherson's writing bears strong marks of the Scottish Enlightenment's empirical poetics: the preference for a simple, concrete language; a turn to sentiment; and an interest in the earliest ages of humanity. On most accounts Macpherson carved out a special, sequestered niche for himself within this intellectual culture: one which, while it was shaped by Thomas Blackwell's poetic theories and publicly defended by Hugh Blair's critical writings, remained primarily a space of aesthetic enjoyment, sublime experience, and cultural nostalgia. On my argument, however, the Ossian poems—*especially* to the extent that they are acts of forgery—explore and test the limits of the Scottish Enlightenment. Specifically, they engage the philosophy of mind that helped cast ancient poetry as a laboratory in which to observe the mind in its early, pristine stages.

Inquiries into brains, nerves, and vital spirits were in full force at this time, and the mind's operations formed the basis of study across the Aberdeen curriculum. For Reid and his colleagues, empirical investigations of the mind were more difficult than those of the body. Alexander Gerard, for instance, in his *Plan of Education*, notes the comparative ease of anatomy:

> We can put *bodies* in any situation that we please, and observe at leisure their effects on one another; but the phoenomena [sic] of the *mind* are of a less constant nature; we must catch them in an instant, and be content to glean them up by observing their effects, as they accidentally discover themselves in the several circumstances of life. (25)

Though Gerard was at least nominally a dualist, the salient aspect of the mind for him is its fleeting nature, its tendency to elude observation. The mind is "less constant" and harder to pin down. He describes the mind's obliqueness in a language of "accidental discovery"—of reasoning backward from effects to causes—that would have been second nature to him. A professor of Natural Philosophy and then Divinity, Gerard outlined Aberdeen's new curriculum as a progression from sensory concreteness toward the abstract principles of logic and "natural theology" (33). From its humble beginning in "pneumatics" (which Gerard defines interchangeably as the study of "spirits" and "the phoenomena of the *mind*"), the curriculum reflected the Enlightenment project of deriving all knowledge from sensation. In Gerard's words, a

---

18. Saunders, *The Life and Letters of James Macpherson* 40.

course of knowledge must begin with "the constitution of man, and his several active powers" (25, 23). Yet knowledge about the mind, the foundation of the empirical sciences, remains dependent upon indirect strategies, secondary circumstances and the instantaneous "gleanings" of the observer.[19]

Gerard was almost certainly in the audience when Reid first lectured on the principles of common sense. "All that we know of the body," Reid explains, "is owing to anatomical dissection and observation, and it must be by an anatomy of the mind that we can discover its powers and principles."[20] Reid is writing figuratively here. An "anatomy of the mind" would not explain the mind by turning to physiology but would seek the mind's own constitutive principles. This is possible, Reid thinks, only through introspection. He notes that while an anatomist can study a wide variety of cadavers, the anatomist of the mind has only himself: "It is his own mind only that he can examine [. . .] He may, from outward signs, collect the operations of other minds; but these signs are for the most part ambiguous, and must be interpreted by what he perceives within himself" (13). However intimate the connection might be between mind and body, mental investigations do not happen in the laboratory. They are restricted to the kind of "armchair philosophy" practiced by John Locke, that mental anatomist who was his own best subject and who turned to introspection to "catch" or "glean" the mind's inner workings.

But introspection is impressionistic. The mind is unwieldy; it often appears as one big, slippery entity and resists being parceled out into analyzable units. This is what Descartes called "unity of mind": The mind appears to be one thing, with no physical extension. It cannot be divided into parts. The body, on the other hand, has a physical extension, and consequently it can be divided into many parts. Furthermore, introspective studies of the mind do not permit the scientific method. Good science would entail the comparison of "bodies of all different ages," as Reid notes, as well as those in variously "defective," "obscure," or "perfect" states (13). Such standards of comparison elude the "anatomist of the mind."

Students of poetry, however, *do* have more than simply introspection into their own minds. As the previous chapter showed, belletristic writers on ancient poetry frequently cast it as evidence from the past ripe for comparison with the present. For many of the period's leading lights, poems were textual artifacts by which voices reach out into futurity and through which future readers encounter, in spectral form, the expressive content of the past. In fact, poetry from earlier ages offers a particularly helpful kind of reportage,

---

19. On "pneumatics" and "pneumatology" in their connection to aesthetics and literary criticism see Landreth, "Breaking the Laws of Motion."
20. Reid, *An Inquiry into the Human Mind* 12.

since the primitive mind was taken to be free of those cultural accretions with which centuries of development had covered over our "original constitution." In the Enlightenment's early version of the debate between "nature" and "nurture," primitive society offered subjects closer to the mind's natural condition.

Thus, for a host of writers—Robert Lowth and J. G. Herder on Hebrew poetry, Paul Henri Mallet on Scandinavian poetry, and Herder and Hugh Blair on Ossian—ancient poetry offered a special kind of language.[21] This is the sensuous language of thought that Herder praised as not yet doomed to the "dead letter" of abstraction. For some theorists, it also implied a privative, rudimentary language restricted to concrete images derived from the five senses. In Mallet's words, early minds are limited by "the paucity of their ideas and the barrenness of their language," and those limitations "oblige them to borrow from all nature, images fit to cloath their conceptions in" (393). Antiquarians like Mallet took the texts they studied to be remnants of a primitive, philosophically impoverished era. That explained both the simplicity and the concreteness of the poets' diction and their penchant for analogies and metaphors in lieu of complex concepts. For Mallet, as for Thomas Blackwell, Robert Lowth, and even Herder, the benefits of philosophical impoverishment were primarily aesthetic: "How should abstract terms and reflex ideas, which so enervate our poetry, be found in theirs?" (393). Primitive poetry—and, by extension, the best modern poetry—was thus far better at expressing sensuous particularity and emotional excess than philosophical nuance. At Aberdeen, the major proponent of this poetic school was Thomas Blackwell, who tutored Gerard and perhaps Macpherson himself.[22] Certainly Macpherson retained Aberdeen's focus on what he termed a "sentimental" aesthetics, one focused on the language of primitive sensation and feeling.

Macpherson would later retail much of this theory as his own, including the assertion that primal, sensory language told readers about the basis of their own, modern minds. As he writes in *Introduction to the History of Great Britain and Ireland*, "The sentimental is peculiar to no age; it suits the inherent feelings of the human mind" (214). Because it spoke from what Blair called, in his *Critical Dissertation on Ossian*, humanity's "most artless ages," primitive poetry revealed the mind at its barest: stripped of the accretions of culture and closer to its natural state (345). Blair writes that "mankind will never bear such resembling features, as they do in the beginnings of society," though what we would now call cultural difference "divert[s] into channels

---

21. Lowth, *Lectures*; Herder, *The Spirit of Hebrew Poetry*; Paul Henri Mallet, *Northern Antiquities*; Herder, "Extract from a Correspondence on Ossian"; Blair, "Critical Dissertation."

22. On Blackwell's relation to Macpherson see Stafford, *Sublime Savage* 28–33, and Trumpener, *Bardic Nationalism* 78.

widely separated, that current of human genius and manners, which descends originally from one spring" (347). This stadial model of sociocultural development came to prominence at the hands of Scottish Enlightenment writers like Adam Ferguson and Adam Smith. Since all minds begin identically, the story goes, each society looks the same at its beginnings. Societies then progress from primitive hunting groups—the earliest stage, in which Blair sets Ossian's Highlanders—through pastoral life, agriculture, and ultimately commercial society. Since each individual is substantially shaped by culture, cultural development drives or constrains cognitive development. Moreover, since societies modernize at different rates, either vast populations can mature quickly, entering by adulthood into the highest forms of commercial modernity; or whole societies could languish in the earliest, primitive ways of living and thinking. While the further reaches of such history were beyond the scope of archival records and antiquarian documents, they were presumed to be continuous with the basic, unchanging foundations of human nature, and so could be imaginatively explored from the armchair using the speculative technique Dugald Stewart would term "conjectural history."[23]

I want to suggest that we read Macpherson's forgeries as conjectural history of this sort. By offering "evidence" of what life was actually like in ancient settings, Macpherson reframed the primitive poem as a venue for experimental engagement with the primitive mind. As such, the Ossian poems pave the way for what Noel Jackson has called "the experimental lyric of early Romanticism" by blending the work of philology with the lure of sentimental immediacy.[24] By my argument, this model of poetry has its origins in an antiquarian turn to the poetic mind, concerned not just with the primitive mind's empirical makeup but its habitual, even superstitious, modes of thinking about other minds. William Collins had already, in 1748, turned to Highland superstitions for their aesthetic value. In the *Fragments*, popular superstitions offer more than aesthetic gains. They embed within the poems a primitive philosophy of mind.

FROM ANIMISM TO MATERIALISM

Macpherson models his first two fragments after the biblical Song of Songs but moves the lovers' dialogue to a new historical setting, one on the point of

---

23. See Stewart, "Account of the Life and Writings."
24. Jackson, *Science and Sensation* 105. Jackson reads Coleridge's "Frost at Midnight," for instance, as a sustained engagement with Reidian self-observation.

being torn apart by the "the wars of Fingal."[25] In the volume's recurrent pattern, the poems move between private affective exchange and public catastrophe. The plot is simple: Shilric must go off to war and knows he will likely die. Vinvela speaks as if Shilric's death is inevitable, and she promises that he will live on in her memory:

> Yes!--I will remember thee—indeed my Shilric will fall. What shall I do, my love! when thou art gone for ever? Through these hills I will go at noon; I will go through the silent heath. There I will see the place of thy rest, returning from the chace. Indeed, my Shilric will fall; but I will remember him. (8)

Vinvela's preemptive lamentation—and later the posthumous regret she expresses from beyond the grave—gain their cultural efficacy from their claim to be records of sentiment that speak to modern readers. Fragment two dramatizes this by beginning with a nameless speaker, who seems to be Vinvela mourning for Shilric. ("I sit by the mossy fountain; on the top of the hill of winds.") Part of the real confusion produced by this poem is whether we are supposed to read it as a continuation of the first fragment at all. We only find out for sure when Shilric is named. A great deal goes into the production of this initial perplexity. For instance, when the second fragment's nameless speaker says, "No hunter at a distance is seen," he echoes Vinvela's description of his absence in the first fragment: "The hunter is far removed" (8, 7). The reasonable inference is that Shilric has not returned from the wars. In fact, though, it is Shilric who is speaking and who is about to see a ghost. The fragment's framing makes the reader's encounter with him similarly phantasmal, as if he is a voice from beyond the grave.

Macpherson occasionally sought to explain his supernatural content by turning to the poetic theory in which he had been educated. In his *Introduction to the History of Great Britain and Ireland* he claims:

> In the infancy of philosophy it is difficult for the human mind to form any distinct idea of the existence of an immaterial Being. We are not, therefore, to wonder that the northern nations carried the business and pastimes, though not the miseries, of life into their future state. Without being acquainted with the PALINGENESIA of Pythagoras and his followers, they clothed departed spirits with bodies not subject to decay. (177-78)

---

25. Macpherson, *Poems of Ossian* 7. On the first two fragments as a "grimly ironic" reworking of the Song of Songs see Stafford, *The Sublime Savage* 102–3.

Primitive subjects lack the more advanced philosophy of Greece or, more to Macpherson's point, Hellenic Christianity.[26] Ideas about the immaterial soul, he argues, arrive comparably late in the history of philosophy and require a level of abstraction that primitive societies lack. As a result, they approximate the idea of the soul by telling tales of ghosts and immaterial spirits.

For poetic empiricists, this philosophical impoverishment was a good thing, since it led to more gripping and moving language. For Macpherson, though, such impoverishment is desirable, paradoxically, for *philosophical* reasons. The primitive mind's dependence on the concrete and the sensory does not just conduce to appealing literary subject matter but also performs a philosophical work of its own by reopening the discussion of materialism. Macpherson's language, of course, concedes that a mature philosophy will ultimately possess a theory of the immaterial spirit. The poems themselves, however, open up the possibility that mind might be more intimately connected to body. If the mind outlasts death, it does so in bodily form.

This location of mind in matter has long been seen as a desire for later eighteenth-century literature, and the possibility of situating the spirit firmly in the body—correlating mind and matter—proved both dangerous and fascinating. The most ambitious way to bring mind and body together was to make a claim about the mind's underlying ontology. In order to explain how mental states inhere in the body, we need first to explain how they can be a property of matter at all. Spinoza had made a particularly influential version of this claim with his monistic account of the universe, in which the one existing substance ("God, or nature") possesses the radically different attributes of thought and extension, mind and matter. Spinoza's influence was on the rise by mid-century. Within a few decades, monist-inflected controversies would erupt between Reid and Priestley—occasioned by the latter's scandalous 1777 *Disquisitions Relating to Matter and Spirit*—and soon thereafter in the German *Pantheismusstreit*.

This set of debates about how matter can think or be understood as vital would seem to be what McGann has in mind, since he claims that "the world of Ossian appears to subsist," at base, "as a complex affective system" (38). Yet there is a substantial difference between this position—which typically goes by the name *panpsychism*—and the more modest, descriptive approach known as *animism*.[27] Animism names a human psychology: The primitive speaker loses track of his own mental states and projects them onto the landscape.

---

26. In the preface to the 1760 *Fragments*, Ossian's resistance to Christian evangelism is framed as evidence of his antiquity (Macpherson, *Poems of Ossian* 5). For the much-remarked Christian use of the Greek term *palingenesia* see Matthew 18:29.

27. On panpsychism's history see David Skrbina, *Panpsychism in the West*.

Panpsychism, on the other hand, alleges that the mental is at least potentially a characteristic of all matter. When William Wordsworth declares his "faith that every flower / Enjoys the air it breathes," he gestures toward a variety of panpsychism that had taken on particular revolutionary associations in the 1790s.[28] A few years after that, he turned to a reactionary animism in an equally well-known exclamation:

> Great God! I'd rather be
> A pagan suckled in a creed outworn,
> That I might, standing on this pleasant lea,
> Have glimpses that would make me less forlorn.[29]

That later sonnet conveys nostalgia for a world *perceived as* vital and living, rather than as the inert object of scientific rationality. Animism, on this familiar model, is a mode of enchantment, one that ultimately tells us less about the world than about the psychology of the perceiving subject. Stanley Cavell suggests why this is disappointing when he speaks of Romantic thought as risking a kind of animism, one "already implicit" in philosophical skepticism.[30] Like the Ancient Mariner's "ghastly crew," animism offers only the artificial animation of something always already lifeless. Against this specter of animistic encounter—and the disappointing Kantian "settlement" with it—Cavell sets Romanticism's project of "bringing the world back, as it were, to life."[31]

This is a disappointment that Macpherson shares. For poetic theorists from Blair to Wordsworth, animism offered primarily aesthetic benefits. Animism supposedly captures something genuine about cognition in general, something that endures in the most basic functions of expressive language. Thus Robert Lowth explains that "to those who are violently agitated themselves, the universal nature of things seems under a necessity of being affected with similar emotions" (38–39). For an influential critical tradition, primitive projection continues to explain our own mental functioning, at least for a special category of impassioned thought. It endures into the nineteenth century, where it becomes the habit John Ruskin terms the "pathetic fallacy." And it

---

28. Wordsworth, *Lyrical Ballads* 76.
29. Wordsworth, *Poems in Two Volumes, and Other Poems, 1800–1807* 150.
30. Stanley Cavell, *In Quest of the Ordinary* 55. Cavell remains agnostic whether "the world that poetry (or what is to become poetry) seeks" will ultimately entail "a new animism, a truer one, or whether the concept of animism will fall away, as if outgrown" (65).
31. Cavell, *In Quest of the Ordinary* 31, 52–53.

inflects Paul de Man's brand of deconstruction, where anthropomorphic projection speaks to the most basic of language's figural dependencies.[32]

Macpherson, though, was uncomfortable with animistic projection. In fact, after publishing the *Fragments* he quickly revised the "Shilric, Vinvela" sequence in ways that make it *less* animistic. The second edition of September 1760 advertises that some changes have been made to conform to the more accurate manuscripts Macpherson claimed to have located.[33] In fragment two, Shilric had originally painted a dreary scene: "One tree is rustling above me. Dark waves roll over the heath." The "troubled" lake and strange midday silence anticipate (unremarkably) Shilric's turn inward: "Sad are my thoughts as I sit alone." In September's revised edition, however, that line is simplified to "Sad are my thoughts alone."[34] Originally, there had been some slippage between Shilric's feelings and the natural scene. The new language, in contrast, makes the lone melancholy element either Shilric ("sad are *my* thoughts alone") or mind itself ("sad are my *thoughts* alone"). Either way, the revision strips away the pathetic fallacy that had suffused the natural scene with mental presences. Macpherson's poetry consistently seeks to identify such mental presences and remains rife with ghosts. But here, he recoils from a moment where those presences threaten to dissipate into a psychology of the primitive mind. If Macpherson is interested in pursuing how thoughts exist in nature—not just as projections, but part of the natural surround—animism will not do. What the poem gains by this revision, then, is a new purchase on the "vital and articulate human presences" that McGann identifies "throughout Macpherson's otherwise inanimate, desolate, and purely geophysical places."[35] Animism would tell us primarily about the psychology of the primitive mind, which supposedly projects itself onto inanimate nature. A literal reading of these poems, in contrast, entails a claim about the mind's underlying ontology: Mental states are continuous with that which is outside the head. This opens up a philosophical framework in which spirits—that is, minds—are integrated into the world of natural objects and in which there is a homology between seeing a rock and perceiving or encountering another mind. The implication is that primitive minds are actually more philosophically sophisticated than modern, "philosophical" readers.

---

32. See Paul de Man, "Anthropomorphism and Trope in the Lyric." De Man's turn to the structures of language was one signal of literary criticism's broader turn away from discussions of consciousness—on which see Colin Jager, "Can We Talk about Consciousness Again?"
33. *Poems of Ossian* 3.
34. *Poems of Ossian* 9 and 9n.
35. McGann, *Poetics of Sensibility* 35. For an extension of McGann's argument to the poetics of orality see Mulholland, "James Macpherson's Ossian Poems" 400–401.

By 1760, the lyric was taking on its soon-habitual association with the solitary expressive speaker, based on the mode's close association with the sensory and linguistic forms that condition individual thought. For Blair, Ossian was one such relic of concrete language and strong feeling, a poet of solitude and the sublime.[36] Blair goes on to align higher philosophical abstraction, which these poems lack, with the realm of social life. Ossian's ideas, he writes, "extended little farther than to the objects he saw around him. A public, a community, the universe, were conceptions beyond his sphere" (354). This assessment of Ossian should sound strange to anyone who has read the poems and tried to keep straight the labyrinthine networks of interpersonal relationships they entail. Even the first, simpler fragments hinge on Shilric's relationship to Vinvela, the call of societal duties, and the conflict between those intimate and public modes of social feeling. But Blair's insistence on Ossian's sublimity makes sense within a familiar empiricist story, which reads primitive poetry as the origin of human thought, and so as a pristine faculty of sensation that preexists social engagement with other minds.[37] In the post-Romantic tradition, such arguments can sometimes sequester lyric subjectivity from the messy business of plots, characters, and events that drives popular literary forms—in other words, from what has recently been described as a narrative obsession with "social intelligence."[38] For Blair, in contrast, the broader horizons of sociality were too much for Ossian to conceive in his world of bare, lifeless objects. Blair is wrong about this. To understand why that mistake matters for Macpherson's literary project, I turn to one of the Scottish Enlightenment's predominant ways of talking about other minds.

FROM COMMON SENSE TO FOLK PSYCHOLOGY

The scholarly discourse that framed Macpherson's project frequently offered a solipsistic model of mental life, one with little purchase on other minds as actual, vital presences in the world. The best-known articulation of this "projectivist" stance is David Hume's. His ties to "natural sociability" theories notwithstanding, in his epistemology Hume was adamant that we never really know the world, but only certain qualities that we project onto the world. Thus, in his account of causation, Hume declines to discuss actual causal relations between objects (say, that a bat strikes and propels a baseball) and

---

36. See Frances Ferguson, *Solitude and the Sublime*.
37. On Enlightenment developmental theory's effacing of sociability see Yousef, *Isolated Cases*.
38. See, for example, Vermeule, *Why Do We Care?*

remains restricted to ideas (I find the bat's striking of the ball "constantly conjoined" to the ball's subsequent movement).[39] A version of this projectivism also governs sympathetic relationships with other minds. I know only my own sensations, my own feelings—but I can, through a projective act of sympathy, approximate the experience of others.[40]

For Reid, Hume's projectivist account of the mind proved unsatisfying. Kant, more famously, would go to great lengths to show that human knowledge refers to an actual world (even if, as Cavell suggests, Kant disappointingly forswears the possibility of knowing that world in itself). Reid's "commonsense" response to Hume, by contrast, took the form of a methodological shift. Projectivism, Reid argued, presumed that our commonsense way of thinking about the world was wrong. We take ourselves to perceive actual objects, Hume said, though a close attention to our own minds showed that we speak merely of ideas and impressions. Against this Humean "way of ideas," Reid asserted that commonsense intuitions about external objects were reliable. "We know," he argues, "that when certain impressions are made upon our organs, nerves, and brain, certain corresponding sensations are felt, and certain objects are both conceived and believed to exist."[41] For Reid, that conception and that belief indicate basic elements of the human constitution, which imply a reliable connection between the world, bodily organs, and sensation. Thus, when I perceive an object, I obtain actual, positive knowledge about something in the world. Although philosophers "find inexplicable mysteries, and even contradictions" in these "acts of mind," Reid emphasizes that they "are perfectly understood by every man of common understanding."[42]

Such acts of mind grant knowledge of the world, and—as Reid discusses in his *Essay on the Intellectual Powers of Man*—knowledge of other minds. Acts like willing, judging, and reasoning, Reid concedes, would be possible in a solipsistic universe. But other, social actions—such as promising, or receiving testimony—presuppose "society with other intelligent beings," and presuming this is part of our basic constitution (68). Reid's main evidence for the naturalness of this presumption is its emergence in early childhood. He writes:

---

39. For this account of how an experience of such "constant conjunctions" produces the idea of a "necessary connection" between causes and effects see especially Book I, Part III, Section XIV of Hume's *Treatise of Human Nature* (155–72).

40. See especially Hume's description of the social passions in Book II of the *Treatise*. Compare, though, Pinch's alternative account of Humean sympathy, where feeling originates outside the self and is never quite one's own in the first place (*Strange Fits of Passion* 17ff).

41. Reid, *Essay on the Intellectual Powers of Man* 27.

42. Reid, *Inquiry* 68.

Our social intellectual operations, as well as our social affections, appear very early in life, before we are capable of reasoning; yet both suppose a conviction of the existence of other intelligent beings. When a child asks a question of his nurse, this act of his mind supposes not only a desire to know what he asks; it supposes likewise a conviction that the nurse is an intelligent being, to whom he can communicate his thoughts, and who can communicate her thoughts to him. (69)

This is Reid's argument against other-minds skepticism, one that follows the same logic he had used to counter skepticism generally. Reid goes on to emphasize that the child's "early conviction" is quite striking and demands more attention than it has frequently merited: "How he came by this conviction so early, is a question of some importance in the knowledge of the human mind, and therefore worthy of the consideration of Philosophers" (69). This natural belief is a phenomenon that must be accounted for in its own right, not explained away as an illusion. The premise of common sense is that ordinary people possess an intuitive, largely reliable folk theory. As such, Reid's philosophy represents a third option that avoids both Humean skepticism and a Kantian faculty psychology with its animistic supplement. In recent years, cognitive science has given Reid's theory a new lease on life; his account of the mind's innate social mechanisms bears a striking resemblance to what now goes by the name of "folk psychology," "theory of mind," or simply "mindreading."[43]

The current philosophical usage of "folk psychology" is usually dated to Wilfred Sellars's 1956 essay "Empiricism and the Philosophy of the Mind." Sellars's argument, in brief, is that people hold the tacit theory that other people's behavior is directed by mental states. If asked why someone picks up an apple and takes a bite, most people would answer that this person *wanted* to or that she *felt* hungry and therefore *desired* to alleviate that hunger. If this seems intuitive—as Reid would say, what no one ever doubted—that is just the point. Sellars, like Reid, sought to explain the mind by vindicating the most usual, commonsense theories about it. For Sellars, this "folk" account gives a good description of mental life. What makes his argument provocative is the assertion that people apply such theories to themselves, too. We talk about our own beliefs and desires not because we can "see" them through introspection but

---

43. While "folk psychology" is a coinage of the twenty-first century, it draws on an older concept of "folk belief" or "folk faith," as opposed to more-developed philosophy or science. Reid uses this verbal formula in his attack on Hume, who, Reid notes, occasionally confesses to having "relapsed into the faith of the vulgar" (Reid, *Inquiry* 21). On Hume's relationship to folk psychology see Kramnick, *Actions and Objects* 48ff.

because we can infer their presence using a theory we developed by observing others.

Reid would not run the causal history this way, if only because of the privileged role of introspection in his philosophy.[44] Yet especially in his theory of natural signs, he suggests that reading others' minds is an independent, original faculty. In fact, many recent approaches to theory of mind place special importance on something that Reid noted: This particular set of cognitive abilities develops quite early in childhood, long before an empiricist would predict. Today's nativists have a name for this early emergence. They refer to it as the "poverty of the stimulus."[45] By the age of four, "normally-developing" children can successfully complete complex behaviors, like attributing a false belief (because she didn't see me move it, Sally thinks the marble is still in the blue box), predicting an action (Sally will look in the blue box), or interpreting facial cues (Sally now looks confused). For some, these aptitudes are evidence for an innate, evolved mechanism that performs mindreading behaviors. While Reid did not speak of such mechanisms, he frequently emphasizes the innateness of the same abilities.[46]

In the remainder of this chapter I explore the common ground between Reid's and Macpherson's turns to folk psychology. To be sure, "folk psychology" is a term invented for specific, philosophical usage. It resembles the "ordinary" in ordinary language philosophy, whose major proponents were directly influenced by Reid's claim that philosophical concepts inhere in everyday speech. Macpherson, meanwhile, is associated with the other, literary-cultural sense of the "folk," and indeed, via his influence on Herder, he contributed to the theories of folk literature that would arise in the nineteenth century. One kind of "folk" yields a theory of culture, the other a theory of cognition. Their divergent intellectual careers notwithstanding, however, they come from the same Aberdeen lecture halls and try to answer the same questions. In response to what Stanley Cavell has called the "crisis of skepticism," both Reid and Macpherson turn to the common in order to reinvest intermental relations with an ontological ground. In Macpherson's hands, ancient poetry carries with it primitive models of relationships between minds. For

---

44. Hume, on the other hand, would. See Kramnick, *Actions and Objects* 56.

45. The "poverty of the stimulus" argument is usually dated to Noam Chomsky's 1959 "Review of B. F. Skinner's *Verbal Behavior.*" Linguists in Chomsky's tradition argue that language acquisition—as opposed to knowledge of particular languages—must be innate, since children become fluent so early in the rules of language use.

46. Alan Richardson points to this "inborn ability to read the 'natural' language of facial expressions and gestures" as something that "Herder, Reid, and Darwin all theorized" (Richardson, *British Romanticism* 161). On Reid and mindreading in early childhood see Richardson, *The Neural Sublime* 92–93.

Macpherson, as for Reid, those notions tell us something about minds that exist out in the world. Further, the Ossianic project strives to countenance the common, shared foundations of the human mind: both as a distant origin visible in the records of ancient civilizations and as an entirely *modern* practice that characterizes popular or "low" literature. The antiquarian poetics of Mallet, Lowth, and Blair asked how primitive man thought—and, as a result, how we continue to think in the "infancy" of our thought. Macpherson, per my argument, goes further and asks *what* we think and whether the commonsense picture of the mind is right or wrong. This makes him a theorist of cognition as well as culture.

This is in keeping with the history of empirical conjectures about ancient poetry I laid out in chapter 1, especially in the way that the turn to ballad and folk studies turns up an interest in the mind's universal or cross-cultural properties—in Addison's declaration, for example, that a song "universally tasted and approved by the multitude" must have "in it some peculiar aptness to gratify the mind of man."[47] Seeking information about the mind not in exemplars of literary refinement, but in the simplest productions that have always had a "peculiar aptness" to please the vulgar, linked poetry's claim to be a rival science of the mind to the category of the popular, of "common" or "low" literature—and, accordingly, to a picture of the ordinary mind, and ordinary ways of thinking, that comes to constitute the ground of "folk" knowledge or belief.

That linking together of folk aesthetics and folk knowledge lays the groundwork for the union of the ancient and the popular that drives Macpherson's pseudo-antiquarian practice. Blair, for instance, suggests that in its supernatural portrayal of "departed spirits," Ossian's mythology "is not local and temporary, like that of most other ancient poets," but "the mythology of human nature; for it is founded on what has been the popular belief, in all ages and countries, and under all forms of religion."[48] In turning to the literature of the "common folk," ballad collectors, antiquarians, and, in Macpherson's case, forgers, understood themselves to be turning from the realm of learned dispute to something like common sense.

Unlike Reid's common sense, though, Macpherson's "popular belief" turns up something quite philosophically counterintuitive. He treats the poems not only as sources of information about the simplest, most ordinary ways of thinking, useful for historical comparison, but also as ways to explore the strangeness and the paradox that inhere *within* older ideas (for instance, the

---

47. Addison, *Selections* 378.
48. Blair, "Critical Dissertation" 368.

Celt's simultaneous belief in materialism and a ghostly afterlife).[49] In his turn to popular representations of the mind, Macpherson interrogates divisions between mind and body, and between mind and environment, that Reid never touched. I turn now to one striking example, from the end of the 1760 volume, that seeks to unite bodily experiments—what Gerard calls our ability to "put bodies in any situation that we please"—with that wished-for ability to extract mentalistic information from the accidents of the body.

THE MIND'S "GENUINE REMAINS"

Fragment fifteen is one of the poems Macpherson specifies as the "detached pieces" of the "greater work" he will soon reconstruct as *Fingal* and of which he offers three quick samples at the end of the volume.[50] The plot is a love triangle. Its occurrences are few: Duchommar approaches Morna and reveals that he has killed a rival suitor, Cadmor. Morna tricks him into giving up his sword and stabs him; he does the same to her. The whole scene unfolds in a few short verse paragraphs, formatted as a dramatic dialogue.

> MORNA.
> And is the son of Tarman fallen; the youth with the breast of snow! the first in the chace of the hill; the foe of the sons of the ocean!—Duchommar, thou art gloomy indeed; cruel is thy arm to me.—But give me that sword, son of Mugruch; I love the blood of Cadmor!
> [He gives her the sword, with which she instantly stabs him.]
>
> DUCHOMMAR.
> Daughter of Cormac-Carbre, thou hast pierced Duchommar! The sword is cold in my breast; thou hast killed the son of Mugruch. Give me to Moinie the maid; for much she loved Duchommar. My tomb she will raise on the hill; the hunter shall see it, and praise me.—But draw that sword from my side, Morna; I feel it cold.——
> [Upon her coming near him, he stabs her. As she fell, she plucked a stone from the side of the cave, and placed it betwixt them, that his blood might not be mingled with hers.]

---

49. In this sense, Macpherson's Ossianic project is already an attempt at what Richardson has termed "cognitive historicism." See Richardson, *The Neural Sublime* 1–16.

50. This fragment, originally number fourteen, was renumbered in the September 1760 second edition and in all subsequent editions of the text.

The poem hinges on bracketed moments of third-person description that most closely resemble stage directions. These descriptions would be familiar enough for readers of dramatic poetry, but they are out of place, to say the least, in poetry that stakes its cultural significance on its supposed origins in oral tradition.

First, Morna asks for the sword, pretending to desire Cadmor's blood, after which (in what I am calling a stage direction) she "instantly" turns the weapon on Duchommar. When Duchommar repeats this pattern of deception and Morna is stabbed in return, we read a still more substantial description. The former stage direction described only Morna's actions. But the one that concludes this fragment delves deeper into her character. It even includes a statement of intention, in what is a rather more complex action than the impassioned murders the volume has heretofore displayed. This would, of course, be quite unremarkable in a novel, but it stands out jarringly in the context of this oral poetry of voice, which on empiricist accounts focused exclusively on a primitive, first-person engagement with the external world. The stage direction pertains neither to the bardic voice nor to the performance of quoted speech. Rather, it splits the work of novelistic narration and editorial gloss. This is also the moment at which voice (lyric or dramatic) stops—is stifled and attempts in the process to mark its *own* body, to delimit its own borders and prevent the commingling of blood. Why does such a mark of translatedness and reconstructedness appear at this particular moment? Clearly this is an important passage for those interested in orality and print, as it dramatizes voice giving way to the "dead letter" of the stage direction.

The first phrase of Hugh Blair's anonymous preface to the 1760 *Fragments* emphasizes their authenticity: "The public may depend on the following fragments as genuine remains of ancient Scottish poetry" (5). "Genuine," of course, speaks to the text's historical legitimacy. Yet in the context of Morna's deception of Duchommar, where the text hinges on a question of concealed intentions, or *dis*ingenuousness, it is the bodily remains (of Morna and of the printed text) that ultimately claim to be "genuine." The textual body of the written tradition here becomes the site of the least corporeal, most mentalistic description available. It might appear that Morna attempts to manipulate the body from beyond the grave or at least from a place no longer reliably embodied. And yet this remains one of the most bodily moments to be found in the *Fragments*: a moment of identification with the body, from Morna's request for the blood of her slain lover to her last measures to keep her own blood free from mixture with that of her aggressor. Macpherson brings into play a materialism both "primitive" and modern; he countenances their shared investment in prolonging the reach of the mentalistic beyond the bodily. Morna's death scene manages to retain the sense that the mind is an easily extinguished modality of the body, one that exists within it and yet still outlasts it, if only "gleaned in an instant"—to revisit Alexander Gerard's language—when made available to literary representation.

For a material account of the vital spirits that might still outlast the body, we might consider eighteenth-century discussions of the soul's posthumous endurance. James Chandler has pursued one such theory—the "vehicular hypothesis," which invests the soul more intimately in the body—from Henry More's poetry, through Abraham Tucker's philosophy, and ultimately to Laurence Sterne's sentimental narratives.[51] The "vehicular hypothesis," in Tucker's words, entailed that the spirit "does not go out naked, nor entirely disengaged from matter, but carries away with her an integument from among those wherewith she was before invested" (33). With its language of departed spirits taking with them a piece of their bodily "integument," the vehicular hypothesis calls to mind Macpherson's discussion of pagan materialists, who "clothed departed spirits" with just such integuments (a term that etymologically means "covering").

That is not, however, what happens in the poem. A more likely candidate, I suggest, is the philosophy of Robert Whytt, whom Neil Vickers has called "the most influential British physician of the eighteenth century."[52] Both Whytt and his rival Albrecht von Haller studied under the renowned Dutch physician Herman Boerhaave and were influenced by his theory of fibers. Under a kind of pantheistic sway, though, Whytt desired to show that matter could perform acts usually reserved for mind. Many physicians, including Haller, divided human action into two kinds of motions. The first, "irritability," included automatic bodily motions, from the beating of the heart down to involuntary twitches. These mere mechanical movements were distinguishable from conscious, volitional actions. For Haller, this latter type of privileged activity required a higher faculty, a faculty of perception, feeling, or consciousness, which he thought to be localized to the brain. Whytt, on the other hand, contended that although the brain may well be the privileged location of thought, the entire body is endowed with a power *like* thinking or feeling, a faculty he referred to as "sensibility." Whytt's goal was actually to reassert the central role the soul played in perception and animal motion, against what he perceived as

---

51. James Chandler, "The Languages of Sentiment" 31.
52. Neil Vickers, in "Review of *British Romanticism and the Science of the Mind* by Alan Richardson," uses this phrase to assert Whytt's centrality in eighteenth-century discourse (148). For Vickers's full discussion of Whytt see his *Coleridge and the Doctors, 1795–1806*.

Haller's more materialist and mechanical approach to the human body.[53] But the result made for strange reading.

To support his theory, Whytt kept a running list of anecdotal evidence, a list of strange or prodigious cases, in which animals, upon decapitation, not only remained living, but even continued to pursue certain habitual, apparently intentional actions for some period of time after being detached from their brains. His *Essay on the Vital and Other Involuntary Motions of Animals* (1751) lists these prodigies, some of which he had observed himself, and many of which he had culled from other writers.[54] Whytt's phrasing sometimes suggests that these incidents are universally observed facts about a species. For instance, he writes, "A frog lives, and moves its members, for half an hour after its head is cut off; nay, when the body of a frog is divided in two, both the anterior and posterior extremities preserve life and a power of motion for a considerable time" (384). Others are single occurrences, such as a tortoise which, after having its brain "extracted by a hole made in its scull, in the beginning of *November*," survived until the following May. Another tortoise, decapitated and bled, lived the better part of a month (386). Most important to Whytt were the cases that showed signs of habitual, but on most accounts volitional, action by animals. "A viper," for instance, "after being deprived of its head and intrails, moved towards a heap of stones in a garden where it used to hide itself" (385). Whytt also recounts Boyle's experiments with vipers that, days after being decapitated and disemboweled, responded to experimental pricking, like the sparks Galvani would administer to a detached frog's leg in his 1771 experiments.

Perhaps the most striking example is something Whytt offers as a little-known fact about silk moths. He cites a phenomenon described by Boyle, who claimed that "the female butterflies into which silk worms have been metamorphosed, not only admit the male, after losing their heads, but also lay eggs" (385–86). Here, the overarching project of Whytt's catalog—to demonstrate the continuity between the brain and the body, between sentient action and mechanical irritability—intersects with a focus on the sexualized body. The spectacle of posthumous penetration and reproduction, which is jarring even in a description of animal life, serves as a disturbing if clinical gloss on the sexual aggression Morna dies trying to fend off. So, too, the catalog as a whole offers an interesting analogue to Macpherson's survey of traumatized bodies, which are torn between the domain of political violence, social and sexual confrontation, and the ostensibly private realm of affect. For Whytt,

---

53. For an account of Whytt's theory see Nima Bassiri, "The Brain and the Unconscious Soul in Eighteenth-Century Nervous Physiology."
54. Robert Whytt, *An Essay on the Vital and Other Involuntary Motions of Animals*.

these not-quite-dead creatures demonstrate that there is really just one kind of spirit, which is fully embodied during life, communicates motion throughout the body during its lifetime, and leaves a temporary, posthumous push—a kind of after-charge—upon being extinguished. Whytt's creatures perform an exaggerated version of Morna's posthumous action.

Read alongside Whytt and the antiquarian poetics on which Macpherson was intellectually raised, the fragments begin to look like a kind of science fiction. They slow down quick and unusual natural occurrences to imagine what they tell us about the mind, which, as Gerard and Reid both suggest, still eluded even the closest observation. Remarkably, Morna's death rewrites, at the starkest physiological level, the strangely material phantoms present earlier in the 1760 volume and subsequently in Macpherson's Ossianic epics. Unlike the ghosts that haunt the earlier fragments, Morna's spirit sticks closer to her body.

This entails, moreover, a formal turn from dialogue to stage direction. The poem ends with a narratorial gloss, which conveys the sense that the motions of the body go on after the voice is extinguished. The whole act, it seems, is something Morna accomplishes—to quote the stage directions—"as she fell." As a result, what we read is a kind of externalized introspection, the equivalent of free indirect discourse for this ostensibly oral poetry. Morna's statement of intention migrates from the first person of the lyrical dialogue to the editorial third person, at the very moment when the text confesses its reconstructedness. We could call this a kind of "giving up the ghost," a fall into print conventions. How does one depict mental states in the absence of a lyric voice? Just as free indirect discourse creates an externalized, depersonalized account of thoughts ostensibly going through someone's head, it is unclear whether this stage direction reflects explicit thoughts.

Morna might have simply announced her intentions: "Our blood shall not be mingled"; "I shall place this rock"; and so on. In fact, such autonarration would not be much more strained than the descriptions of landscape that begin the second fragment in the volume: "One tree is rustling above me. Dark waves roll over the heath" (9). That type of soliloquy would fit well with Blackwell's or Lowth's claims about the rhetorical forms conducive to oral transmission, as well as with theories of primitive thought as a language that figures itself as address. Equally fitting, for that matter, would be Duchommar's metaphorical manner: He tells Morna he has killed a deer for her, when in fact he has killed her lover. On a first reading, this figurative meaning is hardly clear. In the absence of additional context, Morna assumes that Duchommar speaks literally. There is no indication that he is speaking of a murder until he spells it out in explicit terms. The ensuing shock serves to defamiliarize the poem's figurative language and renders it jarring. It hardly seems to embody a theory of primitive language as essentially figural.

In the same way, we might read Morna's final, posthumous action figuratively, as a representation of her disdain for the possibility of union, even in death, with her aggressor. But it seems more promising to read this scene literally, as simply enacting Morna's desire to prevent her blood from mixing with Duchommar's. At this literal level, the poem does not channel voices and feelings from the past. Indeed, the turn to the stage direction dramatizes the collapse of that folk model of poetry, which by this point Macpherson seems to have taken as far as it will carry him.[55] The fragmentary form here suggests an experimental breakage of the lyric voice—as when Whytt describes surgically removing a tortoise's brain—to see how intimately the mind is entangled with the body. The poem locates mental states, to be sure—but it locates them in bodily practices: in Morna's one final continuous movement, remarkably sustained even once the mind's guiding force has dropped away.

MATERIALISM AND LITERARY METHOD

Like Whytt's catalog of experiments, fragment fifteen shifts mentality's location beyond the head, beyond the seat of consciousness. Here the poem takes on the aspirations of panpsychism, which extends mindedness from the conscious agent to matter itself. In doing so, the poem allegorizes a persistent desire to establish mental states as real, observable entities. The fragment thus arrives at a different, materialist answer to the question that Reid also pursued: how to put the empiricist sensorium back in contact with a real world, populated by real minds. In particular, the turn from lyrical dialogue to editorial gloss seeks to affirm that Morna's intentions are legible, that they can be read or recognized as such without the intervention of the expressive poetic voice. They can, in other words, be "gleaned in an instant": not through introspection but by bodily observation. The fragment therefore frames the attribution of mental states not as an act of primitive, animistic projection but as an act of reading. That scene of reading, I want to suggest, registers Macpherson's resistance to Hugh Blair's model of the lyric mind. Blair, remember, described Ossian as a primitive poet, whose thoughts "extended little farther than to the objects he saw around him."[56] By contrast, fragment fifteen depicts a lyric

---

55. Ian Haywood reads the poem as a failed literary experiment, since its main claim to authenticity—its fragmentary status—comes into conflict with Macpherson's claim to editorial authority (*The Making of History* 85).

56. Blair, "Critical Dissertation" 354.

mind that exceeds sensory absorption and animistic projection. Instead, it extends everywhere, hungering after a kind of mentalistic access that can only be granted by other means.

Macpherson "found" in his ancient sources an archival record of the early mind. But the poems tell us of more than primitive, sensuous experience: They proceed to the complex business of plotting and posturing in the social world. As subsequent theorists developed Macpherson's line of thought, they tended to push that latter, socially entangled mindedness onto a different, more emphatically narrative model of literature. That emphasis is clear, for instance, in Wordsworth's polemic against "frantic novels, sickly and stupid German Tragedies, and deluges of idle and extravagant stories in verse."[57] To be sure, Macpherson sometimes hews closely to this antinarrative tradition. He disparages "dull narrative[s] of facts in verse," which cannot "take hold of the human mind" sufficiently to endure in an oral culture. He contrasts such dull narratives with the rich formal and linguistic properties of "the rhimes of the bards," those primal, sensory properties of mind that form poetry's proper object.[58] The thinkers Macpherson is echoing here typically had a hard time addressing the question of *other* minds. Attending to the formal properties of language was the period's most tried-and-true method for explaining what textual artifacts reveal about the literary mind.[59]

That eighteenth-century interest in the literary mind is all the more intriguing in light of the recent "empirical turn" in literary studies. In the wake of the cognitive revolution, scholars have begun to ask what literature's ordinary practices tell us about the mind's foundations. The past decades have seen the formation of an array of such critical methods under the general rubric of "cognitive approaches" to literature and culture.[60] Such studies seek to ground our understanding of these literary experiences in a scientific understanding of the mind's abilities and constraints. In his essay "Literary Universals," Hogan argues broadly for such a critical method, one that would situate diverse literary cultures against a broader "background of commonality," commonalities that are cognitively grounded and cross-culturally universal.[61] Hogan enumerates many such universals: For example, throughout world poetry, poetic lines tend with surprising consistency to contain between

---

57. Wordsworth, *Lyrical Ballads* 747. On the influence of Lowth on Wordsworth see Prickett, *Words and the Word* 43.

58. Macpherson, *Introduction* 77.

59. For the term "the literary mind" and the method it implies see Mark Turner, *The Literary Mind*.

60. See Zunshine, ed., *Introduction*.

61. Hogan, "Literary Universals," in Zunshine, ed., *Introduction*.

five and nine words. Likewise, assonance is a verbal pattern to be found in all major literary traditions, as is "verbal parallelism"—the repetition of the same content in a different verbal structure—which Hogan locates in a host of ancient poetries including Chinese, Babylonian, and Hebrew.

The pursuit of such literary universals was already a feature of eighteenth-century antiquarian poetics. In fact, theorizing the "verbal parallelism" was the major achievement of Robert Lowth's treatise on Hebrew poetry. Lowth identified parallelism as the defining feature of poetry in Hebrew, one that distinguished it from the classical forms known to students of Homer and Virgil. Hebrew poetry, he explained, typically structures itself on a repetition between lines. One line will state a description or proposition, and the next will repeat it with a difference. Sometimes this entails what Lowth calls "synonymous" parallelism, which repeats the same or similar content in different verbal garb. Other times, it entails a "synthetic" parallelism, which takes the original content in a new direction. Although the parallelism initially marked Hebrew poetry's difference from classical poetic forms, it soon became a hallmark of a generic, cross-cultural, and preclassical poetics, founded on the principle that the primitive mind tends to be alike in all its geographical iterations. Lowth writes, "A poem translated literally from the Hebrew into the prose of any other language, whilst the same forms of the sentences remain, will still retain, even as far as relates to versification, much of its native dignity, and a faint appearance of versification" (71). While this was received as an iconoclastic move, one result was the casting of Hebrew verse into a prose that was less characteristic of *any* particular culture. Throwing off the classical paradigm means, in large part, throwing off the features of versification, leaving a generic prose in which verse is only a "faint appearance."

Drawing on the cultural background he shared with Lowth, Macpherson crafted his traditional Ossianic poems to *sound* like biblical literature and to *look*, on the page, like prose. The result was something of an anomaly in Gaelic translation. Previously, for instance, in the *Scots Magazine*, Gaelic poems were by and large fitted to "English" criteria, rendered in balanced, rhymed Augustan couplets.[62] Macpherson, on the other hand, often characterizes what he does as "prose" translation, despite the fact that he usually keeps quite regularly to a hexameter line. Vinvela, for example, opens the 1760 volume by saying, "My love is a son of the hill. He pursues the flying deer. His gray dogs are panting around him; his bow-strings sound in the wind." As the poem continues, a Hebraic parallelism gradually emerges. Here is Vinvela, a few lines later, shown as her lines sound and not as they were originally printed:

---

62. See John J. Dunn, "Coleridge's Debt to Macpherson's Ossian."

> Then thou art gone, O Shilric!   and I am alone on the hill.
> The deer are seen on the brow;   void of fear they graze along.
> No more they dread the wind;   no more the rustling tree. (7)

The punctuation and cadence create palpable pauses, which separate the line into three-stress sections. The second half alternates between the "synonymous" and "synthetic" parallelisms Lowth identified. By making his ancient Scottish poems sound like ancient biblical poetry, Macpherson gestures toward the uniform basis of cognitive architecture, which was required of the empiricist mind and those primitive artistic productions that spoke—as Blair understood them to—from the origins of stadial history.

In this sense, Macpherson's Ossianic project draws on some of the same assumptions that drive recent work on literary universals. Hogan's project, for one, owes a clear debt to Lowth, as well as to Macpherson, in whose hands the Hebrew parallelism began to look less like a mark of cultural difference than a cross-cultural feature of the literary mind. If the pursuit of such universals was already a feature of eighteenth-century belletristic writing, then it is necessary to think about how that history continues to condition more-recent critical endeavors. Like the Scottish Enlightenment's conjectural histories, philologists' exploration of cultural differences in poetry served a broader project, which sought to uncover the mind's basic, cross-cultural foundations. Rather than paving the way for cultural relativism, then, Macpherson's poems (and theories of the "folk" more broadly) are part and parcel of that universalist project.

That project began—like Hogan's "literary universals" or Rueven Tsur's "cognitive poetics"—in the study of the single mind and its experience of poetic language.[63] What makes poetry distinctive—and this remains common sense for many of those who teach poetry to undergraduates—is its complex and self-aware treatment of language, its drawing on sensory experience, and its manipulation of sonic and conceptual linguistic effects. Sometime in the nineteenth century, though, storytelling became a cognitive attribute in its own right. Famously, John Stuart Mill identified poetic "feeling" and narrative "incident" as "two mutually exclusive characters of mind." While "all minds are capable of being affected" by both, only advanced societies cultivate true poetry. The earliest stages of life are marked, meanwhile, by the "passion for a story."[64] Like Wordsworth, Mill reviles popular narrative as a vulgar, rudimentary activity. Yet where Wordsworth aligned only poetry with a mental faculty, Mill grants that narrative, too, is a cognitive ability. The result is a compart-

---

63. Tsur, *Toward a Theory of Cognitive Poetics*.
64. Mill, *Collected Works* 1.345.

mentalized picture of two different faculties: one aligned with sensation, passion, and the domain of a singular voice; and the other marked as the domain of narrative, folk psychology, and the doings of other minds.

That compartmentalization remains clear in more-recent approaches to the literary mind, a subset of which focus on the concerns of folk psychology, specifically readers' engagement with fictional minds. Such studies—as indicated by titles like Zunshine's *Why We Read Fiction* and Vermeule's *Why Do We Care about Literary Characters?*—ask what makes mundane, plot-driven literature possible. In order to provide the explanations their titles promise, both of these studies attempt to link how we read with how we countenance other minds in everyday life. As a groundwork for literary studies, the scientific debates around folk psychology tend to position the literary artifact as a vehicle of social information. For Zunshine and Vermeule, novels portray complex networks of social information, which ultimately provoke and "exercise" our mindreading abilities. This includes both our common or "folk" theories about what the mind is like and, more to the point, our ordinary (and, per many versions of this argument, evolutionarily hardwired) methods for recognizing and navigating the social world. These studies typically describe literature in terms of realist narrative or more generally in terms of plot or story. And that equation is particularly stark in work that, seeking a broad, cross-cultural and transhistorical scope, cuts across myth, national epic, folktale, metrical romance, and the realist novel, seeking a more basic and all-encompassing definition of the literary artifact. The result is a model of literature as something like "storytelling," a designation that has particular affinities with theories of narrative and oral culture. Thus John D. Niles defines "oral narrative" as "people's use of the elements of speech to evoke action in a temporal sequence."[65] The openness of that definition intends to make narrative include both cultural institutions (e.g., ritual performance) and the basic tools of everyday social life (e.g., the conversational anecdote). Indeed, such theories can say little about questions of literary genre; the cognitive architecture to which these theories refer has not changed since the Pleistocene era.[66]

This gives the lyric an anomalous place within cognitive literary studies. The origins of the current cognitive revival can be found in the eighteenth century's historicizing theories of poetry, yet the present obsession with narrative reduces poetry to a solitary lyric voice. Macpherson participated in this trend, too, of course. While they are not precisely ballads, the *Fragments* share many of the characteristics that have made ballads hard for literary critics to

---

65. John D. Niles, *Homo Narrans* 1–2.
66. See Kramnick, "Against Literary Darwinism." On the role of oral narrative in such evolutionary-biological approaches to literature see the introduction to this book.

categorize. Largely narrative, populated by stock figures, generic settings, and brief actions, they support the reduction of literature in general to "narrative" or "storytelling." But Macpherson often discussed his poems using antinarrative rhetoric, highlighting primitive linguistic effects and the "rhimes of the bards." In short, Macpherson worked at a moment when two conceptions of literature were diverging, both of which saw the poem as the source of real knowledge about the mind. On the one hand was the empiricist poetics of sensation, which culminated in an introspective poetics and a theory of lyric solitude stretching from Mill to the twenty-first-century classroom.[67] On the other was a more positivistic turn to cognitive "universals," which countenances the social mind, but only by theorizing the literary as something like an "instinct" to tell stories. Macpherson begins to register that divergence as a contradiction within his own poetic practice.

The best emblem for that theoretical knot is Morna's death itself. Fragment fifteen takes the poetics of sensuous expressivity to its point of rupture. It leaves us with the "dead letter" of the stage direction and its descriptive language of mental states, instantiated in behavior and expressed as a function of the body. In that moment of textual and bodily disruption, Macpherson's poetry probes the intersection of two competing paradigms: poetry as a key to the embodied mind, and literature as a reflex of the mind's social operations. The result is a peculiarly ambivalent engagement with the era's scientifically inflected theories of literature, one that sought both to explain literature as an encounter with fictional minds and to ground humanistic inquiry in the material world.

Ultimately, that is a materialism for which literary studies is still looking. As the previous chapter showed, though, it was an approach to mind, body, and artifact that ballad antiquarians and conjectural historians were beginning to map out. And as the next chapter suggests, it was one that lived on after Ossian in the poetics of the British Dissenting tradition, where—specifically in the poetry of Anna Letitia Barbauld—physiological psychology came into contact with conjectural histories of literature, developmental accounts of the human mind, and theories of natural sociability.

---

67. On the Anglo-American tradition's blunting of Mill's initially more nuanced account of lyric solitude see Virginia Jackson, *Dickinson's Misery* 130ff.

CHAPTER 3

Barbauld and the Growth of the Poet's Mind

> The mind is forcibly carried out of itself; and, embracing
> the whole circle of animated existence, calls on all above,
> around, below, to help to bear the burden of its gratitude.[1]

A CURIOUS THING about animism is the way that it came, by the late eighteenth century, to entangle two opposing views of human mental development. On the one hand, as Anna Letitia Barbauld's remarks on social worship here suggest, animism could serve as evidence of a primary social drive. On the other, it became a name for a "primitive" habit that characterized society's early stages and that lingered as a form of mistaken thought particularly associated with poetry—in moods that detected other minds in the wind or that presumed the universe shared one's own feelings. For that argument, shared by Robert Lowth and Hugh Blair, animistic projection is so common in early poetry because the mind, at that stage, does not yet have a concept of itself or of other minds. It has not yet developed or honed its strategies of mental state attribution and cannot draw the line between its own inner properties and the objective features of the external world. As Lowth writes, the earliest poets were egoists who ascribed their own beliefs and feelings to "the universal nature of things." Those egoistic habits endure into the present as a feature of poetry's impassioned style of thinking and as an error only likely to be made by "those who are violently agitated."[2] For Lowth, in other words, poetic animism tells us relatively little about social intelligence and primarily spoke

---

1. Anna Letitia Barbauld, "Remarks on Mr. Gilbert Wakefield's Enquiry into the Expediency and Propriety of Public or Social Worship," in *Works* 2.428.
2. Lowth, *Lectures* 38–39.

to the clouded relationship that the uncultivated mind, or the impassioned mind, has with the object world.

The previous chapter argued that Macpherson's Ossian poems toyed with these ideas about animism in a very different way and sought to make it more than a primitive error. What appeared to be early self-absorption might in fact be a dim but natural awareness of some more authentic and material pathway of inter-mental contact. This chapter examines how, in Ossian's wake, conjectures about the early poetic mind continued to drive theories of sociability and social intelligence. In particular, the idea that poetry arose from an early, social impulse in the primitive mind offered a powerful image to Anna Letitia Barbauld and her circle, who were cobbling together different strands of eighteenth-century benevolist theory and putting them to new purposes. Some of those strands, like Francis Hutcheson's language of innate moral senses, pointed toward innate, embodied accounts of constitutional drives. Others, like David Hartley's association psychology, pushed toward a different picture of the embodied mind, one that remained radically open to the world around it.[3] To Barbauld, this chapter proposes, the eighteenth-century science of poetry seemed to be able to do both of those things at the same time: to look inward toward the underlying, original human constitution; and to look outward, toward the "constitutive outside" of material and social environments.[4]

Conjectures on the early poetic mind were intimately connected with Barbauld's other domains of social and historical inquiry. For example, she wrote one of her most explicit discussions of the early poetic mind not for the purposes of literary commentary but as part of a debate about the proper mode of Christian worship. In almost a point-by-point rebuttal of Robert Lowth's discussion of Hebrew poetry, she writes:

> The devout heart [. . .] bursts into loud and vocal expressions of praise and adoration; and, from an overflowing sensibility, seeks to expand itself to the utmost limits of creation. The mind is forcibly carried out of itself; and, embracing the whole circle of animated existence, calls on all above, around, below, to help to bear the burden of its gratitude. Joy is too brilliant a thing

---

3. For Hutcheson's explicit connection between moral sense and natural sociability see *Logic, Metaphysics, and the Natural Sociability of Mankind*. For Hartley's theory of association see *Observations on Man, His Frame, His Duty, and His Expectations*.

4. The term "constitutive outside" is Jackson's description for the way that the social world, though it remains external to the mind itself, turns out to have provided it with its very powers of perception (*Science and Sensation* 122). This chapter suggests that for Barbauld, the "outside" is "constitutive" in a more direct and material way.

to be confined within our own bosoms; it burnishes all nature, and with its vivid colouring gives a kind of factitious life to objects without sense or motion. There cannot be a more striking proof of the social tendency of these feelings, than the strong propensity we have to suppose auditors where there are none. (*Works* 2.428)

Barbauld is discussing a social component of all joy—ancient and modern—that compels people to imagine other presences about them, even in lonely, unpopulated, or uncultivated spaces.[5] That basic structure of mental experience is, as it was for Lowth's more solipsistic version, rooted in the type of poetic activity that characterizes Hebrew poetry. "Hence," she writes, "the Royal Shepherd, sojourning in caves and solitary wastes, calls on the hills to rejoice and the floods to clap their hands; and the lonely poet, wandering in the deep recesses of uncultivated nature, [. . .] swells his chorus of praise with the winds that bow the lofty cedars."[6]

Barbauld takes some pains here to redescribe animistic projection as a surplus of social sympathy rather than as a deficit. As in Lowth's description, the individual mind imposes itself on the external world. However, where Lowth describes an "agitated" mind overpowered by its own strong feeling, Barbauld sees the ordinary mind as "forcibly carried out of itself."[7] What Lowth describes as an immersion in one's own interiority, Barbauld calls an "embrac[e]" of "the whole circle of animated existence" (428). Projecting these moods is a mistake, to be sure, but it is a mistake that derives very clearly from a positive "social tendency" rather than a narcissistic error or an inability to do anything besides default to one's own feelings. It is the activity of an outward-directed, sociable mind rather than an introspective, self-absorbed one.

Barbauld deployed this reworking of Lowth's poetic theory in her entry into the 1790s "public worship controversy," a pamphlet war about whether and to what extent religious experience required weekly, public church services.[8] Her target was Gilbert Wakefield, who had in 1791 announced his decision to stop attending church altogether and to pursue instead a fully private, individual mode of devotion. Wakefield defended himself by publishing *An Enquiry into the Expediency and Propriety of Public or Social Worship*, which he dedicated to Barbauld's brother, John Aikin. In at least one place Wakefield aimed his argument explicitly against Barbauld's own earlier essay, "Thoughts

---

5. On Barbauld's "joy" see Adam Potkay, *The Story of Joy* 150.
6. *Works* 2.429. Barbauld is likely thinking of Psalms 98:8 and 29:5, respectively.
7. Lowth, *Lectures* 38; Barbauld, *Works* 2.428.
8. On Barbauld's involvement in the "public worship controversy" see Laura Mandell, "Prayer, Feeling, Action."

on the Devotional Taste." In short, Wakefield explains his controversial decision by arguing that public church services were an increasingly obsolete vestige of primitive or unenlightened religion.[9] He offers a broad survey of Christian history, arguing that the continual progress of the faith from the "infancy" of idolatry to its emerging "manhood" would, in the end, arrive at a "pure system of mere rational and intellectual religion."[10] For Wakefield, that purification of religious experience required the sublimation of "material impressions and manual services" and also a turn away from the public, social context in which such "ceremonial observances" took shape (9–10). In short, Wakefield's convictions about a privatized, modern devotion follow a familiar account of secularization: He argues that religion improves over time by becoming less material; less indebted to shared, social ritual; and more tightly linked to inner, private experience.[11] Taking religious experience as an index to human mental development more broadly, Wakefield tells a story that begins in "infancy," in which individual minds lean heavily on the social body, external institutions, and collective ritual; and from which they advance toward an adulthood marked by greater autonomy from the social and material trappings he describes in terms of the "public," the "social," and (more polemically) "fanaticism" (9).[12] The ultimate arrival at maturity, per this account, would not just be a liberation from materiality, ritual, and dogma, but an individual's disentanglement from a herdlike social body.

Wakefield's picture of a reformed future state grated strongly against the benevolist principles of his Dissenting compatriots. As a result, many of his critics found themselves making uncharacteristically reactionary defenses of public ritual and tradition. Mary Hays, for example, emphasized the continued usefulness of materiality and ritual and proposed that the sort of secular sublimation Wakefield proposed, while conceivably a worthy goal, was far too ambitious for the average person.[13] Barbauld had elsewhere made a similar, surprising defense of material religion in her defense of monastic insti-

---

9. For a concise overview of the argument and its background, including Wakefield's engagement with Aikin and Barbauld see William McCarthy, *Anna Letitia Barbauld* 312–19.

10. Wakefield, *Enquiry* 7–8.

11. For an influential challenge to this idea—that secularization entails as the privatization of religion—see José Casanova, *Public Religions in the Modern World*.

12. Wakefield still frames this maturity in terms of social relations: The modern religious subject still cultivates philanthropy and has a relationship with the deity that does not resemble that of "a *master* with his *servant*" but of "a *parent* with his *child*" (6–7). Nevertheless, for Wakefield, primitive sociability is something that needs to be refined, reduced, and reoriented.

13. On the relation between Barbauld's and other responses, including Hays's see McCarthy, *Anna Letitia Barbauld* 313.

tutions.[14] In this case, though, what Barbauld found most dangerous about Wakefield's argument was his dismissal of the social and collective scene.[15] In response, she does not merely assert the continued usefulness of "public or social worship" but also revises Wakefield's account of the history of civilization. Sociability—even apparently excessive or confused sociable acts like animistic projection—are not primitive errors to outgrow but a foundational part of the mind's origin it must retain. In the language of developmental theory, earlier developmental phases could not be fully outgrown or definitively set aside.

At issue, then, was a disagreement about the natural history of sociability. Unlike Robert Lowth and Hugh Blair, who tended to picture the primitive mind as originally solitary or egoistic, both Wakefield and Barbauld saw the human mind as originally sociable. For Wakefield, though, that meant that exuberant sociability was a feature of humanity's childhood, something that needed to be tempered, restrained, and to some degree outgrown. Barbauld, on the other hand, thought that the unthinking, confused social urges of an uncultivated mind were actually compelling evidence that sociability was a fundamental or foundational part of the human frame, something it could never outgrow. This is the commitment that lies behind her turn to the figure of the ancient poet, projecting feelings onto the landscape. In her descriptions of the "Royal Shepherd" who "calls on the hills to rejoice and the floods to clap their hands," and of "the lonely poet, wandering in the deep recesses of uncultivated nature" who "swells his chorus of praise with the winds that bow the lofty cedars," Barbauld is careful to avoid Lowth's implication that these are merely narcissistic errors (428–29). Instead, she sources such projections of emotion both to the sheer strength of overflowing feeling, and to the mind's basic, foundational impulse to share feeling with a social audience.

As this introductory example shows, Barbauld was among those eighteenth-century thinkers who made ancient poetry into evidence about the mind's foundational powers. Yet she was also deeply committed to a tradition that saw the early existence of sociability in quite different, less innatist terms, like those of Adam Ferguson. Accordingly, this chapter will be equally indebted to scholarship on Barbauld's benevolism (her conviction that the mind has native propensities that motivate it, via social feeling, toward moral

---

14. See Barbauld's essay "On Monastic Institutions" in Aikin and Aikin, *Miscellaneous Pieces in Prose* 88–118.

15. Among Wakefield's critics, as McCarthy has shown, Barbauld was the most invested in rescuing the social facet of worship, as evidenced by the way her response, unlike others, turned to moral sense theory (McCarthy 313).

relations with others), and to scholarship on her broader interests in the history and development of society, from conjectural histories of language and literature to progress-oriented histories of civilization.[16] Her poetic career blends the study of the mind's inner, socially capable structure with the more externalist focus on how minds develop by utilizing cultural scaffolding.

The argument of the chapter, then, is that Barbauld and others in her circle tried to balance their commitment to innate sociability—which could commit them to a logic of innate abilities or drives—with this more radically open or contingent account of mental functioning and growth. Nancy Yousef has described this alternative to Enlightenment autonomy as a precursor to more recent "relational" or "communitarian" theories of personal identity.[17] In my argument, Barbauld's particular reworking of Scottish Enlightenment developmental theories does something slightly different and winds up picturing the mind as what philosophers would now call *embedded*: Rather than an inner, discrete, and separate processing center, Barbauld and others in her circle saw the mind in both internalist and externalist terms—as physiologically rooted but nevertheless dependent on external scaffolding structures and on the social and technological environment.[18] To that end, the first section of the chapter will establish a philosophical and medical context for Barbauld's ideas about the mind's structure and development. The second section turns to her engagement with conjectural histories of language and of poetic development. The final section examines her imitations and reworkings of oral poetics in ways that brought together her understanding of the originally social mind and the socially scaffolded mind.

"MIND, EMBODIED AND EMBEDDED": BARBAULD, AIKIN, PRIESTLEY

While Barbauld's writings on mental development are often seen primarily as theories of pedagogy, they were rooted in, and contributed to, a broader dis-

---

16. On Barbauld's links to the benevolist tradition see, for example, Anne Janowitz, "Amiable and Radical Sociability," and Isobel Armstrong, "Anna Letitia Barbauld." For a study of Barbauld in relation to Adam Ferguson and other historians of civil society see Jonathan Sachs, *The Poetics of Decline in British Romanticism* 103–18.

17. Yousef, *Isolated Cases* 14ff.

18. The term "embedded mind" dates back at least to John Haugeland's "Mind, Embodied and Embedded." I use the term "scaffolding" here in keeping with its usage in embedded theories of mind, a usage that in turn derives from the way psychology and pedagogical theory have developed Lev Vygotsky's theories of learning. For a foundational example see David Wood, Jerome S. Bruner, and Gail Ross, "The Role of Tutoring in Problem Solving."

course about the mind's physiological foundations and social entanglements. The wider purchase of these writings has been better recognized in recent years, as the notion of a Barbauld circle (or, sometimes, a "Barbauld-Aikin" or "Aikin family" circle) has become an anchor for studies of Dissent as an interdisciplinary network. The groups of writers connected to the Dissenting academies at Warrington and Palgrave included poets, physicians, scientist, theologians, and educationalists, including those who, like John Aikin (Barbauld's brother) or Joseph Priestley (their close acquaintance), produced work under almost all of those headings.[19] Increased attention to the networked nature of knowledge, and the way it cross-pollinated the work of the different disciplines then still in formation, has made it easier to see a writer like Barbauld as central to scientific discourses rather than as merely engaging with them at arm's length. It is not merely that Barbauld wrote poems addressing Joseph Priestley in his laboratory; or, to use a different case, that Joanna Baillie compared dramatic spectatorship to medical observation.[20] Nor is it even merely that both of them had brothers who were practicing surgeons, and that they therefore lived on the periphery of the medical world. Rather, it is becoming easier to see poetry, cultural history, and natural philosophy as fundamentally overlapping discourses and as occupying the same shared interdisciplinary spaces. As Noah Heringman has noted, the whole orientation of the Warrington Academy curriculum—including Barbauld's framing of it in her poem "The Warrington Academy"—"integrates natural history with literature and the professions" in the manner traditionally associated with polymaths like Erasmus Darwin.[21] In a similar spirit, Jayne Lewis has examined the close connection between Priestley's chemistry and his theory of grammar.[22] Kathryn Ready has likewise examined John Aikin as a "literary physician" who saw the sciences and poetry as intimately linked and who announced that connection in his *Essay on the Application of Natural History to Poetry*.[23] Aikin, moreover, wrote in similar ways about the history of literary form and the history

---

19. For examples of the ways Barbauld's circle (or the Aikin family circle) has been placed at the center of British Dissenting culture see Daniel E. White, *Early Romanticism and Religious Dissent*, and Felicity James and Ian Inkster, eds., *Religious Dissent and the Aikin-Barbauld Circle, 1740–1860*.

20. See Baillie, *Plays on the Passions* 67–113.

21. Heringman, *Romantic Rocks, Aesthetic Geology* 207. For John Guillory's reading of Barbauld's "The Warrington Academy" in terms of canonicity and the professions, to which Heringman is here responding see Guillory, *Cultural Capital* 103–7. On Erasmus Darwin as offering an integrated account of the arts and sciences see Martin Priestman, *The Poetry of Erasmus Darwin*; Griffiths, *The Age of Analogy* 51–82; and Dahlia Porter, *Science, Form, and the Problem of Induction in British Romanticism* 73–112.

22. Lewis, *Air's Appearance*.

23. Kathryn Ready, "'And make thine own Apollo doubly thine.'"

of medicine, and he prescribed best practices for maintaining the sanitary airs of hospitals as well as for improving poetic diction.

The synthesizing spirit of these writings has been framed not as a new, emerging interdisciplinarity but as a set of "predisciplinary encounters" between disciplines still relatively early in their professional separation.[24] But there is evidence that such crossings within the Barbauld circle were already experienced as the production of a new interdisciplinary synthesis. In her 1825 memoir of Barbauld, for example, Lucy Aikin could retrospectively describe her aunt's most innovative teaching methods as creating such moments of confluence. Barbauld framed geography (which Lucy Aikin calls "a study seldom interesting to children") as a unifying field of sorts, one that encompassed "the connexion of this branch of knowledge with the revolutions of empire, with national manners, and with the natural history of animals."[25] This broadly integrated view of cultural history and natural history came, in large part, from Scottish Enlightenment writers such as Adam Ferguson and Adam Smith, whose developmentalist accounts of society's progress and decline provided a vocabulary for weaving together individual mental development and broader cultural development.

Barbauld was also immersed throughout her life in specific discussions about the mind's physiological growth and its physical foundations, discussions that were rooted in both philosophy and practical medicine. During the years in which the Aikin siblings were most active in their literary collaborations, John was also undertaking his medical training and, subsequently, practicing as a physician. In 1781, he printed "A Sketch of the Animal Economy," a short primer written for use by students at Warrington's Dissenting academy. The "Sketch" provides a basic outline of practical anatomy and physiology, beginning with the announcement that the medical field has reached a basic consensus that the mind is intimately connected with the body's organs. He notes that "it is agreed that the brain is a gland for the secretion of the *animal spirits*" which are then conveyed by the nerves. Then he more tentatively puts forth the latest, equivocal word on the material hypothesis: "It is conjectured that these spirits are a very subtle fluid; but no such has ever been discovered by the senses" (23–24). There is a gap, it seems, between the medical community's consensus that the brain "secrete[s]" the animal spirits, and this type of ensuing "conjecture" that the spirits themselves were material. More prag-

---

24. See Calè and Craciun; and Heringman, *Sciences of Antiquity*. As Michael McKeon has put it, formative moments of disciplinary division, in which scholars stake out their own disciplinary territory, frequently "appear intertwined with a synthesizing counter-movement" ("The Origins of Interdisciplinary Studies" 18).

25. In Barbauld, *Works* 1.xxvi–xxvii.

matically speaking, Aikin then describes the nerves first as a system of tubes that convey a vital fluid to all parts of the body, and subsequently, using the language of energy and impression, states, "The nerves are a set of conductors, by which the energy of the brain is conveyed to all parts of the body, and which carry back to the brain the sense of all impressions made upon those parts" (24). This picture of the brain and nervous system would have been generalized enough to allow for David Hartley's model of the nerves as a vibratory medium, or to allow for the beliefs of the previous generation of Leiden-educated physiologists, like Robert Whytt and Albrecht von Haller, who pictured the nerves as fluid-filled tubes.

This physiological psychology was consistent with the way that Barbauld, and the broader Dissenting network in which she lived and worked, understood human mental action. Crucially, its effect was not just to enclose minds in particular, self-contained bodies and bundles of nerves. Rather, the mind's close connection with the body was also the basis for seeing it as extending *beyond* the confines of the individual corporeal frame. A decade earlier, in 1771, Aikin had published his *Thoughts on Hospitals,* a brief for reforming hospitals on the principle that the vital spirits of the brain were intimately connected with, and could be contaminated by, "the corrupt air of a crowded hospital" (27). To that end, he writes:

> The danger of bad air in fractures of the skull, is a particular observation of antient date. These have not only the general unfavourable circumstances of compound fractures, but the aggravated evil of a disordered brain and nerves. The fatality of this accident in private practice is melancholy, but to a much greater degree in hospitals. (26)

According to Aikin's account, hospitals are spaces in which the mind is, in a very literal and material way, opened up through injury and in which damage to the body's physical integrity (here, the "fractures of the skull") threatens to influence and "disorder" the mental operations via the "brain and nerves." In fact, Aikin writes, the body in general can have its "fluids vitiated by steeping in a morbid atmosphere," until "the whole body will become in some measure assimilated to the putrefactive ferment in the mortified parts and will readily imbibe and spread its contagion" (27). The fact that the hospital is "crowded"—that it is a social space of interpersonal contact—heightens the basic, physiological fact of the body's entanglement with its environment, and its existence as a system of circulating and mixing fluids, be they the subtle fluids of the nerves, the circulation of the blood, or the surrounding and commingling airs.

As Jayne Lewis has shown with regard to Joseph Priestley's experiments with oxygen, thinking about airs, atmospheres, and environmental mediation had ready-made links in these circles because of David Hartley's approach to mental vibrations. Hartley's name was linked to an ecological account of the mind, which saw minds as immersed in a social and material environment. Thinking is tied to and mediated through the brain and nerves as, for Aikin, health is mediated through airs.[26] Isobel Armstrong has helpfully explained how Hartley made possible a porous or open picture of the mind—in specifically literary terms—by turning to the discourse of the sublime. Armstrong argues that, unlike the Burkean sublime—an encounter with something that exceeds the mind's physiological capacities—Barbauld tends to picture sublime experience as an occasion for the mind to stretch and reshape itself as it forges a new associative frame of reference for the previously unconceivable. Accordingly, in Barbauld's poem "A Summer Evening's Meditation," contemplating the night sky is not the occasion for sheer stupefaction, but for a pleasing "vastness that expands the mind."[27] As in Joseph Priestley's writings on the subject, the sublime is not "an agent of terror and oppression" but an agent of the mind's growth and expansion (66).

I would add to Armstrong's account that the most sublime experience Barbauld invokes in "A Summer Evening's Meditation"—the contemplation of the infinite—helps bring about not just a new frame of reference for thinking about the cosmos but also a new kind of social, interpersonal attitude. What the poem forges in its climactic moment of starry conjecture, after all, is a new mode of relating to God as experienced *in* the cosmos, a personal deity addressed via the apostrophe "oh thou mighty mind!" (96). This type of interpersonal, relational stance was fundamental to Barbauld's writings on religion, which often drew on the analogical reasoning of the natural theology but which first and foremost saw religious devotion as grounded in the social affections, or "devotional taste."[28] To that end, the poem also describes the stretching, enlarging mind in terms of the "swelling heart"—a sensibility carried out of itself in the same way as the animistic poet, by a disposition to view the system of nature as a mind like its own.[29]

---

26. Jayne Lewis, *Air's Appearance* 190–218.

27. Isobel Armstrong, "Anna Letitia Barbauld" 66–67. See Barbauld, "A Summer Evening's Meditation," in *Selected Poetry and Prose* 98–102.

28. See "Thoughts on the Devotional Taste," in *Selected Poetry and Prose* 209–34.

29. Arguments of this sort existed on a wide spectrum, from Hutcheson's "moral sense" theory (based on a sentimentalist theory of the moral passions) to the teleological argument on offer in William Paley's *Natural Theology*. Barbauld's writing shows marks of both, though she eventually "lost much of her faith in Hutcheson" and "inscribed Paley's name, not Hutcheson's, in *Eighteen Hundred and Eleven*'s pantheon of British greats" (McCarthy, *Anna Letitia Barbauld*

David Hartley had a term for this emergent, personal stance people learned to take toward the world. He termed it *theopathy*, a cultivated social feeling directed toward the deity.[30] In fact, Hartley saw all such social attitudes as emergent properties of the mind—as things that were in no way present in early life but that became possible only as associations accrued in the sensorium, and experience built up an increasingly complex and ordered system. For Hartley, we begin with bare object-sensation and basic feelings, and gradually our storehouse of ideas becomes more complex. At those higher-orders of complexity, in turn, we become capable of new feelings. Read this way, the sublime would be the aesthetic property that attended those moments of emergence: in the scene rehearsed in "A Summer Evening's Meditation," a new type of social orientation.

Yet another impulse at work in this Dissenting approach to the open mind—overlapping at times with Hartley's developmental account of the mind but in many ways incompatible with it—can be sourced back to the "moral sense" school of Hutcheson and, more recently still, the "common-sense" school of Reid. Hutcheson's influence on the Aikin-Barbauld circle is well documented. He was the major influence on their benevolist habits of argument, which frequently argued from the premise of natural sociability and philanthropic feeling.[31] Hutcheson held that the mind possessed basic abilities or predispositions that were like "internal senses" and that made possible the kinds of thinking required both for aesthetic judgments (the sense of beauty) and for interpersonal relations (the moral sense).[32] A Hutchesonian reading of the social sublime would see those moments of stretching not as ruptures or moments of emergence, but as the exercise of faculties that were always already there; or, to adapt a metaphor Hutcheson and Barbauld both frequently use, that resembled the plantlike growth of properties latent, but already present, in the seed. That version of a social sublimity has very different stakes. The difference is between, on the one hand, theories of the mind's eventual, emergent, and (with Hartley, at least) providential and inevitable capacity for benevolent feeling; and, on the other hand, theories that altruistic motivation and social concern were primary and foundational to cognition in general.

Barbauld's more overtly benevolist, Hutchesonian writings, such as her essay "Thoughts on the Devotional Taste," place greater emphasis on the mind's

---

459). For a reading of natural theology as it operates in Barbauld's broader poetic output, including "A Summer Evening's Meditation," see Colin Jager, *The Book of God* 73–101.

30. "Pleasures and Pains of Theopathy," in David Hartley, *Observations on Man* 1.486–92.

31. See McCarthy, *Anna Letitia Barbauld* 15–16.

32. Francis Hutcheson, *An Inquiry Concerning Beauty, Order, Harmony, Design.*

original, innate principles and dispositions. In that essay, Barbauld argues that religious devotion was and ought to be grounded in the natural, benevolent emotions and in dispositions and propensities that were not merely developed later through experience but were "in a great degree constitutional."[33] A glance back at John Aikin's *Thoughts on Hospitals* shows that there, too, the language of a Hartleian providential future was commingled with the language of implanted or foundational principles—terms that, even more readily than to Hartley, would have been second nature to Aikin given his commitments to medical philanthropy and the spirit of universal benevolence. Specifically, Aikin draws an analogy between the airs that circulate in a hospital and an atmospheric description of society at large, where shifting, commingling airs become a model of social reform and reorganization. "The universal diffusion of this amiable spirit," he writes, is what will ultimately conduce to the improvement of hospital conditions, as the contagious spirit of philanthropy opens up a utopian horizon of social amelioration (6).

This conviction in the inevitable and universal progress toward social perfection overlapped substantially with Hartley's own "system of optimism."[34] But Aikin goes on to write in quite different terms about the reason why such a universal diffusion is inevitable:

> To counterbalance the various evils and miseries of life, Providence has planted in our natures a benevolent principle, which, without waiting for duty to incite, or reason to approve, inclines us by an involuntary emotion to relieve the distresses of our fellow-creatures, and gives us the purest and most sensible pleasure for our reward. (5)

It is possible that the differences between Hutcheson's and Hartley's brands of providentialism may not matter for Aikin's purposes here or that asserting the naturalness and innateness of benevolent motivations is simply more rhetorically useful. But it also suggests that, at least to its later eighteenth-century adherents, it was easy to blend a Hartleian "ecological" account of mental development with an older, Hutchesonian language of innate abilities. Moreover, while this language of an implanted benevolent principle was a phrasing

---

33. Barbauld, *Selected Poetry and Prose* 211.
34. The "system of optimism" is Samuel Taylor Coleridge's shorthand for the necessitarian system of Hartley and Priestley, with which he had a notoriously inconsistent relationship. On Coleridge's relation to the "system of optimism" see David Vallins, *Coleridge and the Psychology of Romanticism* 103ff. In terms of Hartley's attractions and shortcomings for Coleridge see Richardson, *British Romanticism* 9–12.

Hartley himself pointedly objected to in his remarks on the human frame, it was a terminology he flirted with in the second volume of his *Observations on Man*—the half of the treatise that was famously dedicated to theological and providential speculations and that Priestley omitted in his 1775 abridgement.[35] Hartley writes there of "The Voice of Conscience, or the moral Sense, within a Man, *however implanted or generated,*" and, after leaving that method of generation open, suggests that the ability itself "bears Witness [. . .] to the moral Rectitude of that universal Cause from whom it must proceed ultimately" (2.40, my emphasis). Passages like this show how Hartley was actively accommodating an older benevolism into a new language, one that made the moral dimension of the universe a matter of final causes, not something internal to the mind's original, internal makeup.

Peter Kivy has argued that, in the long run, "associationism was instrumental in rendering obsolete" that older vocabulary of an innate moral sense, since it made social and moral capabilities emerge from the raw materials of sensation rather than positing numerous, additional inner senses.[36] However, in practice, as the Barbauld circle's writings show particularly clearly, the two paradigms continued to have considerable overlap for quite some time. For Priestley, Hartley seems to have offered a way to do justice to both the mind's inward embodiment and its environmental contingency. To John Aikin, associationism was able to loosen the boundary between mind and world without completely letting go of the anatomist's more essentializing desire to map out the mind's physiological basis and its built-in dispositions. He could read Hartley as bridging anatomy and natural benevolence. In other words, in arguments about moral philosophy and political reform, there remained a strong drive among Dissenters to assert that principles like sociability or philanthropy were, indeed, implanted or innate parts of the human frame. While we have good accounts of the way that the Barbauld circle understood the mind to be mediated, or predicated on Hartleian expansion and growth, those porous or networked accounts of the mind did not preclude them from also hanging onto an older, more internalist Hutchesonian account of native propensities or abilities.

---

35. Hartley explicitly rejects the idea of "an original, instinctive, implanted Nature" in *Observations on Man* 1.455.

36. For the argument that associationism spelled the doom of moral sense theory see Peter Kivy, *The Seventh Sense* 182.

INWARD FACULTIES, OUTWARD SCAFFOLDING: FROM REID TO BARBAULD

The desire to have it both ways—to affirm the inwardly grounded, "constitutional" nature of social and moral feeling and at the same time to picture the mind's basic activities as *less* internal—led Barbauld and others to retain the language of moral sense in a new intellectual microclimate increasingly focused on associationism. It would also explain why Barbauld often echoes the commonsense philosophers for whom her friend Joseph Priestley had so little patience. For both Reid and Barbauld, this section of the chapter will suggest, moral sense theory needed to be updated. For both of them, updating it in the right way could actually open the mind up to the world further, in ways that even Hartleian associationism could not.

As the previous chapter described, Reid took aim directly at what he called the "way of ideas," the assumption that the mind's main vehicles of knowledge were representational tokens in the sensorium. Instead of that type of inner processing, Reid proposed a "direct realist" account of perception: The basic array of mental acts—perceiving an object, attributing an intention to another person, making moral judgments—were better described as transactional relationships between the mind and the world.[37] The "conceptions" with which Reid replaces "ideas" are, after all, a peculiar type of mental content—one that that by definition exists only partly in the mind itself and, more properly speaking, resides in the external object. For all that it seems to be a more strongly internalist or nativist theory, then, Reid's account of the power of "conception" also made it possible to see mental content as partly external to the mind itself. Reid's enumeration of those abilities was aimed, in the first place, to explode the notion that the mind processes inner representations of outward events and to entangle the mind and world more thoroughly than any theory that relied upon representational ideas.

We might, then, see the debate that ensued between Reid and Priestley in terms of a conflict between two competing ways of bringing the mind back into contact with the physical world around it. It makes sense that Priestley, the defender and popularizer of Hartley's associationism, reacted so strongly against Reid's common sense: What Reid derided as the "way of ideas" was the very model of the mind that Hartley was suturing to the nerves. Priestley followed Hartley by picturing the sensorium as a single, streamlined processing

---

37. On the relation between Reid's nativism and his natural realism see Edward H. Madden, "Was Reid a Natural Realist?" On his realist theories of perception see Keith Lehrer, "Conception without Representation, Justification without Inference," and Keith DeRose, "Reid's Anti-Sensationalism and His Realism."

center, which was corporeally influenced and shaped by the external environment. Reid's theory of direct perception, in contrast, makes all of the mind's activities more external, but at the cost of building in a wide array of foundational, built-in abilities—what Priestley, in his 1774 critique of Reid's *Inquiry*, called "unconnected instinctive principles."[38] Priestley went so far as to produce a "Table of Dr. Reid's instinctive principles" which maps out the array of abilities Reid had posited, including specialized faculties for detecting external properties of the world like "hardness"; the ability to use "articulations of the voice, and attitudes of the body" to recognize other people's mental states; and the "sense of credulity, or a disposition to believe others."[39] As the focus on "credulity" indicates, one of Priestley's suspicions was that Reid had simply added these innate faculties into his account of human nature as an excuse to leave received views unchallenged. For Priestley, Reid's major liability was his easy confidence that the world works the way we have always assumed it to work, and this was a type of confidence that went right down to Reid's core epistemological claim that an object "compels our belief."[40]

This relationship to belief characterizes Barbauld's writings, too. This way of looking at Reid has led some to connect him to more recent "reliabilist" philosophies of knowledge, which are grounded in a basic commitment that our processes of knowing the world and other people (while not infallible) can at least be trusted, in principle, as plausible modes of transaction. Tim Milnes has glossed Reid and other eighteenth-century writers in just this way, as part of a later eighteenth-century turn away from skeptical empiricism and toward a hermeneutics of "trust."[41] That "reliabilist" attitude is one of the main things Barbauld shares with Reid and is the main reason she so often seems to echo his argumentative strategies. While she does not name Reid in her writings or have a particular stake in his mechanics of perception, Barbauld's writings on the mind and its growth are broadly infused with the principles of common sense. First, her nods toward natural sociability regularly make benevolence and credulity into "constitutional" parts of the human frame. Second,

---

38. Priestley, *An Examination of Dr. Reid's Inquiry* 7.

39. Priestley, *Examination* 7. For an overview of this debate see the chapter "'Common-Sense' and Associationism," in Robert E. Schofield, *The Enlightened Joseph Priestley* 43–58. On "credulity" see Schofield 49.

40. Reid's statement "Sensation compels our belief of the present existence of a thing" is the first direct quotation Priestley makes from Reid's *Inquiry* following the table of instincts (Priestley, *Examination* 10). For a discussion of Reid's relationship to reliabilist epistemology see Philip de Bary, *Thomas Reid and Scepticism*.

41. On Romantic theories of communicative rationality as proto-pragmatist see Tim Milnes, *The Truth about Romanticism* (especially 45–46). On the idea of a hermeneutics of "trust" see Milnes, "Beyond Excess."

her turn to native faculties was very often a way to describe the mind as less self-contained and autonomous and more reliant upon the world around it. As for Reid, many of the mind's most important powers are versions of the same power: an underlying ability to rely upon a world that it trusts is there.

Barbauld adopts a stance that is, in that respect, much like Reid's; but she blends it with a Hartleian approach to the mind's embodied and environmental contingency and with Adam Ferguson's focus on the role of technological and social scaffolds in cognitive development. The result is a picture of the mind's thorough embeddedness in its natural and social environments. For Barbauld, in fact, some types of thought or belief need to be offloaded onto artifacts or other people. This picture of the mind's reliant or dependent nature is particularly clear in her writings on Enlightenment education and religious "prejudice," to which I now turn.

In March of 1800 the *Monthly Magazine* published an essay of Barbauld's titled "On Prejudice."[42] Like her other short essay, "What Is Education?" (1798), "On Prejudice" is an entry in late-century debates about pedagogical theory. The most surprising thing about the essay is that it is a *defense* of prejudice, in much the sense that Edmund Burke had used and defended that term in his *Reflections on the Revolution in France*.[43] Barbauld opens by criticizing those innovators who pursue progress for progress's sake: She alleges that the very reformers to whom "the world is ever to look for its improvement" are, paradoxically, those who are most liable to endanger the accomplishments of the past. Their problem, Barbauld writes, is that they "have divested their minds of that reverence which is generally felt for opinions and practices of long standing" (334). As she turns to the essay's primary subject, Barbauld recruits this Burkean traditionalism to a more targeted argument about the best means of educating children. While she is a proponent of experiential education, she is opposed to the idea that children ought to exercise full intellectual autonomy and is especially critical of recent arguments that educators ought to take pains to avoid prejudicing a child. "On Prejudice," in contrast, argues that children cannot always think for themselves and should certainly not be left to form their own opinions: Their physical and intellectual safety requires that they let others do a good deal of their thinking for them. Barbauld's rationale is that there are some types of knowledge that do not permit experimental discovery: "A child may be allowed to find out for himself that boiling water will scald his fingers," she writes, "but he must be *prejudiced* against rats-bane," or other poisons, "because the experiment will be too costly" (344).

---

42. See Barbauld, *Selected Works* 333–45.

43. Burke's *Reflections* presents his defense of prejudice—indeed, his insistence that the English "cherish" their prejudices precisely "because they are prejudices" (87).

For Barbauld, "prejudice" thus conceived is not just a developmental stage marked by a lack of maturity or independence. It is also a positive principle and a constitutional part of the way the mind works and grows. Barbauld specifies that there are "two principles deeply implanted in the mind of man, without which he could never attain knowledge—curiosity, and credulity" (341). "Curiosity" was the core mental principle Burke had earlier, in his inquiry into the sublime and beautiful, identified as "the simplest emotion which we discover in the human mind."[44] While Burke, too, had there identified numerous "ideas, axioms, and rules" that had been "implanted in us by Providence," by coupling Burkean curiosity with Reidian credulity here, Barbauld is grafting together Burke's traditionalism and Reid's common sense. As William McCarthy has suggested, Barbauld deploys the term *credulity* precisely in Reid's sense. Moreover, he suggests that Barbauld may have even been the anonymous author of the more targeted "Remarks on the Principle of Credulity" that appeared in the *Monthly Magazine* in 1803.[45] Lest we mistake what she means by calling credulity an "implanted" principle in "On Prejudice," she goes on to assert its innate, constitutional character by asserting that "the credulity of a child to those who cherish him" is an "instinct" and moreover "one of the most useful instincts he has" (341).

This turn to the external domain of prejudice—and its surprising link back to an inner domain of instinct—was not a new development for Barbauld, or really even a departure from her earlier empirical, sentimentalist account of religious feeling. It had long had a place in that sentimentalist theory, by the same logic according to which Burke had made sentiment the grounds of trust in tradition. In 1775 Barbauld had published her "Thoughts on the Devotional Taste" as the preface to a collection of psalms.[46] The essay became controversial because of the way that it sought to naturalize religion by rooting it in principles of taste. In the year following Priestley's attack on Reid's system, and the year he began proselytizing Hartley's, Barbauld wrote "Thoughts on the Devotional Taste" to defend innate moral feeling (it is here that she first says that such feelings are "constitutional") and a Reidian propensity for trust.[47] Here in 1775, as later in "On Prejudice," Barbauld argues that overindulging in theological dispute or free-thought can damage the mind's built-in propensities. It disrupts the natural feelings on which devotion ought to be based and

---

44. Burke, *Philosophical Enquiry* 27.
45. See McCarthy, *Anna Letitia Barbauld* 380. For the anonymous piece see Anonymous, "Remarks on the Principle of Credulity." For McCarthy's tentative attribution to Barbauld see 624 n28.
46. In *Selected Poetry and Prose* 209–34.
47. Ibid. 211.

can thus be "prejudicial to the feelings of a devout heart" (213). "Prejudicial" is an interesting word to choose here, since it can alternately mean simply "detrimental or damaging" or can more specifically invoke external suasion, in the style the later essay recuperates.[48] One implication of Barbauld's argument is that the free-thinking debaters, more so even than dogmatic conservatives, are eviscerating the mind's natural resources. In her words, "a disputatious spirit, and a fondness for controversy, give the mind a sceptical turn, with an aptness to call in question the most established truths" (213). Importantly, then, for Barbauld the mind's natural disposition is to lend credence to those "established truths." This is the habit of belief that she will later, in "On Prejudice," align with a child's entirely appropriate and well-founded tendency to trust parental wisdom. In short, Barbauld's writings on prejudice combine a Reidian "commonsense" approach to innate credulity with a Burkean approach to the external, traditional, and culturally embedded institutions on which minds must rely and which they are constitutionally framed to require: parental prejudgment, traditional or "established" opinions, and other means by which already existing social structures scaffold and support the individual mind's growth. Remarkably, what Barbauld found in Hartley was something she also found in Burke.

For William McCarthy, the general tenor of Barbauld's thinking here makes her a forerunner to Heidegger, insofar as both are interested in thought's "enmeshment in time and place."[49] That "enmeshment" is increasingly a concern in the cognitive sciences, too, though, and Barbauld's remarks on education have much in common with recent "embodied-embedded" approaches to thinking and learning.[50] Theorists of the embedded mind argue that many cognitive tasks do not just draw on inner processes but are shaped and scaffolded by their social environment, as mediated through particular artifacts. Some paradigmatic examples in the literature include the way that tutors provide models and examples that a student can learn and internalize; or the way a bartender remembers a long list of drink orders by lining up the proper glassware in the proper order, treating the glasses as an external set of memory aids; or the way that actors in Shakespeare's Globe Theatre used the space of the theater itself as a set of prompts and cues that help them turn an only

---

48. "Prejudicial, adj., 1." *OED Online*, Oxford University Press, March 2007.

49. He suggests, in particular, that her remarks on Samuel Johnson's *Rasselas* could "read as a forecast of Heidegger" because of her focus on thought's "enmeshment in time and place" (642 n26).

50. For a deployment of Heidegger in the context of "embodied-embedded" approaches to cognitive science see Michael Wheeler, *Reconstructing the Cognitive World*.

partially seen script into a complete play.⁵¹ In each of these examples, the mind has its own internal resources, but also depends upon the affordances of the built environment and on learned traditions. More than some other varieties of "distributed" cognition, theories of the embedded mind seek to explain how individual thinkers make use of inherited or traditional resources. As philosophers Michael Wheeler and Andy Clark put it, the "cognitive niche" in which an individual develops involves "the cultural transmission of knowledge and practices resulting from individual lifetime learning," as those previous generations' learning is concretely instantiated due to the "physical persistence of artefacts."⁵² Hartley's associationism may have already been a theory of the embedded mind, since for him the material world does not merely impress itself on the sensorium but reshapes and restructures it in ways that grant it new, emergent abilities. By emphasizing the mind's reliance upon existing cultural institutions, and the beliefs supplied by one's parents and educators, Barbauld goes further and builds inherited, traditional, and artifactually mediated knowledge into her account of the mind's foundational powers.

A similar approach to cultural scaffolding is present in Barbauld's essay "On Monastic Institutions" (1773).⁵³ There, she turns to the gothic monastery, and medieval social institutions more broadly, as a progressive engine of development rather than a dark age of intellectual backsliding. While the monastery has been viewed as an oppressive institution, she argues, it was also an important repository of books and learning and functioned, in the long run, as a site of collective memory. So, she writes, "It is owing, to the books and learning preserved in these repositories, that we were not obliged to begin anew, and trace every art by slow and uncertain steps from its first origin. Science, already full grown and vigorous, awaked as from a trance [. . .] nor was she entirely idle during her recess"; but monastic practices of transcription, translation, and education were proceeding all the while (93). The monastery still stands, for Barbauld, as a vacant interval or a pause in the progress of knowledge. Yet it is as if "we," partaking in a collective progress of

---

51. On the skilled bartender see Michael Wheeler and Andy Clark, "Culture, Embodiment and Genes" 3564. On Shakespearean acting and distributed memory see Evelyn Tribble, *Cognition in the Globe*.

52. Wheeler and Clark, "Culture, Embodiment and Genes" 3564. The term "cognitive niche" comes from evolutionary biology but echoes the way that Barbauld and other eighteenth-century writers were seeking to integrate two different focuses of the Scottish Enlightenment human sciences: the mind's physiological development, on the one hand, and its scaffolded, culturally mediated development on the other. For an early formulation of the "cognitive niche," and the term's coinage, see John Tooby and Irven DeVore, "The Reconstruction of Hominid Behavioral Evolution through Strategic Modeling."

53. In Aikin and Aikin, *Miscellaneous Pieces in Prose* 88–118.

intellect, had been placed in a type of suspended animation from which we suddenly awaken. The collective knowledge of the monastery scaffolds and supports the development of individual thinkers, ensuring that "we" moderns did not have to "trace every art by slow and uncertain steps from its first origin." If parental prejudice is cognitive scaffolding for Barbauld, it is a very locally instantiated one. The monastery is a broader scaffold, with a wider historical and geographical ambit. It plays into a story about the resources available to a whole society and helps connect Barbauld's remarks on embedded learning to the broader histories of civilization and the idea of a "progress" of intellect. Ultimately, that Enlightenment discourse made both levels of scale part of the story: If society progressed over time, or passed through successive developmental stages, an individual mind's development could be accelerated by the cumulative weight of inherited artifacts, traditions, and tools. For Barbauld, as for Aikin and Priestley, this is where poetry enters the story most concretely.

DISSENT'S CONJECTURAL HISTORIES: LANGUAGE, LITERATURE, SCAFFOLDING

In Barbauld's intellectual networks, the approach to language itself as a scaffolding technology came to characterize a vast range of arguments about the origin and history of language and, more specifically, about the origin and history of poetry. Two representative texts that came from the Warrington circle, in particular, are Priestley's *Course of Lectures on the Theory of Language and Universal Grammar* (1762), which frames language as a tool for thinking that improves and drives social development; and the Aikin sibling collaboration *Essays on Song-Writing* (1772), a history of poetry by John Aikin to which Barbauld contributed some original poems. In an extension of the project of Percy's *Reliques,* Aikin's essays correlated minor forms of poetry with a society's increasing mental capacities. These histories of language and writing kept intellectual company less with Hutcheson's moral sense than with natural histories of society, like those by Rousseau, Herder, and Ferguson.

Discussions of the origins of poetic style in this period could be contentious. Some writers, in keeping with Lowth, argue that such patterned language arose early because of the primitive mind's weakness and need for memory aids. Priestley, for his part, says that they arise later, once language has grown more "copious." As for Herder, cries and gestures are natural, but, unlike Herder, for Priestley poetry is not really attached to human origins in any meaningful way. It develops only in comparatively advanced stages of society—that is, in highly developed oral cultures on the cusp of developing a culture of writing—and should be understood as the *result* of mental cultivation, not one of its foundational causes.[54] This argument is very different from the one Ferguson would make a few years later, when he declared that "art is natural to man" and that "the skill he acquire[s] after many ages of practice, is only the improvement of a talent he possessed at the first."[55] Priestley strongly denies that poetry captures, in any relevant sense, the earliest stages of language and thought. For Priestley, poetry was a mark of cultural development—a language that had grown "copious" enough to permit rhyme, variation, and formal complexity. In his *Course of Lectures* he writes:

> It cannot be supposed that *metre,* or *verse,* should have been introduced till a considerable time after prose had been in use. The latter is a matter of necessity, the former of ornament only. For *metrical composition* requires that words be placed in some regular order: so that the pronunciation of them may yield a kind of harmony. This, it is easy to see, requires some choice of words. Language, therefore, must not only have been formed, but have become pretty copious before it would admit of verse. (239)

When Priestley does sign onto the idea that poetry captures early phases of cognition, it is in the style of Blackwell and Lowth, who (as chapter 1 showed) align poetry's loose transitions and figurative tendencies with language's early sparseness. For Priestley, almost everything about poetic language serves a similar function: Poetic transitions between ideas are blunter because rude practitioners were not yet capable of smoother ones (159–60). To some degree, these aspects of poetic language are names for a linguistic crudity that is no longer permitted in cultured speech and that in more recent ages has been relegated to the domain of the literary. The result, then, is that poetry takes on a strange, intermediate temporality. It is the mark of a culture that has developed its language to a significant extent but is still restricted in its vocabulary; that has some measure of conceptual sophistication but is still primitive in its ideas and in its manner of connecting them. It comes down, as it so often does, to the passive-aggressive way conjectural history deals with Hebrew poetry and with Hebrew culture more broadly: as a celebrated cultural point of origin that also needed, in Christian supercessionist theology, to be marked as primitive or incompletely developed. For Priestley, biblical Hebrew marks a moment in linguistic development that was at once cultivated enough to

---

54. See Priestley's *Course of Lectures* 159–60.
55. Adam Ferguson, *Essay* 257.

produce poetry but that had still, paradoxically, "received little or no improvement" (160). The result, I would suggest, is a theory that makes poetry less an origin point, or a mark of the "natural" mind's original ways of thinking and feeling, and more a scaffolding technology, a mark of a still "barbarous" mind's gradual, incipient development.[56]

The Aikin siblings' collaborative entry in this conversation—the anonymously published *Essays on Song-Writing* (1772)—echoes both Priestley's *Lectures* of 1762 and Ferguson's *Essay* of 1767. The volume signs onto a dominant narrative of progress and decline influentially articulated at the end of Ferguson's *Essay*.[57] It also leaves behind any nostalgia for a heroic, precommercial society. The whole purpose of the volume is to defend song as a minor, intermediary form: unheroic but embellished; cultivated but not yet decadent. In short, the volume celebrates "song-writing" as a salutary middle state of intellectual, social, and poetic development. Accordingly, *Essays on Song-Writing* is not a collection of ancient poems or popular ballads but an attempt to develop an English canon of minor poetry. Aikin notes that "the chief sources of good songs, are the miscellany poems and plays from the time of Charles the second to the conclusion of Queen Ann's reign" (vi). This is the same era that Priestley had proposed the English language was "fixed" in a more stable, enduring form.[58] It also follows Priestley's conviction that poetry and music were coeval in all societies and thus work to two different, somewhat contradictory aims: Each essay is framed partly as a conjectural history of the origin of verbal art and partly as a manifesto for a particularly cultivated style of minor, musical poetry—"lyric," in other words, in that term's broader, eighteenth-century sense, which Virginia Jackson and others have aligned with a proliferation of minor forms and genres.[59] The fact that "song" had so far been neglected as poetry, Aikin writes, "will appear the more extraordinary when we reflect that some of the most excellent productions in the former"— presumably he is referring here to epic and dramatic poetry—"have been the spontaneous growth of a rude and uncultivated soil, whereas the latter have

---

56. We might, then, classify Priestley's theory of poetry as modernist (in the relevant sense of the term), since the value it placed on ancient poetry nevertheless looked toward a modernizing or developmental trend of which the arts were one manifestation and which continued developing into modernity. There is no theory of postclassical decline, and, in fact, *Course of Lectures* posits that language is still continuing on its course to a perfect "*philosophical and universal* language, which shall be the most natural and perfect expression of human ideas and sentiments" (7–8).

57. See Sachs, *Poetics of Decline* 63–64.

58. On Priestley's notion of language becoming "fixed," in connection with his chemical approach to "fixed airs" see Lewis, *Air's Appearance* 207–8.

59. See Virginia Jackson, *Dickinson's Misery* 7–8.

never flourished without acquired richness in the soil and the fostering hand of art" (1–2). Indeed, he goes on, it has been easier to class minor poems "under the general title of *Songs*" than to develop a nuanced taxonomy "of the minor classes of poetry" beyond "the long established divisions of ode, elegy and epigram" (2).

Like Priestley's, Aikin's orientation toward poetry here is firmly "modernist": Rather than return us to the earliest moment in human history, poetry arrives late and tracks the cultivation of mind, language, and manners. But this does not mean that Aikin can do without a conjectural history of human origins. His story still depends upon them. In fact, he states at the essay's outset, "The task of determining with exactness the nature of song-writing, and the various distinctions of which it is susceptible," requires that he return readers to an earlier moment in cultural history and, crucially, even to the mind's origins: "to go far back into the origin of poetry in general, and to recur to those first principles existing in the human mind, which alone can give a firm foundation to our deductions" (3). The allusion to first principles of mind affiliates the project of the *Essays on Song-Writing* with the empirical aesthetic tradition of Burke's *Enquiry*—and, moreover, with the Burkean-influenced essays in the following year's *Miscellaneous Pieces in Prose*. But Aikin is more explicit even than Burke that such a project requires a kind of conjectural time travel, "to go far back" into a story of origins. If it is a work of Burkean aesthetics, *Essays on Song-Writing* is after all more closely affiliated with the collections and theorization of "Ancient" poetry, songs, and ballads that proliferated in the wake of the Ossian phenomenon.

Barbauld contributed several songs to the *Essays on Song-Writing* volume, trying her hand at this state of cultivated but not quite modern verse. These were of a piece with her other experiments with the aesthetics of society's different developmental stages, whether in her celebrations of modern technology ("The Canal and the Brook," "Inscription for an Ice-House"), her gothic medievalism ("On Monastic Institutions," "Bertram: A Tale from the Gothic"), or her imitations of classical forms of ode and epic.[60] In the poetic texts to which I now turn, she also pushed back further in time to explore moments closer to a conjectural origin point. While her poem titled "The Origin of Song-Writing" gestures toward that idea, it actually offers a light-

---

60. Fiona Price notes that "though Barbauld, like Macpherson, Ferguson, and Blair, is drawn to the aesthetic qualities of an imagined 'primitive' society, she is also interested in the aesthetic appeal of later social stages, with supposedly more complex ideological and social structures," such as the gothic setting of "On Monastic Institutions" (*Revolutions in Taste, 1773–1818* 32).

hearted reworking of the idea of "origins."[61] In contrast with that mythic etiology, her poem "Seláma, an Imitation of Ossian" revisits and reimagines the early moment of poetic history Macpherson had brought into vogue with his 1760 *Fragments*.

BARBAULD'S ORALITY

JoEllen DeLucia has described how Ossianism (the popular imitation of Ossian and more general vogue for pseudo-antiquarian poetics in the later eighteenth century) carved out a particular space for women writers to experiment with the past and to produce alternate histories of society on antifoundationalist premises. For DeLucia, the appeal of Ossian was the way that it made it possible to imagine "an alternative British women's history located in the distant Scottish past."[62] For Barbauld, in her Ossianic poem, that meant sharpening the focus on female mourning and female agency that was already on offer in Macpherson's *Fragments*. Formally speaking, Barbauld's poem "Seláma" follows Macpherson's model of what these earliest poetic records ought to look like. Her poem has particular resemblance to the opening "Shilric, Vinvela" sequence of the 1760 *Fragments*.[63] The prose poem opens with a suggestion of a ghostly or animistic landscape: "What soft voice of sorrow is in the breeze?" (47). The speaker recognizes the title character, named as "maid of the mournful look," who is addressed or invoked as if a muse but whose voice, song, or cry remains an indirect background noise, heard on the wind. The dialogue is unmarked, and the reader must work to attribute voice to character in what turns out to be a dialogue. Seláma's tragic backstory is an ill-fated love intrigue with a characteristic Ossianic emphasis on weird, over-the-top forms of social intelligence already hyperactive at this primitive stage. For example, a jealous lover says to himself, thinking of his rival, "Seláma dwells in thy dark bosom—shall my steel enter there?" as if to suggest he intends to injure an inner representation of the beloved (51). Overall, the poem offers a variation on Ossianic melancholy and feminine disaffection in a culture of militaristic and amatory aggression.[64]

---

61. The poem is explicitly addressed "to the Author of Essays on Song-Writing" but presents a mythological origin story in which Cupid takes up music (*Works* 1.67–72).

62. DeLucia, "'Far Other Times Are These'" 45.

63. On that opening sequence see chapter 1. For Barbauld's "Seláma," see Aikin and Aikin, *Miscellaneous Pieces in Prose* 47–58.

64. For a reading of how Barbauld's "Seláma" "manipulate[s] tradition by emphasizing female agency" see Price, *Revolutions in Taste* 29–31.

As the above-quoted lines demonstrate, "Seláma" is written in what Blair called Ossian's "measured prose."[65] In Macpherson's poems, that had usually meant prose sentences whose grammatical clauses each contained three strong stresses and resembled a hexameter line with a medial caesura. As chapter 2 showed, the Ossian poems' resemblance to Lowth's Hebrew translations was alternately made evidence for their antiquity or their forgery.[66] Barbauld's "Seláma" keeps to the same general plan as Macpherson, with prose that falls into the rhythms of accentual meter. Her clauses vary more widely, containing anywhere from three to five stresses.[67] At Warrington in the 1770s and 1780s, the phrase "measured prose" meant something like the bare minimum that could count as prosody, a poetry that is just barely beginning to keep a pulse. The world of "Seláma" is already marked by complex social structures and modes of social recognition, and it shows the marks of a mind already thinking in measure and leaning upon emerging generic conventions. But for Barbauld, at least, measured prose stood for a moment in the history of poetry where there was a looser fit between the mind's rhythms and its collective, received forms.

Interestingly, Barbauld herself used Blair's phrase "measured prose" to describe her 1783 *Hymns in Prose for Children,* with which this chapter will conclude.[68] If "Seláma" replays an early, already sociable, and linguistically scaffolded moment in cognitive development, the *Hymns in Prose* use their "measured prose" to replay that early moment for modern children and to put scaffolding processes into practice. As previous sections of this chapter have shown, Barbauld (like many others in her intellectual network) put forward a developmental account of the mind that looked in two directions at once: inward, to the mind's material substrate and its innate or "implanted" abilities;[69] and outward, to the social and technological scaffoldings that guided and fed the mind's growth. That dual interest is clearest in her writ-

---

65. Blair, "Critical Dissertation" 399. Indeed, since it is a prose poem, and was designated as such by its inclusion in Aikin and Aikin, *Miscellaneous Pieces in Prose,* it has usually failed to make its way into accounts of Barbauld's poetic output or to be included in editions of Barbauld's poetry. Her *Works* (1825) includes it not under poetry but under "Miscellaneous Pieces."

66. See chapter 1.

67. See, for example, the three-stress clause and subsequent five-stress clause in the line "Thy grey locks are scatter'd, as a wreath of snow on the top of a wither'd trunk" (51). This approximation of accentual meter would become important to the gothic ballad revival, to which one of Barbauld's students—William Taylor—made an important early contribution with a translation of Gottfried August Bürger's "Lenora." On Taylor's appreciation for Barbauld as an instructor see Lucy Aikin's memoir in Barbauld, *Works* 1.xxv.

68. In Barbauld, *Selected Poetry and Prose* 234–60.

69. *Implanted* was a common term, especially among fans of moral-sense philosopher Francis Hutcheson, for built-in or divinely ordained features of the human constitution.

ings for children: namely, *Lessons for Children* (1778–79) and *Hymns in Prose for Children* (1781). This pair of texts roughly corresponded to the common schoolroom format in which basic reading lessons would be followed by the more complex business of religious instruction. Both books used simple language in order to meet children more or less at their own level.

In *Hymns in Prose*, in particular, Barbauld explicitly links this simple language to the mind's developmental stages and frames her educational text as offering a kind of guided recapitulation of society's development. Rowland has put this succinctly in her study *Romanticism and Childhood*, arguing that "a notion of infancy as the developmental origin of language and literature thus works to bring infants and infant language into the larger field of literary culture at the same time that it establishes the unspeaking, *infans* state of infancy as the original mystery of culture and communication" (135). Barbauld had in mind a language that would recapitulate early or rudimentary forms language—the "childhood of humanity," as well as the language of actual, eighteenth-century children—and would also provide a scaffolding structure to guide the further growth of the child's mind.

Barbauld justified her choice of prose style, as opposed to verse, by arguing that verse is a mark of more advanced linguistic and conceptual development, and that children are not yet ready for it. She writes, for example, that "it may well be doubted, whether poetry *ought* to be lowered to the capacities of children, or whether they should not rather be kept from reading verse, till they are able to relish good verse."[70] We can read this a few ways. Perhaps poetry did not exist in primitive society, if (as Priestley had argued) the early mind was incapable of verse in the same way that Barbauld supposes modern children to be. Or, in contrast, perhaps poetry does emerge during society's childhood, and children need to experience that process at their own pace. That would be in line with many theories of religious development: As in Wakefield's remarks on public worship that opened this chapter, or in Priestley's history of language, early societies were frequently said to have lacked concepts of divinity or to have passed through various material, superstitious, and idolatrous stages on their way to a mature theism. Yet according to Barbauld's argument, in the *Hymns in Prose*, parents should not require their children to recapitulate each stage of that earlier history for themselves.

Instead, as Barbauld had also suggested in "On Prejudice," parents and tutors should enable children to leap directly from infantlike thinking (a childlike obliviousness to God and poetry) to mature thinking (an awareness

---

70. *Selected Poetry and Prose* 237.

of God's presence and the ability to "relish" poetry). Indeed, on the former, theological point, Barbauld asserts:

> The peculiar design of this publication is, to impress devotional feelings as early as possible on the infant mind; fully convinced as the author is, that they cannot be impressed too soon, and that a child, to feel the full force of the idea of God, ought never to remember the time when he had no such idea. (*Selected Poetry and Prose* 238)

The logic here, in 1781, previews the basic argument that would structure "Of Prejudice" almost twenty years later. The young mind, too early in its development to conceptualize an idea as complex as a deity, needs to have that idea supplied externally in the meantime. Barbauld's phrasing in *Hymns in Prose* is some of her most explicitly associative and empiricist: Feelings must be "impressed' upon the individual mind, and the ultimate goal is to create a healthy, devout state of association by "connecting religion with a variety of sensible objects; with all that he sees, all he hears, all that affects his young mind with wonder or delight" (238). From one angle, this passage divulges the secret that the "natural" or instinctive nature of religious feeling is actually engineered, not "implanted" by God but "impressed" by parents and educators. From a different angle, though, Barbauld is emphasizing that association, as a theory of mental development, is not a purely natural or reliable process. It must be carefully managed. Like the different, instinctively credulous mind of "On Prejudice," the child reading hymns must rely not just on sensation, but on prejudices.

The very first hymn in the volume announces this plan, and this set of convictions, by catechistically placing it in the child's own mouth:

> I will praise God with my voice; for I may praise him, though I am but a little child.
>
> A few years ago, and I was a little infant, and my tongue was dumb within my mouth:
>
> And I did not know the great name of God, for my reason was not come unto me.
>
> But now I can speak, and my tongue shall praise him; I can think of all his kindness, and my heart shall love him. (239)

The child-speaker says (or rather is ventriloquized as saying) that the hymn is an expressive vehicle for spiritual knowledge and feelings, which the child is only just now able to understand and verbalize. From the point of view of the Christian pedagogue, this would have had particular implications both for the hymn's relation to Hebrew poetry and for its status as an instrument of public Christian worship.

That type of history, and the relation between Hebrew poetry and Christian public worship, invokes both the broad arc of history and the particular, local ways that poetry served as a technology of mental growth, as seen in the *Essays on Song-Writing* and Priestley's *Theory of Language*. Priestley, in particular, identifies Hebrew poetry as crucially important in the development of a language for religious concepts, yet as written at a point when "their language had received little or no improvement."[71] Lowth had gone to great lengths to vindicate the characteristic formal properties of Hebrew poetry, notably the use of parallelism between consecutive lines, and to set up Hebrew literature as an achievement in its own right, comparable to Greek or Latin literature. Hebrew poetry was indeed a complex poetry, Lowth argued, if the reader could see those formal features that were hidden in plain sight and that might appear as prose to the untrained eye. In Priestley's hands (and arguably Barbauld's, too), that proximity to prose could be made into evidence for a developmental arc, in which Hebrew literature shows the incipient marks of both "true religion" and authentically poetic diction.

In particular, this is the quasipoetic effect of the lines for which Barbauld adopts the term "measured prose," which she calls "nearly as agreeable to the ear as more regular rhythms" (238). A similar emphasis on parallelism and measured cadence rather than accentual-syllabic metrics had, we have seen, marked studies of Hebrew poetry and Macpherson's experiments in translating or imitating ancient Scottish poetry. In the opening lines of *Hymns in Prose*, in fact, "measuredness" looks like it might well mean parallelism, represented here by long lines divided by a caesura. That opening passage frequently deploys what Lowth called a "synthetic" parallelism: The second half of the line elaborates upon or extends, rather than merely repeats, the first half. The final line quoted above is a good example of more straightforward repetition-with-a-difference. Reformatted as two poetic lines, it would appear as:

> But now I can speak, and my tongue shall praise him;
>   I can think of all his kindness, and my heart shall love him. (239)

This does indeed resemble the form of the Psalms in many eighteenth-century translations. Yet the very idea of "measured prose" was meant to sig-

---

71. Priestley, *Course of Lectures* 156–60.

nal an argument about the progress of language, and to mark a transitional moment in literary development: a moment, that is, aligned with an early stage of cultural development; with universal properties of the mind, rather than the particularities of any given culture; and with only a rudimentary handle of verse form or philosophical concepts—though it showed incipient signs of both.

That was also at stake in the poems' relation to oral culture. Barbauld's assertion that these hymns are printed works meant to simulate or remediate an originally oral form of linguistic scaffolding. They are not simply primers meant to be read, but "are intended to be committed to memory, and recited" (238). While eighteenth-century poetry was still very frequently read or recited in group settings, in this case Barbauld felt the need to insist on the text's orality.[72] She needed to be explicit about this because even if the text offers a modernization of the oral psalm or hymn, its engagement of "secondary orality" plays into the way it guides and shapes the child's mind through language, meeting the child at (and recapitulating) an earlier developmental stage.[73] The hymns are supposed to meet children where they are and equip them to move them through the next stages of intellectual development. At the same time, like the parents and tutors of "On Prejudice," they are meant to supply theological attitudes that operated according to a different temporal logic and that were dramatically accelerated compared with the historical moment they mimicked.

In the section of his *Observations on Man* that discusses "theopathy," Hartley describes the concept of a deity to be a particularly difficult stretch of the early imagination. Eventually, though, he thinks it is a concept that all minds will inevitably develop and understand. For Hartley, all social feelings, but particularly one that blends sociability with concepts like infinity, were not accessible at earlier stages. Barbauld's *Hymns in Prose* explicitly positions theological concepts in a similar way. Yet, insofar as the book seeks to cultivate theopathy (as Barbauld states, in her own terminology, in the book's preface), it does so by relating the dimly understood concept of deity to already familiar concepts: in "Hymn 1," greatness, praiseworthiness, and feelings of relatedness and solicitation. The formula "Let him call me, and I will come unto him," for example, is not just a mode of interaction that children would have already

---

72. For an overview of the controversies around eighteenth-century oral recitation practice see McDowell, *Invention of the Oral* 177ff. On the prevalence of oral recitation see John J. Richetti, "Performance in Eighteenth-Century English Verse." For a discussion in connection with Barbauld see Elizabeth Kraft, "Hearing Eighteenth-Century Occasional Poetry by and about Women."

73. On "secondary orality" see Walter J. Ong, *Orality and Literacy* 2.

experienced, but one that, as Barbauld argues in "On Prejudice," was a way they were innately predisposed to think about the world around them and about their caretakers (239). The poems themselves continue that process by which a caretaker supplements and scaffolds the child's development, supplying external, theological concepts by depicting them in terms of an already familiar sociable attitude.

In her reading of the *Hymns in Prose*, Lisa Zunshine has glossed Barbauld's tension between familiar and unfamiliar knowledge in explicitly cognitivist terms. For Zunshine, the hymns are rhetorically persuasive because they invoke and play with children's evolved, cognitively universal categories of thought: specifically, an evolved tendency to distinguish between "natural kinds" and "human-made artifacts."[74] "If we adopt the cognitive anthropological perspective," Zunshine writes, then it appears that Barbauld's rhetorical force comes from her hymns' cognitive "shock value" (131–32). That is, they present humans as if they were artifacts, made by God, in ways that provoke an innate predisposition to distinguish between persons and things. In short, this argument goes, to say that children are "made" to praise God provokes a category crisis, and that crisis can be resolved only if those children reorient themselves conceptually. The idea of God emerges as a way to resolve what would otherwise be a contradiction.

There are authentic echoes of Hartley's theory of mind in this cognitivist interpretation, but Zunshine's bigger point is a methodological one: that any ideological text must interact with, and can be read in tandem with, what evolutionary psychology tells us about the mind-brain's evolved structures and categories. While that is not a methodological aim this book shares, what is interesting about Zunshine's analysis is that it seems true to Barbauld's own frame of reference for thinking about education and child development. Though Zunshine reads Barbauld's own theory of knowledge mainly in terms of the Lockean blank slate, there is good evidence that Barbauld did, in fact, think about her hymns as working with and building upon the mind's basic predispositions. Moreover, while it is true that Barbauld was working in a different paradigm and "did not think in terms of natural kinds and artifacts when she wrote *Hymns*," she *was* thinking in terms of the difference between objects and persons and of a natural ability to approach those categories differently (133). In her more Hartleian moments, after all, Barbauld might have imagined that the young child's conceptual frustration about these matters is inevitable but will be righted in later years. But because she also believed the

---

74. Lisa Zunshine, "Rhetoric, Cognition, and Ideology in A. L. Barbauld's *Hymns in Prose for Children* (1781)" (129–30).

child had naturally social dispositions, she would have also seen these hymns as drawing out the implications of something deeply familiar. The felt distinction between persons and things would have been, for Barbauld, a familiar, childlike point of reference, which could be used as a bridge to the more complex methods of conceiving of a deity or developing a teleological view of the universe. Scaffolding "theopathy" in early childhood, finally, is actually one of the most interesting ways that Barbauld revises Hartley's system: Rather than wait for its natural development, Barbauld advocates—in "On Prejudice" and more palpably and rhythmically in the poetic scaffolding of *Hymns in Prose*—that it can be supplied externally for children who had the seeds within them but were not yet fully capable of that attitude on their own.

CHAPTER 4

Wordsworth's Scattered Minds

> That aught *external* to the living mind
> Should have such mighty sway! Yet so it was—[1]

THIS CHAPTER revisits the central tension in Wordsworth's poetry, which the "yet" in the above passage signals: his reluctant but abiding commitment that the activities of the "living mind" included the agency of external things. The previous chapter showed how Barbauld and her circle began to develop an account of a culturally scaffolded mind. To suggest how Wordsworth pushes that logic further, I begin by turning to a more recent, controversial thought experiment.

In 1998, philosophers Andy Clark and David Chalmers published a controversial paper arguing for what they call an "active externalism." By the 1990s the cognitive sciences had begun to leave behind an older model of cognition as symbolic processing or computation and were beginning to picture it instead as a thoroughly embodied process. In that context they posed a question: What if cognition was not just distributed throughout the body but also extended beyond its bounds altogether? According to their argument, philosophers of mind also needed to consider "the active role of the environment in driving cognitive processes."[2] To explain what they mean, Clark and Chalmers tell a story about two characters, Inga and Otto. Both of them are in New York looking for the Museum of Modern Art. Inga is able-minded. She

---

1. William Wordsworth, *Prelude* 8.701–2. Unless otherwise noted, all references are to the 1805 text.
2. Clark and Chalmers, "The Extended Mind" 7.

thinks back, remembers that the museum is on 53rd Street, and goes there. Otto, on the other hand, "suffers from Alzheimer's disease" and "relies on information in the environment to help structure his life. Otto carries a notebook around with him everywhere he goes. When he learns new information, he writes it down. When he needs some old information, he looks it up" (12). Their point is that the way "remembering" works for both of these characters is structurally analogous. At least in theory, there might not be a compelling reason to think that consulting one's internal memory and consulting a notebook are different types of cognitive activity. "For Otto," they write, "his notebook plays the role usually played by a biological memory" (12). Though they invoke biological memory loss here to make their point, Clark and Chalmers go on to suggest that any case of "reliable coupling" with an assistive device or environmental resource might create a similar situation, and might give external content the same functional role as inner mental content (11).

This "extended mind" thesis is a more radical proposition than the one that the previous chapter aligned with Anna Letitia Barbauld's theories of the scaffolded mind. Barbauld's boldest claims about the mind's dependency upon the environment—for example, the way she offloads knowledge onto parents and tutors in "On Prejudice" and onto institutional repositories of memory in "On Monastic Institutions"—do sometimes sound like they are pointing toward a theory of external mental content, like the one the extended-mind thesis advances.[3] Yet Barbauld's primary interest is in the way that the social environment structures and shapes the individual mind, providing it with a template that can foster its own growth and that it eventually internalizes. What Clark and Chalmers are suggesting—and what this chapter suggests was also a driving force in William Wordsworth's poetry—is that the environment thinks for us in more fundamental, constitutive ways. For example, the very concept of "belief" might have to change if beliefs need not be lodged in internal representations or in biological memory. To return to Clark and Chalmers's thought experiment, as long as the information in Otto's notebook is "reliably there when needed, available to consciousness and available to guide action," it works "just the way that we expect a belief" to work (13). The thought experiment, which Clark has since developed into a broader theory of cognitive extension, goes beyond the developmentalist paradigm that this book has aligned with the Scottish Enlightenment human sciences.[4] It imagines that minds and their processes spread out into the world around them.

---

3. See chapter 3.
4. See Clark, *Natural Born Cyborgs* and *Supersizing the Mind*.

There are glimmers of a similar desire in some of the early Romantic writers this book has discussed so far: Herder's conviction that thinking actually happens both in language and in linguistic artifacts; Macpherson's vision of a material mind that circulates in an affectively charged landscape; or Barbauld's supplementing of the enlightened, autonomous mind with externally derived beliefs. It is hard to read about Otto's notebook, though, without thinking about a different Romantic-era notebook: In fact, it would be remarkably easy to revise the thought experiment by replacing Otto with William Wordsworth, and the notebook with Dorothy Wordsworth's *Grasmere Journals*. It has long been a commonplace that Wordsworthian poetics is the joint product of multiple minds rather than just one, with poems and journal entries interwoven to the point that Susan Levin has called the poetic corpus "a communal act of perception."[5] In a similar vein, Wordsworth's proposed, unfinished project *The Recluse* has frequently been described as one he felt unable to complete without consulting Coleridge's philosophical notes.[6] These actual, interpersonal collaborations line up with one of Wordsworth's most consistent conceptual interests: the way that he pictured mental experience as a collaboration between mind and world.

That proposition has been at the center of Wordsworthian scholarship for quite some time, from M. H. Abrams's focus on the mind's "holy marriage with the external universe" to Geoffrey Hartman's description of the major Wordsworthian tension between the mind's independence from or dependence upon nature.[7] This chapter argues that those impulses in Wordsworth's poetry build on the kind of "scaffolded" cognition he found in ballad traditions; in Enlightenment anthropology; and in poetic precursors like Barbauld. Yet Wordsworth often makes a stranger claim that nature does some of his thinking for him. While he was just as committed as Barbauld to the cultivation of the mind's own inner resources, he returns again and again to the idea that in order to capture the way mind and world interact, the boundary line between them needs to be moved or rendered porous. Many of Wordsworth's most paradigmatic "credal declarations" seek to bring the mind more durably into contact with the world. The Prospectus to *The Recluse* celebrates "how exquisitely [. . .] The external world is fitted to the Mind"; so, too, the fragment "There is an active principle" asserts that

---

5. Susan Levin, *Dorothy Wordsworth and Romanticism* 34.
6. See, for example, Magnuson, *Coleridge and Wordsworth* 13.
7. Abrams, *Natural Supernaturalism* 28, 61.

> All beings have their properties which spread
> Beyond themselves, a power by which they make
> Some other being conscious of their life.[8]

That "active principle" can be glossed in a few different ways, whether in terms of a Platonic apprehension of truth, Locke's account of "active power," or the pantheistic premise of a minded nature.[9] This idea of perception as a fundamentally collaborative activity has also led David Miall to identify Wordsworth with more recent approaches to "embodied enactivism," an approach to distributed cognition that sees even basic acts of perception as an interplay of mind, body, and world.[10] As a more recent approach to mind, body, and world, enactivism captures a recurrent Wordsworthian argument about the active mind: that the mind half-creates what it perceives and in return remains open to solicitations from the object world. Yet even enactivism fails to explain other aspects of Wordsworth's poetry, from the *Lyrical Ballads* to *The Prelude,* where he is more interested in offloading mental processes onto environmental agents: vagrants, inscriptions, particular localized spots, or—in short—anything that might do the mind's work for it.[11]

Rather than focus on "enactive" moments where the mind co-creates the world it perceives, this chapter proposes to unpack moments in Wordsworth's poetry that work more pointedly from the outside in—moments that make the external environment play an active, constitutive role in mental life while remaining fundamentally and permanently outside the head. Alan Liu has recently pinpointed one such moment, in Book 2 of *The Prelude,* where Wordsworth describes his creative habits in very externalized terms, as something operating alongside him. Wordsworth calls this power "a forming hand" that "abode with me":

---

8. See Wordsworth, *The Major Works* 676. The term "credal declaration" is Simon Jarvis's term for this characteristic type of Wordsworthian confession (*Wordsworth's Philosophic Song* 31).

9. On the various approaches to this passage see Tim Milnes, *William Wordsworth—The Prelude* 56. For Locke's discussion of "active powers" see *Essay Concerning Human Understanding* 2.21.2. On Wordsworth and Spinoza see Marjorie Levinson, "A Motion and a Spirit."

10. See especially Miall, "Wordsworth's 'First-Born Affinities.'"

11. Some of this argument hinges on the difference between the (admittedly overlapping) categories of enactive and extended cognitive processes. Both extended and enactivist views posit that the world can be understood as a storehouse of information; the salient difference is whether the knowledge in question should be understood in terms of navigating and manipulating an environment (e.g., moving around a cube-shaped structure or learning to judge the size of distant objects) versus a process that uses information stored out there (e.g., the paradigmatic cases of calculators and notebooks).

A local spirit of its own, at war
With general tendency, but for the most
Subservient strictly to the external things
With which it communed. (2.381–87)

There are many such moments in Wordsworth's poetry where he looks to this type of external action and where what matters most seems not to be his own agency but a different, more impersonal power that Liu terms "local agency." In such moments, Liu writes, there seems to be "no one at the control stick," and the poet's agency comes to appear nothing but "a cascade of local agencies."[12] Interestingly, Liu glosses that dependency of agency upon local agencies in terms of "emergence," a paradigm that sees mental processes arising from (and reducing to) simpler, lower-level processes. For all the similarities between Liu's "emergence" and Miall's "enactivism," the focus on "local agency" holds out at least one additional possibility.[13] Instead of a celebration of the mind's remarkable power to receive, reconfigure, and collaborate with the environment, what Liu pinpoints is a poet strangely less eager to identify his creative powers as his own and more open to the possibility that they may be performed externally on his behalf.

Recent years have provided a number of new names for this revisionary account of Wordsworthian agency, for example, in what Khalip glosses in terms of the impersonal or the "anonymous"; or what Anne-Lise François terms "recessive action"—a sense of entitlement to that which is freely given and done on one's behalf.[14] These additional proposed vocabularies ("local agency," "dispossession," "recessive action") suggest that we do not yet have, and indeed may continually need to update, our language for Wordsworth's abiding interest in opening the mind up to the world. The "extended mind" may not be quite the right term either. However, I argue that the question it asks about the mind's entanglements with the world—is thinking influenced by the environment, or does it actually happen out *in* that environment?—can help to clarify and name one of the particular questions Wordsworth was asking too. As such, it represents an approach that ought to be included among the diverse, overlapping, and even contradictory ways that he talked about the mind's dependencies.

---

12. Alan Liu, "A Forming Hand: Creativity and Destruction from Romanticism to Emergence Theory" (cited with permission). For previous engagements with this passage of Liu's unpublished essay see Khalip, *Anonymous Life* 15–16, and Jager, "Can We Talk?" 29.

13. Miall plausibly glosses the "forming hand" passage in terms of the paradox that the "active mind" nevertheless acts sometimes "without our knowledge" (707).

14. See Khalip, *Anonymous Life,* and Anne-Lise François, *Open Secrets.*

To that end, this chapter traces the way that, from the *Lyrical Ballads* self-declared "experiments" to the sustained self-experiment of *The Prelude*, Wordsworth tries to bring external assistance—from cultural scaffolding to nature's peculiar, distributed "ministry"—into the work of cognition. The first section of the chapter reads the *Lyrical Ballads*, and the debates about rustic language it produced, as a negotiation with the collective scaffolding of the ordinary mind. It then turns to a transitional moment, in some poems of 1802, where Wordsworth strenuously tries to reframe those cultural scaffolds as features of the mind's interaction with the *natural* world—that is, as a way in which the mind might let nature act for it and might leave its mark on nature in return. From the *Lyrical Ballads*' depictions of social encounter to Wordsworth's later mingling of mind and landscape in poems like the sonnet "To Toussaint L'Ouverture," the faculties that drive social encounter are the same ones that the individual mind relies upon to perform the basic, situated work of thinking and feeling. Wordsworth's poetry is, therefore, one clear place where theories of social intelligence come into contact with theories of environmentally situated cognition. Finally, I suggest, Wordsworth's major work, *The Prelude,* experiments with a few different ways to make that faith in inter-mental relationships into an account of nature's cognitive agency. Ultimately, what the extended mind thesis brings into view is one of Wordsworth's career-long efforts: to experiment with just how far "aught external to the living mind" could be said to be a *part* of the mind rather than simply holding "sway" over it.[15]

WHERE DOES THINKING HAPPEN?

I begin this section with a quick turn to Coleridge—not because he actually thought for Wordsworth but because he offers a helpful picture of what Wordsworth was pushing against. For the 1800 edition of *Lyrical Ballads,* Wordsworth moved Coleridge's "Rime of the Ancient Mariner" from the front to the back of the volume and replaced it with a very different opening: the pair of poems "Expostulation and Reply" and "The Tables Turned." The 1798 "Advertisement" had specified that these two poems were aimed at "a friend who was somewhat unreasonably attached to modern books of moral philosophy" and who is generally taken to be William Hazlitt. Yet the poems' argument—especially the injunction in "The Tables Turned" to "quit your books"—works equally well as a response to Coleridge.

---

15. *Prelude* 8.701–2.

Coleridge was very interested in the ways that the individual, ostensibly private mind was actually heavily mediated by language, by ideas or ideologies, and by institutions. One of his favorite ways of framing this embeddedness was hierarchical: He frequently pointed to a class of people—church clerics, philosophers, or secular elites he would eventually term the *clerisy*—who condition a population's thinking. In a February 1801 letter to Josiah Wedgewood, Coleridge describes such conditioned thinking more explicitly in terms of using books of philosophy. After lamenting the errors that Locke and his followers had introduced into philosophy, he argues for the necessity of "mak[ing] ourselves accurately acquainted with the opinions of those who have gone before us." After all, he writes:

> Life is short, & Knowledge infinite; & it is well therefore that powerful and thinking minds should know exactly where to set out from, & so lose no time in superfluous Discoveries of Truths long before discovered. That periodical Forgetfulness, which would be a shocking Disease in the mind of an Individual relatively to its own Discoveries, must be pernicious in the Species. For I would believe there is more than a metaphor in the affirmation, that the whole human Species from Adam to Bonaparte, from China to Peru, may be considered as one Individual Mind.[16]

According to this passage, philosophy is a species-level project that is *like* an individual mind. Losing the insights of the past, or failing to stand on the shoulders of giants, is *like* a form of memory loss, or *like* a "shocking Disease." On Coleridge's argument, we need to understand the loss of collective textual knowledge as being similar to physiological memory loss.

And yet at the same time, this sort of offloaded thinking is, Coleridge emphasizes, "more than a metaphor." The passage invokes the Unitarian language of the "one life" in which Coleridge was still immersed at the time, and which, as he puts it himself in his poem "Religious Musings," saw "God / Diffus'd thro' all" the universe "one Mind, one omnipresent Mind" (139–40; 114).[17] Coleridge would officially renounce Unitarianism within a few years' time, and the 1801 letter to Wedgewood gives an inkling of how the "one life" argument would adapt in the more orthodox context of his later writing. The implied narrative of philosophical progress relies on specific moments

---

16. Coleridge, *Collected Letters of Samuel Taylor Coleridge* 2.701. For a reading of the letter to Wedgewood in light of the "One Mind" and transcendental philosophy see Milnes, *The Truth about Romanticism* 181ff. For my reading of it in light of Coleridge's other gestures toward distributed cognition see John Savarese, "Cognitive Scaffolding, *Aids to Reflection*."

17. *Poetical Works* 171–91.

of textually embedded thinking to help individual thinkers execute complex conceptual moves. Individual thinkers have access to a wider, textually distributed thought process. They can offload their personal mental labor onto the texts and arguments of the past. Losing or ignoring those texts and arguments would *actually* represent a loss of memory, insofar as it would mean losing an important cognitive apparatus. On Coleridge's argument, we need "lose no time" working out the foundations of a philosophical problem, since the process can be accelerated with the help of textual artifacts that solve preliminary problems in much the same way that a calculator speeds up the solution of a complex equation. Like Otto losing his notebook, the philosopher who loses the texts and arguments of the past loses the external repository of valuable (here, collective) memory. In both cases, minds are not bounded or self-sufficient.[18]

Wordsworth would later echo this argument in *The Prelude*. In the long philosophical passage that builds up to the identification of a "forming hand" operating alongside him, Wordsworth addresses Coleridge directly on this subject: "Thou, my Friend! art one / More deeply read in thy own thoughts," he says, punning on Coleridge's publication *The Friend*, but also capturing the entanglement of knowing one's own mind and reading. He continues:

>   To thee
> Science appears but, what in truth she is,
> Not as our glory and our absolute boast,
> But as a succedaneum, and a prop
> To our infirmity.[19]

Wordsworth's vocabulary here is worth unpacking. *Prop* is a common word for him and one he uses for the supports and walking sticks of aged beggars, discharged soldiers, and rural wanderers in his poems of social encounter. As in Coleridge's letter to Wedgewood, "science" comes to appear as a similar kind of prosthetic. "Succedaneum," a synonym for *supplement* or *replacement*, has a long history in medical terminology where it would usually refer to a medicine or treatment used in place of the customary one. It often named

---

18. Coleridge's focus on the mind that need "lose no time" echoes Barbauld's essay "On Monastic Institutions," which like Coleridge, was also addressing the idea of a "progress of intellect" (Aikin and Aikin, *Miscellaneous Pieces in Prose* 88–118). On that essay, and Barbauld's treatment of external repositories of knowledge, see chapter 3.

19. *Prelude* 2.211–15.

an inferior substitute.[20] Both Coleridge and Wordsworth, then, are willing to frame "science" as a textually mediated ground of collective knowledge and as a prosthetic supplement to the individual mind's "infirmity." The implication is that the progress of knowledge should be understood not in triumphalist terms but as the basic condition of mental functioning in the first place, without which minds could accomplish very little.

In its foregrounding of specific cognitive aids, this model of philosophical progress resembles the model of linguistic change that Coleridge describes with his coinage *desynonymization*: Language, as a tool for thinking, becomes more precise over time as former synonyms take on more particular, pointed meanings. Coleridge relates desynonymization to "an instinct of growth" he sees "in all societies," an instinct that operates via language: "a certain collective, unconscious good sense working progressively to desynonymize those words originally of the same meaning."[21] Framing linguistic change this way implies that in order to think clearly, one must have adequate terms to work with. Just as (for stadial theorists of cultural development) societies move from hunting with spears to farming with plows, so for Coleridge knowledge progresses by improving the tools people use to think.

This picture of a "socially scaffolded" mind was not just a matter of abstruse philosophy. It was part and parcel of the poetics that emerged from the collaborative project of the *Lyrical Ballads,* in which the relation to "traditional" knowledge had already been mediated by ballad antiquarianism and language theory.[22] That model of the mind informs the core argument between Wordsworth and Coleridge, which we glimpse in *Biographia Literaria,* when Coleridge flatly denies Wordsworth's position "that the words and combinations of words derived from the objects, with which the rustic is familiar [...] can be justly said to form the *best* part of language" (53). He echoes Charles Burney's review of the *Lyrical Ballads,* which accuses Wordsworth of valorizing solitary, rustic life "as if men were born to live in woods and wilds, unconnected with each other!"[23] Coleridge builds on Burney's assertion that it is "to education and the culture of the mind that we owe the raptures which the author so well describes" in the contemplation of rural scenery and solitude.[24]

---

20. While it has become customary among editors to footnote this passage with a warning that Wordsworth is using *succedaneum* incorrectly here, his usage is actually fairly appropriate if, as I am suggesting, he is claiming that "science" functions as a prosthetic aid.

21. Coleridge, *Biographia* 1.82–83.

22. See Mary Jacobus, *Tradition and Experiment in Wordsworth's Lyrical Ballads (1798)*; and Maureen N. McLane, *Romanticism and the Human Sciences,* especially 43–53.

23. Burney's unsigned review appeared in the *Monthly Review* of June 1799. See Robert Woof, ed., *William Wordsworth: The Critical Heritage* 74–78.

24. Burney, in Woof, *Critical Heritage* 78.

Yet, while he emphasizes that the best part of language is not derived from a bare engagement with the object world, Coleridge does not write off rural thought and language altogether from poetic diction. Rather, he suggests that what appears in rustic life as a solitary act of thinking is already profoundly social. In the *Biographia,* he puts this explicitly in terms of social scaffolding:

> The thoughts, feelings, language, and manners of the shepherd-farmers in the vales of Cumberland and Westmoreland, as far as they are actually adopted in those poems, may be accounted for from causes, which will and do produce the same results in *every* state of life, whether in town or country. (54)

Geoffrey Hartman reads this passage as Coleridge merely "claiming that whatever poetic merits can be found in ordinary rural language derive from the Bible read in church," for which reason he "simply missed the point" Wordsworth was making about oral forms of transmission.[25] But for Coleridge that dispersal of aids to reflection does not simply equate to education or instruction, since, he notes, in Britain's remaining oral cultures, even "the most uneducated share in the harvest which they neither sowed nor reaped" (54). The seeds of that "harvest" are specific verbal phrases, which are sown in ordinary language, and Coleridge remarks that the casual observer "would be surprised at finding so large a number" of words "among our peasants" that were once "the exclusive property of the universities of the schools." In fact, he argues, the dispersal of verbal nuance begins with the Reformation, by which it is "transferred from the schools to the pulpit," but the effect is that the resulting concepts "gradually passed into common life" (54). The "best part of language"—which Coleridge agrees is what poetry crystallizes—is not a return to language's origins but an accretion of this kind of socially scaffolded thinking.

Framing things this way offers to turn a good deal of Romantic language theory on its head. Especially following James McKusick's *Coleridge's Philosophy of Language* (1986), it has been customary to associate Coleridge with a linguistic essentialism that would purify and return language to its divinely instituted origin, with Wordsworth (in contrast) on the side of linguistic conventionalism and "the real language of men." Yet both Wordsworth and Coleridge framed ordinary language in terms of a built environment that structured and scaffolded the individual mind. Coleridge tended to frame the mind's linguistic abilities in terms of supplements and divided labor.

---

25. Geoffrey Hartman, *The Unremarkable Wordsworth* xiii.

Sometimes, to be sure, it was the divine supplement of revelation (by way of "Adamic" language). But he frequently pointed, too, toward the hierarchically divided labor of pastor and philosopher.[26] Wordsworth, for his part, sometimes appears equally essentialist, for example, if we take at its word his declaration that rustic minds recapitulate language's origins through communion with the "great and permanent objects" of nature.[27] Yet in practice, as James Chandler has shown, Wordsworth's true point of reference is often not nature itself but a Burkean "second nature," a naturalized account of the built social environment.[28]

Coleridge recognized the mismatch between the language theory in the preface to *Lyrical Ballads* and Wordsworth's own poetic practices. Like the philosopher who desynonymizes terms, and thereby hones the tools that individuals use for thinking, what Wordsworth actually *does*, according to Coleridge's argument, is craft newly refined verbal formulations, which possess an "independent weight or beauty" sufficient to make them endure in the reader's mind and to spur on, by their own momentum, certain trains of thought. As evidence for this, Coleridge relates anecdotally that several "persons of no every-day powers and acquirements" have attested that "from no modern work had so many passages started up anew in their minds at different times, and as different occasions had awakened a meditative mood."[29] Beyond the mnemonic function Coleridge attributes to meter, which aids in the recollection of particular words or expressions, Wordsworth's poetry refines or improves upon vernacular speech to form micro-units of thought that get stuck in readers' heads and encourage or "awaken" a particular kind of thinking.

Not too long before he added the words *prop* and *succedaneum* to that address to Coleridge, Wordsworth also revised the preface in ways that more explicitly emphasize the divided labor of the professional knowledge disciplines and the way that the poet's task was to graft that type of thinking into readers' bodies. The 1802 additions to the preface make a slightly different case, one closer to Coleridge's later rebuttal, as they frame poetry as a kind

---

26. For an alternative reading of Coleridge's linguistics as both more empiricist and progressive see Paul Hamilton, *Coleridge's Poetics*.

27. *Lyrical Ballads* 747.

28. For the argument that Wordsworth turned fairly early to Burke, "for whom use, custom, and habit constituted a second nature to rival the first," see James Chandler, *Wordsworth's Second Nature* xviii. Levinson has recently offered a reminder that such deferral to external determination can just as easily invoke Spinoza ("A Motion and a Spirit"). For my purposes, it is enough to note that, as a philosophy of mind, Wordsworth's externalism cuts across these political affiliations.

29. *Biographia* 2.106.

of folk knowledge rather than a mere reflection of primitive wisdom. The relevant passage hinges on Wordsworth's opposition of poetry to science, and of the poet to the "man of science":

> The knowledge both of the Poet and the Man of Science is pleasure; but the knowledge of the one cleaves to us as a necessary part of our existence, our natural and unalienable inheritance; the other is a personal and individual acquisition, slow to come to us, and by no habitual or direct sympathy connecting us with our fellow-beings. (752)

Poetry, in other words, distinguishes itself from scientific knowledge by its thorough integration into "our existence," a vague phrase that Wordsworth affiliates with physiology but also seems to associate with social being: with automatic, reflexive, or unthinking knowledge, as opposed to the "slow" labor of individual knowledge.

Accordingly, this later development of his argument for ordinary language reframes poetry as an engagement with intimate forms of common knowledge, knowledge that becomes a part of (or, in Clark and Chalmers's terminology, "couples" with) people's basic mental makeup:

> If the time should ever come when what is now called science, thus familiarized to men, shall be ready to put on, as it were, a form of flesh and blood, the Poet will lend his divine spirit to aid the transfiguration, and will welcome the Being thus produced, as a dear and genuine inmate of the household of man. (753)

Wordsworth frames poetry as thinking in this common medium, and poets as professionals who are doing their part, like the man of science, within a modernizing division of labor.[30] The poet's task is to hone and improve that intimate medium, as Wordsworth emphasizes when he envisions a time when those more abstruse sciences "shall be manifestly and palpably material to us as enjoying and suffering beings," becoming a science "familiarized to men" that has "put on, as it were, a form of flesh and blood." It is the poet's job to "aid the transfiguration" of abstract knowledge into embodied form (753). Wordsworthian poetry, like Coleridgean desynonymization, is an activity of refining thinking in the vernacular. In this respect, Wordsworth agrees with Coleridge that we shortchange poetry if we understand it simply as a return

---

30. Much has by now been said about Wordsworth's relation to the intellectual disciplines. See especially Thomas Pfau, *Wordsworth's Profession*; Valenza, *Literature, Language, and the Intellectual Disciplines in Britain*; and Klancher, *Transfiguring the Arts and Sciences*.

to human origins (as an illumination of what elementary "acts of mind" *are*) rather than as a tool for extending them further. In short, Wordsworth's chief disagreement with Coleridge seems not to have been about whether cognitive labor of this sort was divided or "offloaded," but with the idea that such divided labor should be the top-down prerogative of sanctioned institutions. In that sense, Wordsworth hybridizes the positions of Percy and Ritson in their debate about the "minstrel" as a figure of distributed intellect. Like Percy, Wordsworth emphasizes the poet's special role in cultivating feeling and improving or educating inferior minds. But, like Ritson, he suggests that poetry as a medium is distributed and antihierarchical.[31]

In this light, the 1800 volume's opening pair of poems, "Expostulation and Reply" and "The Tables Turned," might be read not as a polemic against books, per se, but as an attempt to claim for the mind's own relationship to nature the same sort of scaffolded or "offloaded" function performed by textually mediated learning. Like Coleridge, the poems' dramatized interlocutor first frames books in traditionalist and organicist terms as a communal "spirit breath'd / From dead men to their kind" and then, much like Coleridge's language of "shocking Disease," reframes them as prosthetic aids for those who are otherwise "forlorn & blind" (6–8).[32] The speaker defends himself against the charge of neglecting books (and of living as if "none had lived before" him) by insisting that he had that kind of relationship not with books but with nature (12). As the speaker elaborates on the analogy between books and nature in "The Tables Turned," the claim moves beyond a commitment to sensation or natural education and carries with it the idea that a natural "impulse" (21) can perform a similar role for the mind by delivering "spontaneous wisdom" (19).[33] For all their ostensible vitriol against books, the effect of the poems is to frame nature itself as being more like a book—not in the way that natural theology framed nature as readable as God's book, but as a medium for intellectual content that remains available to the wisely passive mind.

FROM OTHER MINDS TO DISTRIBUTED MINDS

Read in that light, many aspects of *Lyrical Ballads* that we might attribute to an organic vision of society, or to a defense of embedded, traditional ways of life, also have particular things to say about the division of cognitive labor. If Wordsworth's theory of poetic language is oriented toward theories of linguis-

---

31. On Percy and Ritson's dispute see the introduction.
32. *Lyrical Ballads* 107–8.
33. Ibid. 108–9.

tic "scaffolding," the *Lyrical Ballads* themselves frequently blend the idea of cognitive scaffolding with scenes of interpersonal encounter and social sympathy. "Simon Lee," for example, sets up an analogy between the ostentatious performance of physical labor on behalf of the "overtasked" title character and the speaker's apparent discomfort with doing similar work for the reader (81).[34] The speaker urges readers to cultivate better, more active reading habits. Yet such readerly self-exertion continues to depend on the poetic work of selection, framing, and marking unapprehended relations, which the speaker has already performed on our behalf. Just as Simon Lee's powers, had he not allowed them to atrophy in his younger years, would have allowed him to live "upon the village common" in older age, so too would readerly self-cultivation empower us to receive properly what poetry has already partially processed for us (40). There is an echo of the active mind's ability to "half-create" what it perceives; but narrative framing ("perhaps a tale you'll make it") is a different type of thought-work, one explicitly indebted not to the world's collaborative action but to the poet's specialized labor (72).

In "The Idiot Boy," Wordsworth revises Enlightenment histories of language and society to tell a different story about interpersonal entanglements.[35] That poem has long been seen as paradigmatic for the *Lyrical Ballads*' general project of using ballad traditions to reimagine the "primitive" mind. Indeed, as Bewell has argued, the poem strategically deploys and burlesques Enlightenment theories of "idiocy," a category construed, from John Locke onward, as an inability to form durable ideas or representational signs. On Bewell's reading, the poem recapitulates the origin of language as it moves from Johnny's silence to his nonverbal "burr" and finally to his metaphorical reply, at the poem's end, to a request for what happened to him while lost:

"The cocks did crow to-whoo, to-whoo,
"And the sun did shine so cold."
Thus answered Johnny in his glory,
And that was all his travel's story. (460–63)

As Bewell argues, Johnny's non-story here makes figural language antecedent to narrative and "suggests that the world that first appears to human perception is fundamentally metaphoric. Only later, as language (and with it knowledge) develops, do 'moons' and 'owls' displace the cold suns and hooting cocks of primitive perception."[36] The poem thus revalues idiocy pre-

34. Ibid. 68–70.
35. Ibid. 91–104.
36. Bewell, *Wordsworth and the Enlightenment* 69.

cisely by affiliating it with the deep history of human cognitive and linguistic development. It follows in the footsteps of many eighteenth-century theorists of poetic language, from Lowth to Priestley, who attribute early poetry's penchant for metaphor to the paucity of a language that had not yet grown "copious."[37]

However, if "The Idiot Boy" begins from the premise of poetry's affiliation with human cognitive origins, and its ties to metaphor in particular, one of the most fascinating things the poem does is to experiment with a picture of that early mind's *social* entanglements.[38] Like "Goody Blake and Harry Gill," "The Idiot Boy" is a medical poem about psychosomatics: As Susan Gale's "mind grew worse and worse, / Her body it grew better" (425–26).[39] Accordingly, the poem renders porous the boundary between mind, body, and environment. In lieu of the doctor who never arrives at his destination, the social body regulates itself through a series of distributed tasks. Rather than go herself to fetch assistance for Susan, Betty sends Johnny, "her idiot boy," for the doctor (80). Johnny, in turn, the speaker tells us, "seems [. . .] the rein to give" over to his horse (363); and the chain of events he sets off serves as the catalyst for the social body to return itself to equilibrium. Johnny is given a task to accomplish for someone else and accomplishes it in a roundabout way that makes the poem appear a study in unintended agency and unsought effects. Tellingly, it still calls its outcome a "merry meeting" of minds (440).

Rather than read the poem metaphorically, in terms of the way an organic social body resembles an individual organism, I suggest that "The Idiot Boy," like Coleridge in his letter to Wedgewood, wants to see "more than a metaphor" at work. "The Idiot Boy" may not posit that its cast of characters, or the society they live in, coheres together as "one individual mind." However, it does focus on the way that inner, embodied components (Susan Gale's "very life") are continuous with that wider causal network (31). Moreover, it foregrounds the distribution of its tasks among a set of discrete actors, from Betty to Johnny to his "horse that thinks" (122).[40] Navigation, in fact, has been a

---

37. Priestley, *Course of Lectures* 239. On Priestley's theory of language see chapter 3.

38. For a further gloss on the poem's negotiations with theories of primitive poetic origins and its relation to disability, in the context of Walter Scott's response to Wordsworth, see chapter 5.

39. For "Goody Blake and Harry Gill" see *Lyrical Ballads* 59–62.

40. It would be right to hear an echo of actor-network theory, with its particular brand of distributed action, in this formulation. However, I am less interested in the broader concept of agency (how things get done) and more interested in particular tasks that "count" as part of an individual's cognitive loop regardless of where among an actor-network (or in how many different places) the thinking takes place. For an introduction to actor-network theory see Bruno Latour, *Reassembling the Social*.

paradigmatic case for distributed cognition, in terms of a ship's crew or in terms of the horse and rider as a coupled system.[41] The poem provocatively connects the distributed action of the community to the material makeup of Susan Gale's mind and body. Perhaps still more important, if it tells a story about a so-called primitive mind, or if it reenacts early moments in a conjectural history of human cognitive origins, it builds distributed cognitive acts—strategizing, decision making—directly into that history. This differs sharply from accounts that emphasize primitive poets' animistic projection onto nature, like Lowth's picture of an early mind so egotistical that it remains unaware of other minds and is prone to think of its own emotions as ontological facts about the environment.[42] The alternative that "The Idiot Boy" offers is a poetic mind that is already socially aware and socially entangled. Rather than seeing his own feelings in the landscape or losing track of his own mental states, Johnny offers an image of a mind that distributes itself in a different way, by giving over the reins and trusting in the judgment of others, including the "horse that thinks" for him (122).

The association of the poetic mind with the socially distributed mind becomes clearer in the more starkly Burkean poems Wordsworth adds to the 1800 volume, poems that frame individual memory as delegated across social networks. Figures of such distribution include the old Cumberland beggar, whose habitual rounds serve as an anchor and "record" of the whole village's habits of moral reflection (81); and the priest of "The Brothers," who reframes the second volume's various epitaph- and inscription-poems as written technologies for offloading memory, for which a village like his would have no need: "We have no need of names and epitaphs, / We talk about the dead by our fire-sides" (176–77).[43] Wordsworth's nostalgia for traditional and oral culture often hinges on the way he relates internal and external memory. It might seem that oral cultures place higher demands upon people's internal or biological memory, and Wordsworth's remarks about the enervation of the modern, media-saturated mind in the 1800 preface to *Lyrical Ballads* do play that argument out. Yet poems like "The Brothers" also show that in "traditional"

---

41. Edwin Hutchins's *Cognition in the Wild*, one of the landmarks in the theory of socially distributed cognition, characterized nautical navigation as a cognitive process distributed among a ship's crew. Karen Raber makes a similar point about horse-rider relations as a collaborative mode of embodied thinking, a trope that had become commonplace by the early modern period (see *Animal Bodies, Renaissance Culture*, especially 13–15 and 75–102).

42. See chapter 1.

43. See "The Old Cumberland Beggar" in *Lyrical Ballads* 228–34 and "The Brothers" in *Lyrical Ballads* 141–59. I make this argument about "The Old Cumberland Beggar" in John Savarese, "Wordsworth between Minds." On Wordsworth and epitaphic "mediation" see especially Kevis Goodman, *Georgic Modernity* 106ff.

societies, memory is still buttressed by collective practices and depends upon continued, reliable access to those who have and tell the stories. In the same way that early modern critics saw commonplace books as eviscerating individual memory, or indeed that Wordsworth saw idle and extravagant print materials eating away at the nation's attention spans, "The Brothers" characterizes Leonard's removal from a traditional set of memory practices as leading to a profound type of memory loss.

ALMOST DOUBLE: THINKING WITH NATURE AROUND 1802

The 1802 preface addition about the poet and the man of science was at that point Wordsworth's most explicit published statement about the division of labor he envisioned for poetry. It clarifies both the way that poems performed knowledge-work like the sciences and the fact that the poet's medium was not the individual reader but a common medium that structured thinking for broad swaths of society. Describing it as embodied knowledge with "a form of flesh and blood" ties the mind to the rhythms of the body, as Alan Richardson has helpfully connected to Wordsworth's theory of poetic rhythm (753).[44] Yet such embodied knowledge is equally a part of human physiology and cultural scaffolding. In other words, Wordsworth thought people's basic mental makeup could be changed because he habitually thought of "the mind" as both embodied and extended, composed of vital blood as well as cultural extensions. The conviction that the poet's task was to add to that common medium persisted into the 1805 *Prelude,* when, in the *ars poetica* embedded in Book 12, Wordsworth announces his hope

> that a work of mine,
> Proceeding from the depth of untaught things,
> Enduring and creative, might become
> A power like one of Nature's. (12.309–12)

Before turning to *The Prelude* itself, I will look at a transitional moment around 1802, during which (alongside the "man of science" addition) Wordsworth composed a number of poems that try to move beyond the language of cultural "scaffolding," and that try to read that distributed agency into nature itself.

---

44. On Wordsworth and embodied thinking see Richardson, *British Romanticism* 66–92.

One of those poems is "Resolution and Independence," which we might read as an attempt to draw together the various concerns at play in *Lyrical Ballads*: social concern for the mendicant poor; the encounter with the rustic mind; and the logic of disability and infirmity, to name a few.[45] As earlier in the lyrical ballad "Lines Written in Early Spring," the poem opens with a glimpse of something like a social intimacy with nature, as if able to peer into the joy of animal and vegetable life.[46] In the same way that in the earlier poem "pleasant thoughts / Bring sad thoughts to the mind" (3–4), here the speaker describes a moment in which

> as it sometimes chanceth, from the might
> Of joy in minds that can no farther go,
> As high as we have mounted in delight
> In our dejection do we sink as low,
> To me that morning did it happen so;
> And fears, and fancies, thick upon me came;
> Dim sadness and blind thoughts I knew not nor could name. (22–28)

The poem aligns such dejection, once more, with a sense of humanity's difference from the nature he beholds. But those "blind thoughts" are different, and he attributes them to habits of thought he suspects he has picked up from his poetic predecessors, namely, Chatterton and Burns: "We Poets in our youth begin in gladness; / But thereof comes in the end despondency and madness" (48–49). The speaker suggests, in other words, that his melancholy train of thought is intertextual in character, a habit of thinking he has picked up from poetic precedent.

The "leech gatherer" himself enters the poem, like the old Cumberland beggar, as an immobile, aged figure in the landscape. In fact, the poem immediately attempts to make the leech gatherer a part of the natural world: He seems "not all alive nor dead":

> As a huge Stone is sometimes seen to lie
> Couch'd on the bald top of an eminence;
> Wonder to all who do the same espy,
> By what means it could thither come, and whence;
> So that it seems a thing endued with sense:

---

45. *Poems in Two Volumes* 123–29.
46. *Lyrical Ballads* 76.

> Like a Sea-beast crawl'd forth, which on a shelf
> Of rock or sand reposeth, there to sun itself. (71, 64–70)

The leech gatherer appears to be a vestige of something, though it is not clear exactly what. He might remind the poet of a brute nature, which only *seems* (as if by animistic projection) to have human qualities; or else, he might represent a recapitulation of life's initial emergence out of inorganic nature. Yet the poem's irony is that the leech gatherer turns out to be not an example of "natural man" at all but an example of socially embedded man. When the leech gatherer starts speaking, Wordsworth depicts himself as receiving correction or "admonishment" from the man's mental fitness, and from his use of a more refined language ("choice word and measured phrase; above the reach / Of ordinary men; a stately speech!") than might be expected from a rural mendicant subdued by animal decay (119, 102–3). The concluding sentiment that "I could have laugh'd myself to scorn, to find / In that decrepit Man so firm a mind" might be read as a concession to Coleridge's argument that the "real language" of rural life is a figment of Wordsworth's imagination and is, in fact, caught up in a broader movement, whether one characterized as "civilizing," philosophizing, or socially extended (144–45). The poem is notable for its attempt to reframe the philosophical problem of the mind's place in nature in terms of spontaneous, rural, or "natural" linguistic production. In both cases, the solitary absorption in the object world gives way to the supplements of culture and to the ways that minds depend on other minds.

It is telling, then, that to the extent that Wordsworth felt the poem to mark a crisis, he found resolution to the crisis by looking to his sister and her journal. "Perplexed, and longing to be comforted," he turns to memory in the distributed sense her notebook afforded. At the introduction of the leech gatherer, at the transition between stanzas 7 and 8, the poem opens out to incorporate features and phrases from the *Grasmere Journal* and becomes a collaborative thinking-through of a shared episode. As it happens, that episode, recorded in the *Grasmere Journal* entry for October 3, 1800, was a story about the fracturing of a skull. After a rainy morning, William and Dorothy "met an old man almost double."[47] His reduced physical stature, the journal records, was the result of a debilitating accident: "He had been hurt in driving a cart his leg broke his body driven over his skull fractured—he felt no pain till he recovered from his first insensibility" (24). At first, the poem is invested in the leech gatherer's insensibility, where (like the "insensibly subdued" character described in the earlier poem "Old Man Travelling") age

---

47. Dorothy Wordsworth, *Grasmere Journals* 23.

and hardship have returned the man to the state of "animal tranquility," here imaged in a sea beast: a stripped-down form of mind described as if it were just emerging from brute, primeval nature. Ultimately, though—after the speaker's correction—it becomes clear that the old man's debility has actually forced him into a state of *inter*dependency that parallels the poem's recognition about the rustic mind: That private mental life extends beyond the skull. In that respect, as an engagement with early nineteenth-century models of the mind, the leech gatherer stands in sharp contrast to another character with a head injury, Louisa Musgrove in Jane Austen's *Persuasion*. Louisa's character, it has been noted, is "'altered,' remarkably and apparently for life, by a single incident, a severe knock on the head."[48] Where Louisa offers a reminder that Austen had available models of an embodied mind, the leech gatherer offers a somewhat different model: one that is still fundamentally embodied and dependent upon its material substrates, but that does not stop at the body's limits.

Ultimately, of course, the poem buries or elides the journal's specific reference to a fractured skull and moves from its opening gestures toward the pathetic fallacy and its fantasies of primeval, seaborne life to its culminating picture of a much more ordinary (and less specifically cognitive) type of dependency. By his own telling, the leech gatherer depends on the environment for economic subsistence, though that dependency is upon a species of worm that is itself parasitic, suggesting a mutual dependency. If the poem makes any thematic use of leeches' role in the medical profession, it seems to remain at the level of a more general association with the life's blood or with healing contact.[49] If the old man's moniker derives from those leeches, the image with which he is most frequently associated is his staff, with which, the speaker tells us, "Himself he propp'd, his body, limbs, and face" (77). In addition to being a simple bodily prop, supporting the old man's back and (more unusually) his head and face, the staff is the instrument of his trade, which he uses to stir the waters in pursuit of leeches. The poem's main image of the old man "almost double," then, like that phrase "grow double" in "The Tables Turned," invokes dependence and reduced stature as well as expansion via prosthetic supplements. It highlights the continuity between his (perhaps) fractured head, his physically supportive staff, and the watery habitat of the leeches that sustain him. A different way to put this would be that the poem reduces the man's head injury to a metaphor. The speaker merely conjectures:

---

48. For this reading of Louisa's fall as a depiction of character's dependence on "an embodied mind," see Richardson, *British Romanticism* 97.

49. On the poem's relation to healing—including the way it casts the leech gatherer himself as the antidote to a solipsistic attitude—see Jackson, *Science and Sensation* 153–55.

The man is bent double, "as if some dire constraint of pain, or rage / Of sickness felt by him in times long past, / A more than human weight upon his frame had cast" (75–77). As in "The Idiot Boy," it seems, Wordsworth's tendency is to make disability metaphorical for general conditions of cognitive interdependency.

The published poem also effaces the leech gatherer's books. In the fair copy, written in Sara Hutchinson's hand, the leech gatherer speaks at greater length and gives more of the speech recorded in the *Grasmere Journal*:

> Feeble I am in health these hills to climb
> Yet I procure a Living of my own
> This is my summer work in winter time
> I go with godly Books from Town to Town
> Now I am seeking Leeches up & down
> From house to house I go from Barn to Barn
> All over Cartmell Fells & up to Blellan Tarn.[50]

The reference to books shows that Wordsworth is still thinking about a more explicit analogy between the vital matter of the mind and the cultural artifacts that inform the mind: "Procuring a Living" puns on the acquisition of economic sustenance and the acquisition of the life processes, as if directly, from without, whether in terms of the manipulation of the vital blood with leeches or in terms of the cultivation of the mind with "godly Books." This earlier, effaced version of the leech gatherer cuts quite a different figure, one who is gathering and selling leeches to the medical establishment in summer, and in winter selling reading material to strengthen people's minds. That alternation between leech and book, blood and pneuma, seems momentarily to offer a way to perform what Wordsworth that same year, in the 1802 additions to the preface, called a "transfiguration" by which knowledge can "put on, as it were, a form of flesh and blood." The published version of the poem effaces that analogy between leech and book and leaves traces only of the naturalized linguistic scaffolding: the speech patterns that structure the old man's thought patterns, and Wordsworth's own immersion in poetic precedent—Chatterton and Burns—that seems to have become part of the second nature that surrounds him.[51]

Another key work of 1802 worth noting here is the sonnet sequence Wordsworth wrote a few months later and also included in *Poems in Two Volumes*

---

50. For a facsimile of this draft see *Poems in Two Volumes* 316–23.
51. See Chandler, *Wordsworth's Second Nature*.

(1807). Wordsworth composed these sonnets in the context of Napoleon's declaration as consul and his own return to France, which he undertook to settle his affairs with Annette Vallon before his marriage to Mary Hutchinson. The sonnets address political progress and liberty and frequently locate history's movement in collective life, in political institutions, even (most notably in the sonnet "To Toussaint L'Ouverture") in the sympathetic forces of nature.[52] The sonnet to Toussaint is well known for displacing Toussaint's agency onto nature. The poem attempts to cheer the jailed revolutionary by reminding him:

> Thou hast left behind
> Powers that will work for thee; air, earth, and skies;
> There's not a breathing of the common wind
> That will forget thee; thou hast great allies;
> Thy friends are exultations, agonies,
> And love, and Man's unconquerable mind. (9–14)

A common and useful way to read these lines is to find in them an organic vision of the harmony of humanity and nature, whereby "collective life," including the natural world, "is in solidarity with" Toussaint.[53] But the "powers" Toussaint leaves behind are also a set of ideas, convictions, and beliefs that Wordsworth sees as gaining footholds and gradually seeding ideological change.

Wordsworth is heavily invested in this idea that mental phenomena (and their political ramifications) can be offloaded onto nature's elements or that nature might continue to do the work that people begin. We might compare the sonnet to Toussaint to "The King of Sweden," the poem that precedes it in the 1807 volume.[54] That sonnet, about an empowered king who builds upon the work of his ancestors, sets up a strong contrast with the following poem to Toussaint, a disenfranchised populist figure. King Gustavus is framed as a ruler who is continuing the work begun by his "glorious Ancestors," work that the poem also casts, unironically, as the work of providence (13). Taken together, though, the two sonnets juxtapose Gustavus, an empowered and enfranchised world-historical individual, with Toussaint's more distributed, naturalized mode of historical change. One way to read this would be that the sonnet to Toussaint moves from the historical agency of particu-

---

52. *Poems in Two Volumes* 160–61.
53. Joshua Stanley, "Wordsworth and 'the Most Unhappy Man of Men': Sentimentalism and Representation" 188.
54. *Poems in Two Volumes* 159–60.

lar great men—like the revolutionaries *The Prelude* will call "powers, / Like earthquakes" and "shocks [. . .] felt through every nook of town and field"— to a focus on the dispersal of ideology through society as a whole (9.180). More concretely, the nods to natural forces can be read as reaching for the material base through which such collectively held ideas can be stored. Stanley is surely correct to read the poem's reference to "Man's unconquerable Mind"—an allusion to Thomas Gray's "The Progress of Poetry"—as resisting Gray's "primitivist vision of the innate freedom and poetic impulses of the human mind."[55] For Wordsworth, the human mind is "unconquerable" not because of its innate freedom but because it can be externalized and (at least in the naturalistic fantasy of "air, earth, and skies") hidden away for later use. I would agree, therefore, that Wordsworth opposes the primitivism on offer in Gray's ode with a more fundamental vision of modernization and change. Yet I would take the allusion in a similar spirit to Wordsworth's dalliance with conjectural history in "The Idiot Boy." In both cases Wordsworth stakes a great deal on there being an original, physiological "mind of man" that houses the possibilities of human action. In both cases he alludes to developmental histories that posit a link between those physiological underpinnings and poetic utterance. Yet in both cases as well he pictures human agency as exceeding that physiological frame and spilling over into the environment: Nature is "allied" with human action and thinks and acts for us. But the sonnet to Toussaint imagines that humanity changes nature, too, in substantive ways that reshape the way it can work for people going forward.[56]

A POWER LIKE ONE OF NATURE'S

The ability to think in and through nature—an ability, or at least a felt need, to imprint socially transformative powers into nature itself—becomes particularly important in *The Prelude*. Although it is only in Book 12 that Wordsworth announces his wish that his poetry could "become / A power like one of Nature's" (12.310–11), he offers a fairly explicit imagination of what it might mean to become such a power in Book 5, the section of the poem titled simply "Books." The occasion is a lament for the frailty of human media—books, but presumably also language in general and, more broadly still, the collective productions of the human intellect. Much like Coleridge's lament for those

---

55. Stanley, "Wordsworth and 'the Most Unhappy Man of Men" 189.
56. For a reading of Wordsworth's changing natures in light of natural history, ecology, and colonialism see chapter 6 of Bewell, *Natures in Translation*.

modern philosophers who throw off the long-accrued intellectual labor of the past Wordsworth grieves for

> Those palms atchieved [*sic*]
> Through length of time, by study and hard thought,
> The honours of thy high endowments. (5.7–9)

In the first draft of this passage, in 1804, Wordsworth grieves not for the mind's accomplishments (its "palms atchieved") but "for thy powers," as if to suggest some slippage between these achievements of the past and what they make available to present thinkers, or the constitutive abilities that would make use of them.[57] As in the sonnet to Toussaint, "powers" here seems to refer both to human capabilities and to the distributed agencies that make them possible. While the 1805 text revises this into a general lament for humanity's collective intellectual achievements, the focus on what the archive makes possible persists in the apocalyptic vision that follows:

> A thought is with me sometimes, and I say,
> "Should earth by inward throes be wrenched throughout,
> Or fire be sent from far to wither all
> Her pleasant habitations, and dry up
> Old Ocean in his bed, left singed and bare,
> Yet would the living presence still subsist
> Victorious, and composure would ensue,
> And kindlings like the morning—presage sure,
> Though slow perhaps, of a returning day."
> But all the meditations of mankind,
> Yea, all the adamantine holds of truth
> By reason built, or passion (which itself
> Is highest reason in a soul sublime),
> The consecrated works of bard and sage,
> Sensuous or intellectual, wrought by men,
> Twin labourers and heirs of the same hopes—
> Where would they be? Oh, why hath not the mind
> Some element to stamp her image on
> In nature somewhat nearer to her own?

---

57. *Five-Book Prelude* 4.335. All references to the 1804 text are to that volume, which is Duncan Wu's conjectural reconstruction of what such a transitional edition might have looked like.

Why, gifted with such powers to send abroad
Her spirit, must it lodge in shrines so frail? (5.28–48)

This passage is frequently read as a vision of human extinction, with its focus on the mismatch between the sovereign mind and the ephemerality of its bodily materials and artifacts.[58] It is striking, however, that, as in Coleridge's letter to Wedgewood, Wordsworth is envisioning one more instance of catastrophic collective memory loss, via "inward throes" (5.29) or (in an earlier 1804 draft), by "dislocation on this star of ours."[59] No longer focused on how an individual might arrive at a particular level of reasoning, Wordsworth is here concerned with how intellect itself might be preserved for a future repopulation of the earth in humanity's absence. How could some future species pick up, to echo Barbauld and Coleridge, without losing any time? For Wordsworth, the answer is presumably not far off from the "one life" doctrine, where human intellect represents a high point in the development of the spirit's self-awareness. Indeed, after humanity "the living presence" would somehow "still subsist / Victorious, and composure would ensue." The 1804 text has a slightly different reference to "the vital spirit of our frame" persisting.[60] Besides being a possible allusion to Coleridge's "Frost at Midnight," that earlier phrase was also a closer echo of vitalist physiology than the phrase "living presence" to which it was revised in 1805. So, too, the 1805 text's imagination of a future return to planetary "composure," as opposed to 1804's more terminal "peace," suggests both the calmness of animal decay (as the "mild composure" of the *Lyrical Ballads*' "Old Man Travelling") and a return to order, as the "living presence" began composing new species, new knowledge, and ultimately new texts once more.[61] Between drafts, in other words, it is not clear whether Wordsworth is referring to an underlying spirit of humanity, coded into a providential order; a desire for specific human knowledge and artifacts to persist after the species' collapse; or some combination of the two.

The problem the poem here envisions—which Redfield has called the impossibility of "imagin[ing] the survival of the archive"—is that it seems impossible for people to make their cultural and intellectual achievements parts of nature, in any sense that could exist in the absence of other people (64). This is a new challenge, even a crisis, in Wordsworth's now longstanding claim that poetic knowledge "put[s] on a form of flesh and blood"

---

58. See, for example, Mary Jacobus, "Wordsworth and the Language of the Dream"; Morton Paley, *Apocalypse and Millennium* 166; and Marc Redfield, "Wordsworth's Dream of Extinction."
59. *Five-Book Prelude* 4.352.
60. Ibid. 4.357.
61. Ibid. iv.358. See "Old Man Travelling" in *Lyrical Ballads* 110.

and becomes "a necessary part of our existence."[62] On the face of it, Book 5's lament for the frailty of the shrines of human knowledge leads to the crucial compromise whereby Wordsworth gives up on the mind's impetus toward transcendence and immortality and reconciles himself to the lesser sort of permanence poetry *can* have, with its "sure foundations in the heart of man" (5.200).

However, one of the most important things this passage does for *The Prelude* is to imagine communication differently: Rather than simply working in the "sure foundation" of the human passions, it imagines a way that receiving collectively accumulated information could look more like a naive encounter with natural objects. This new type of transfigured knowledge aspires not just to a change in human relations or "second nature" but also to a change in nature itself, here pictured in a way that would literalize Toussaint's offloading of his "powers" onto air, earth, and skies. It imagines a form of knowledge that could have a simple or primary causal effect in the world, even in a posthuman future unable to decode human symbols. It is, to be sure, a vision of idealized, unmediated communication, in keeping with the idealized form of inter-mental contact which Virginia Jackson has designated the "lyricization" of poetry (7). But it is also a vision of a different and not necessarily transcendental mode of communication. Its aim is for a type of social transmission that might make human knowledge less like a labored process of what Coleridge called "individual acquisition" and more like an immediate, reflexive engagement with information stored outside the head. Books should be more like nature—accessible, unmediated, and free for the taking; and nature, in a way different from in "The Tables Turned," should be more like a book—or at least should be recognized as providing more of the intellectual content we usually associate with books. That easy model of cognitive availability is not something Wordsworth ultimately holds out as a goal for any actually existing poetry—not something he actually thinks the poet adds to nature. But it helps him point to one of *The Prelude*'s key claims, which is that nature does already think for us in crucial ways.

The Prelude begins as a study of nature's influence upon the growing mind, and its inventory of poetic powers is equally geared toward naming the poet's own inward, "first-born affinities" and those gifts from abroad that contributed to his creative agency. In the two-part *Prelude* of 1799, the chief way that nature became agential was through the Hartleian logic of association. At least in 1799, these moments of givenness are caught up in moments of childlike animism or superstition that made them seem to be the work of minister-

---

62. *Lyrical Ballads* 752.

ing spirits or "beings of the hills" (1799 1.130). Wordsworth writes that these moments made sure his passions were "intertwine[d] [. . .] with high objects, with eternal things" (1799 1.133–36). Even the much-remarked phrase "spots of time," in the 1799 text, seems to be one more name for how certain external states of affairs wind up lodging in the memory and laying the groundwork for imaginative replay and re-association. The "drowned man" episode, for example, which is the occasion for the initial statement, "There are in our existence spots of time," is an episode that becomes "impressed" upon the poet's mind and creates a network of associations "to which in following years / Far other feelings were attached" (1799 1.283–85). It is in the second part of the 1799 text that *The Prelude* comes to suggest that more than just association is at work. That second part moves from early reminiscences of childhood to the poet's "conjectures" about the early "progress of our being" (1799 2.268–69). We might call this a change in methodology: The poem at this point moves from first-person testimony or "self-experiment" to a conjectural history of its own origins and prehistory.[63] It is appropriate, then, that Wordsworth begins this conjectural prehistory with the note to Coleridge on the uncertainty of such knowledge: The 1805 addition that "science" at large is but "a succedaneum and a prop / To our infirmity" seems a fitting description of the turn to conjecture, a fictive method traditionally performed as a substitute where actual empirical evidence was wanting. (2.212, 214–15).[64]

What is most notable about the second part's conjectures is the way they look for a language to describe something other than a creative, active-and-reactive mind working in collaboration with the sensory world, or with the "dark invisible workmanship" of association.[65] Instead, he looks for more and more of the work to be performed by other hands. This happens first in the famous "blessed babe" passage, which Miall has helpfully read in terms of an "enactivist" collaboration between the mind's inborn powers and the world's action upon it. Yet the blessed babe does not just undergo the brute work of associative development. As Yousef has shown, the child is "subjected to the discipline of love," an externally enforced discipline actively performed by another (2.281).[66] So, too, the child may have an innate power to "claim manifest kindred" with other minds, but the idea that the world is a fit home for a

---

63. On Romantic poetry as "self-experiment" see Noel Jackson, *Science and Sensation* 103ff.
64. On conjectural history as a confessedly imperfect method see chapter 1.
65. The phrase "dark invisible workmanship" does not appear in 1799. Its later addition seems not only to allude to the mystery of how associative growth works but also, in making it more mysterious, to suggest that there is something more clandestine at work than the association of ideas. See *Prelude* 2.352–53.
66. On this passage's relation to debates about humanity's solitary or social origins see Yousef, *Isolated Cases* 126.

being like him is something actively demonstrated by a caretaker (2.272). Like Barbauld, in her essay "On Prejudice," for Wordsworth the "first / Poetic spirit of our human life" is sourced back to a dependence upon external agents.[67] So, too, as Liu has convincingly argued, the "forming hand" passage that immediately follows reframes the poet's "first creative sensibility" in largely external, impersonal terms (2.409). The "plastic power" that "abode with me," though clearly an internal operation generating an "auxiliar light [. . .] from my mind" (2.409, 417–18, 414), is also cast as a "local spirit of its own," distanced from the poet's own creative agency. It is one thing to model creativity as the internal play with nature's affordances. It is another to describe creativity as a power that operates alongside or at arm's length from the poet's own agency.

This push beyond association theory became more pronounced as the poem progressed after 1799, particularly with reference to the spots of time. In the earliest version of *The Prelude*, "spots of time" are defined simply in terms of the internal work of memory. That well-known passage reads:

> There are in our existence spots of time
> Which with distinct pre-eminence retain
> A fructifying virtue, whence, depressed
> By trivial occupations and the round
> Of ordinary intercourse, our minds—
> Especially the imaginative power—
> Are nourished and invisibly repaired. (1799 1.288–94)

Certain memories lodge in the mind in such a way that they become, in the language of "Tintern Abbey," "life and food / For future years," providing the imagination with sustenance or reparation (65–66). The expanded definition given in Book 11 heightens the tension between inner power and outer determination, referring to these moments once more in the language of Book 1's ministering spirits or Book 2's "local spirit of its own":

> This efficacious spirit chiefly lurks
> Among those passages of life in which
> We have had deepest feeling that the mind
> Is lord and master, and that outward sense
> Is but the obedient servant of her will.
> Such moments, worthy of all gratitude
> Are scattered everywhere, taking their date
> From our first childhood. (11.268–75)

---

67. Two-part *Prelude* 2.306.

This time around, Wordsworth adds an emphatic note that besides serving as food for the imagination in later years, in the moment of initial occurrence they also provided reassurance of the mind's sovereignty over the world. Yet, as in Book 6 (where he misrecognizes his own imagination as an external "unfathered vapour"), the assertion of the mind's sovereignty happens only under the appearance of encountering an external power, an "efficacious spirit" that mobilizes it, or, alternately, after gathering up found objects "scattered everywhere" and available for the taking. They are not so much food for his own imaginative power as encounters with something else that acts for him and that he had previously called "visitings of imaginative power" (11.252). Wordsworth frames these encounters as acts of imagination, but the vast majority of the work is offloaded onto the environment and very little is left for the poet to do.

In Book 7's London scenes—the part of *The Prelude* that models how a different, more populated, and more constructed environment changes thinking—Wordsworth continues this logic by modeling creative acts in which the poet has some role, but still a minimal one. After describing his encounter with the blind beggar, whom the younger Wordsworth thinks of as a "type" of "the utmost that we know / Both of ourselves and of the universe" (7.618–20), the poem distinguishes that type of emblem-making from a different and more natural type of figurative processing:

> Though reared upon the base of outward things,
> These chiefly are such structures as the mind
> Builds for itself. Scenes different there are—
> Full-formed—which take, with small internal help,
> Possession of the faculties. (7.624–28)

The contrast here is between two types of poetic or figurative "structures" that the mind builds to process the world around it. One is the blind beggar as a trope, which the younger poet made for himself in a high-minded moment and which required a good amount of analogical effort to turn a man into a poetic image, a shorthand for his own future ruminations or a tool to think with. It is a moment that the younger Wordsworth is proud of, and the older, narrating Wordsworth seems embarrassed about. The other type of poetic "structure" of thought is less like a straightforward symbol or allegory and requires very little internal effort.[68] Unlike the blind beggar, they

---

68. The opposition between stylized "emblems" and naturally occurring figures bears some resemblance to Coleridge's better-known opposition of allegory and symbol. Yet while both formulations oppose allegory to something more organic, Coleridge emphasizes the mind's internal creative power of shaping new wholes, where Wordsworth, in contrast, emphasizes the

arise "full formed." This addendum to the blind beggar episode, I suggest, is a description of the kind of poetic "power" Wordsworth is trying to name—one that looks like nature thinking for him and that, while it resembles analogy, emblem, or allegory, is assembled by the world rather than by the mind.

That external location of creative agency—the literalization of what merely *seemed* external in Book 2's "forming hand" passage—takes place, predictably, in the poem's climax on Mount Snowdon. Like the blind beggar episode, what arises is an analogy between the natural scene and the human condition. The "breach / Through which the homeless voice of waters rose" seems to be the chasm in which "Nature lodged / The soul, the imagination of the whole" (13.62–65). This image serves later as a sort of fully formed analogy for "a mighty mind," but one that appears to him ready-made, and highlights the ways that nature "moulds," "endues" "abstracts," and "combines" on behalf of the receiving mind (13.79). The point, unlike what the "spots of time" passage alleges, is not that the mind is lord and master, but rather that there is a power in nature that sometimes does work much like the mind does. If in Book 6 Wordsworth famously misrecognizes as an "unfathered vapour" what he can later call his imagination, Snowdon is where, as Geoffrey Hartman puts it, "the poet comes face to face with his Imagination yet calls it Nature."[69] There might have been many reasons why Wordsworth *wanted* to call his imagination "Nature" at this point. One of them, I have been suggesting, has less to do with his reification of his own powers and more to do with his long-standing conviction that his own poetic agency came from outside.

Appropriately, the culminating image in *The Prelude* as a whole is an image of nature's external agency—an image which is itself made by nature and which confirms the poet's conviction that the power

> which Nature thus
> Thrusts forth upon the senses, is the express
> Resemblance—in the fullness of its strength
> Made visible—a genuine counterpart
> And brother of the glorious faculty
> Which higher minds bear with them as their own. (13.85–90)

This picture of creative agency resembling a primary creative force in the world is hardly an anomaly in the Romantic canon. It resembles that most canonical formulation of creativity, Book 13 of Coleridge's *Biographia Liter-*

---

mind's minimal agency. For a detailed discussion of the Coleridgean symbol and the limits of its coherence as a concept see Nicholas Halmi, *The Genealogy of the Romantic Symbol*.

69. Hartman, *Wordsworth's Poetry, 1787–1814* 226.

aria. Yet in its traditional, Coleridgean formulation, the "echo" of God's primary imagination is, for the creative mind, a very internal affair—the action of a divine spark we all have within us. For Wordsworth, there is a lot more slippage between the individual mind's action and its "genuine counterpart" that acts alongside us. This differs from collaborative co-creation with the world or the affordances of association's collateral interests. The Snowdon passage evinces a faith, tinged by natural theology, that analogies are not mere chance resemblances to be marked between human affairs and natural scenes; but that there are actual, structural reasons why the external world can do some of our thinking for us. If nature is structured by a principle *like* (indeed "a genuine counterpart / And brother of") our minds, then it is only natural that it might do some thinking, too, and that some of our own thinking might therefore come to us fully formed.

It took a lot of blank verse, including the jettisoned "analogy passage" and many other false starts, digressions, and overlapping aims, to get to the point where nature's external contribution to *poiesis* could seem like a viable, consistent possibility. As it stands, the Snowdon scene may well leave things too clean and too consistent, too suggestive of a particular, safe theological framework. But as an endpoint to *The Prelude,* the image of the mind of Snowdon, like the impossible "element to stamp her image on" of Book 5, sets out a goal toward which the rest of *The Prelude*'s less tidy moments aspire. The river's murmurs, the nurse's song, the ministering spirits, and the "forming hand" all serve as influences upon the mind that come to appear more than influences and become instead constitutive parts of the poet's cognitive processing. The poem lodges in the landscape a power Wordsworth also wants to assign to books, creating a homology between a ministry of nature (by which the affordances of sensory entanglement can, by a sort of "ministry more palpable," proceed to perform more complex processing for him) and the "palms atchieved" by the collective human intellect. Whether it looks to books, or nature's ministry, or the second nature of "transfigured" knowledge, the poetic mind depends as much on its own powers as on the external world—on its social supports, as well as on nature—as a "prop / To our infirmity."

CHAPTER 5

"Incoherent Song"

Scott and the Margins of Sociability

> It's the *worst sort* of classroom activity, the rote memorization, that supplies the best model for cognitive science, because it has the nice feature of decoupling memory from understanding. Memory of this sort is just brute storage (like a singer memorizing the lyrics of a Russian song without having the faintest idea what they mean).[1]

DANIEL DENNETT'S offhand remark above about song and memory is a surprising callback to some long-standing Enlightenment and Romantic claims about popular poetry. As Lowth and others emphasized, poetry served a mnemonic function for oral cultures and had a special but often "rote" way of relating individual and cultural memory. Moreover, as a feature of "brute" memory—the underlying cognitive mechanisms that have no necessary connection with reason or understanding—Dennett's turn to "brute storage" echoes those eighteenth-century primitivists who aligned poetry not with the mind's most developed powers but with its earlier and less developed point of origin. Eventually, it seems, such affiliation of poetry with rudimentary, foundational, and unremarkable features of the mind became a "model for cognitive science" and the different sorts of mental activity someone like Dennett is trying to separate.

This chapter argues that Walter Scott, in his first novel *Waverley* (1814), uses poetry and traditional song to accomplish a similar separation of mental faculties. In the character of Davie Gellatley, the Baron of Bradwardine's intellectually disabled attendant with a penchant for memorizing scraps of poetry, Scott brings Romantic-era discourses of intellectual disability to bear directly on the questions of mental development and traditional literature

---

1. Dennett, *The Intentional Stance* 220.

that this book has been tracing from their Enlightenment origins. Scott picks up a conversation that we last saw in Wordsworth's lyrical ballad "The Idiot Boy" and that, on Bewell's reading of that poem, resists Enlightenment discourses of "idiocy" by connecting it to primitive cognition and poetic figuration.[2] Ultimately, the last chapter argued, Wordsworth's picture of the poetic mind escaped that primitivist logic. In a move that "The Idiot Boy" actually anticipates in other ways, Wordsworth searched for a language with which to describe a less bounded, more dependent, and more distributed approach to the mind's basic powers. In *Waverley*, Scott responds to Wordsworth directly and develops his own, rival account of a materially dependent, fragmented, and socially distributed mind.

In the novel, Davie Gellatley is the first character the protagonist Edward Waverley meets upon his arrival in Scotland, and the first local Scottish character who is given dialogue. He is really Waverley's first encounter with "Scotland" in general, aside from the unkempt village of Tully-Veolan and the Scottish girls he sees washing clothes. Davie enters the novel's pages singing "with great earnestness, and not without some taste, a fragment of an old Scotch ditty" (41). Throughout the novel he reappears in several different roles: as a figure of traditional ballad literature; an ironic commentator on the plot's events; and a minor character designed to provoke readerly sympathy. It would be easy, though, to read the narrator's own sympathies as more divided. Early on, the narrator alleges that Davie is a "half-crazed simpleton," possessing "so much wild wit as saved him from the imputation of idiocy" (58). Davie's initial character sketch juxtaposes his talent for the demands of traditional oral literature—"warm affections, a prodigious memory, and an ear for music"—with an eccentricity that runs athwart social norms and manners (58). From the start Davie is marked by "the oddity of [his] appearance and gestures," both in his clothing and in his possession of a "wild, unsettled, irregular expression," an expression that the novel tells us results from "neither idiocy nor insanity [. . .] but something resembling a compound of both, where the simplicity of the fool was mixed with the extravagance of a crazed imagination" (40–41). It is clear enough that *Waverley* makes ballad collection, transmission, and preservation a central theme. But why does it link its chief examples of traditional literature to this particular understanding of disability? To answer this question, this chapter considers how Scott responds to and revises earlier theories of poetry as cognition. From its first Scottish scene, *Waverley* engages with the previous century's arguments about popular poetry and the architecture of the mind. Specifically, this chapter revisits

---

2. *Wordsworth and the Enlightenment* 69. See chapter 4.

a long-standing association of the discourse of Romantic idiocy with poetic theory's arguments about the primitive mind.

As Dennett suggests in the epigraph to this chapter, the cognitive paradigm has a surprising affinity with earlier approaches to popular song. In fact, Dennett suggests that memorized, phonetically learned songs offer a "model for cognitive science" because they highlight the separate, lower-level, subrational processes that are so central to mental functioning. To follow up on that surprising affinity, then, this chapter considers how, for Scott, popular song offers an alternative to the rational, imaginative, or "organic" models of the mind that appear as recognizable commonplaces in Romantic discourse. That insight matches the revisionary account of Romantic poetics that ballad studies has also begun to confirm.[3] Talking about the poetic mind did not always entail a concept of lyric that pointed toward primitive, pristine modes of thinking and feeling. Rather, the ballad tradition Scott invokes also registers the mind's "brute" or "rote" features—features that fit less neatly within Romantic sentimentality and the modes of sociability it entailed.

Scott is frequently aligned with that sentimentality, at least in terms of literary form. In fact, his major literary contribution—his series of Waverley novels—has often been viewed as a "farewell to poetry" and a reckoning with the forms of sentimental history.[4] More pointedly, Ian Duncan has argued that Scott's turn to the novel offers an alternative to the "Kantian-Coleridgean" lyric, which "casts the imagination as a trace of an alienated transcendental cognition."[5] The alternative to this overdetermined model of the lyric, by Duncan's account, is sentimental fiction, which provided the fictional counterpart of Hume's skeptical philosophy. As Hume "traces a skeptical dismantling of the metaphysical foundations of reality and their replacement with a sentimental investment in 'common life,'" so too do "Scott's novels activate skepticism rather than faith as the subjective cast of their reader's relation to history" (29). In fact, Duncan argues, Scott's rise to prominence coincides with a revival of Humean skepticism over Reid's nativist "faith." Yet even as he made his supposed farewell to poetry, this chapter shows, Scott identified the materiality of poetry as a stronghold against the skepticism that sentimental fiction could be seen as accommodating. For Scott, the answer to that skepti-

---

3. On the relation between ballad production and more canonical accounts of Romantic authorship see especially Newman, *Ballad Collecting*; McLane, *Balladeering*; and Simpson, *Literary Minstrelsy*.

4. In contrast, Celeste Langan suggests that if Davie is "a kind of anachronism," he shows how Scott's "farewell to poetry, a farewell supposedly announced with the publication of *Waverley*, need not be complete" ("The Poetry of Pure Memory" 70). On sentimental history see Mark Salber Phillips, *Society and Sentiment*.

5. Duncan, *Scott's Shadow* 124.

cism comes from ballad poetry, which *Waverley* figures as an outmoded and obsolescent form, even as Scott is deploying for the first time the techniques of "historical romance." In *Waverley,* ballad poetry appears as a vestige of an older Scottish popular culture, as something that, like Reid's common sense, was by 1814 increasingly a matter of the past. However, this chapter argues, *Waverley* also looks forward to the materialist recuperations of Reidian common sense that would arise—especially in Scotland—during Scott's most productive years as a novelist. I first contextualize *Waverley* within discussions of Enlightenment idiocy; I then turn to the reception and extension of Reid's philosophy in the Edinburgh phrenological circles to demonstrate a physiological argument about the mind with which *Waverley* has strong affinities. I then read Scott's account of poetry and cognition in light of this alternate tradition before turning to the broader influence of Scott and his early critics on the nineteenth-century scientific community.

"WILD BOYS" AND POETS

Waverley's depiction of Davie Gellatley is only implicitly allusive to Wordsworth until late in the novel, in the chapter titled "Desolation." In the aftermath of the failed Jacobite uprising, stretches of formerly inhabited land are deserted or demolished, and many of the families that supported the Jacobite cause have gone into hiding. At this point, Waverley revisits the ruins of Tully-Veolan and is met by Davie, who initially regards him with suspicion. Eventually, Waverley prompts recognition by whistling a tune that he had taught Davie and had become one of his favorites. That intimation of relationship through significant but wordless tune assuages Davie's fears, and he takes Waverley to the Baron's hiding place. It is there, in a scene of mother and son, that the allusion to Wordsworth's Betty and Johnny Foy takes place. Davie's doting mother Janet praises him for his ability to tend barehanded to the eggs roasting on the fire. This prompts Waverley, and the narrator, to turn to Davie

> with his nose almost in the fire, nuzzling among the ashes, kicking his heels, mumbling to himself, turning the eggs as they lay in the hot embers, as if to confute the proverb, that "there goes reason to roasting of eggs," and justify the eulogium which poor Janet poured out upon
> "Him whom she loved, her idiot boy." (320)[6]

---

6. Scott here paraphrases the often-repeated and -varied line of "The Idiot Boy," which first appears in line 11 of Wordsworth's poem (*Lyrical Ballads* 91–104).

Scott's allusion here serves as much as a commentary upon Janet Gellatley's maternal style as upon Davie himself. From Coleridge to John Wilson, Wordsworth's readers had complained of the difficulty they had sympathizing with Betty Foy's maternal affections.[7] Most important, though, the allusion to Wordsworth serves as a late confirmation that Scott is joining a conversation about poetry and disability. As the previous chapter noted, "The Idiot Boy" was Wordsworth's most explicit engagement with the discourse of Enlightenment idiocy, and it makes a polemical claim for the importance of the lyric and its figurative modes of expression. In *Wordsworth and the Enlightenment*, Bewell identifies Johnny as an example of idiocy and, more generally, of the Enlightenment category of "marginal people," the "'idiots,' 'wild children,' blind, deaf, and mute people'" who offered a particular kind of evidence about the early mind (39–40). Writers like Locke, Monboddo, and Condillac understood "idiocy," in particular, as the condition of being stuck with one's original blank slate. Those who were deaf and mute, or the so-called wild children who seemed to have been raised away from human society, were seen as offering valuable evidence of human mental life in its earliest, presocietal stages, and thus of what all our minds were like before our educations at the hands of an advanced culture.[8] Wordsworth's achievement, in Bewell's argument, is to identify with marginal figures rather than instrumentalizing them. In "The Idiot Boy" Wordsworth celebrates the marginal by aligning idiocy with a lyrical mode, a mode that the poem asserts as valuable over and against its own narrative frame. The previous chapter discussed that poem in light of its models of social intelligence and social entanglement. But because Scott engages at length with its depiction of poetic "idiocy," that aspect of the poem deserves some further discussion here.

"The Idiot Boy" tells the tale of Betty Foy, who sets her son Johnny ("her idiot boy") off on horseback to bring home a doctor for their neighbor, Susan Gale. When Johnny fails to return, Betty grows worried and after much searching discovers the horse standing idly, feeding by a waterfall, as Johnny sits calmly or, as Wordsworth suggestively puts it, "as careless as if nothing were" (360). It is the poem's conclusion—in Johnny's answer to his mother's

---

7. Coleridge complained that the poem offered "disgusting images of *ordinary, morbid idiocy*," which, when coupled with the "folly of the mother," made the poem seem "a laughable burlesque on the blindness of anile dotage" (*Biographia* 2.48). In response to John Wilson's similar complaint, Wordsworth asserted that "the Boy whom I had in my mind was, by no means disgusting in his appearance quite the contrary and I have known several with imperfect faculties who are handsome in their persons and features" (Wordsworth and Wordsworth, *The Letters of William and Dorothy Wordsworth* 357).

8. For a detailed discussion of the eighteenth century's "feral children," see Harlan Lane, *The Wild Boy of Aveyron*.

entreaty to tell the tale of "where all this long night you have been, / What you have heard, what you have seen"—that the poem resists narrative in favor of the lyrical:

> "The cocks did crow to-whoo, to-whoo,
> "And the sun did shine so cold."
> —Thus answered Johnny in his glory,
> And that was all his travel's story. (460–63)

After Betty's tense, counterfactual conjectures as to Johnny's fate, the poem comes to a carefully prepared anticlimax that amounts to a refusal of plot or story. This is to the narrator's own ostensible regret, since reporting Johnny's adventures would have made "a most delightful tale" (326). In short, Betty has a narrative, the tale of "maternal passion" that Wordsworth emphasizes in the 1800 preface.[9] Johnny, in contrast, has only an elliptical attempt to report certain enigmatic sensations. "The Idiot Boy" makes the lyric a primal and first-person category against the third-person accumulation of narrative "incident."

This non-narrative emphasis makes sense on most accounts of Enlightenment idiocy. Since idiocy was understood as a slowness of the faculties, and as an impairment of memory, it implied a continual flow of sensations the memory could not catch, which for that reason could not take a narrative structure. In Bewell's argument, the very fact of Johnny's reporting *anything* offers a retort to Enlightenment constructions of idiocy. His ability to articulate his experience retrospectively would have been remarkable to a "philosophical reader," Bewell argues in *Wordsworth and the Enlightenment*, since "to an age that saw idiocy as a state excluded from language and memory, its very existence would have seemed to offer rare empirical support for an investigation of the origin of language and memory" (68). Ultimately, though, Bewell thinks that Wordsworth intentionally frustrates that Enlightenment impulse, since the evidentiary narrative Johnny would provide is something that the poem flatly refuses. Instead of delivering that impossible narrative of origins, Johnny's reply "suggests that the world that first appears to human perception is fundamentally metaphoric. Only later, as language (and with it knowledge) develops, do 'moons' and 'owls' displace the cold suns and hooting cocks of primitive perception" (69).

Poetic language, however, cannot be made a separate matter and cannot be so neatly bracketed from the broader Enlightenment stance toward cognitive origins. While Bewell argues that Wordsworth defies his philosophical

---

9. *Lyrical Ballads* 745.

reader's expectations, it is important to recognize that the poem's alternative—its privileging of primitive, figural cognition—keeps it entangled with a quest for origins. Richardson reinforces that alignment with origins when he notes that Johnny has "a knack for figurative language" (*British Romanticism* 168). Wordsworth's identification with marginal figures may be preferable to their instrumental treatment at the hands of earlier practitioners. Yet, despite what chapter 4 saw as the poem's other, more "distributed" interests, the concluding moment of "The Idiot Boy" remains bound up with the Romantic construction of poetry (and idiocy) as a return to the early mind. Through theories that correlated cognitive function with the development of language in the individual mind, many of these accounts celebrated the lower ranges of cognitive functioning by associating them with poetic language and, as previous chapters have shown, with the early "paucity" of language that generates metaphorical figuration. In other words, for many language theorists, figural language *was* the origin of language. If Wordsworth's Johnny Foy strains to describe his experience, then at some level he is recapitulating that same early phase of cognitive development.

At stake here is the principle of Enlightenment thought that Bewell, for his part, finds "ironic"—namely, "that empirical philosophy," which aimed for a description of "normal" functioning, became "preeminently a discourse about marginal people" (25). Besides the general logic of the statistical norm, there was also a methodological reason that this happened. By the same logic as the study of physiology and pathology, the best way to learn about the body in health, it seemed, was to study disease. The best way to study how the body worked was to study examples in which it did not work as it should. It is worth noting that this principle still applies broadly in experimental psychology, specifically in cognitive neuroscience. The principle is that if a biological *mechanism* is what enables a particular ability, then studying cases where that ability is impaired will show us what and where the mechanism is. In studies of social intelligence—which this book has been tracking in terms of debates about theory of mind or mindreading—this principle has been important to many of the researchers who posit an innate mechanism associated with social intelligence. For example, Baron-Cohen has influentially (though problematically) proposed that a specific kind of impairment may be the key to locating the innate mechanism that drives mental state attribution: He has hypothesized that autism is an impairment of a "theory of mind mechanism" in a particular region of the brain.[10] While "normally developing" (that is, neu-

---

10. See Baron-Cohen, *Mindblindness*. For a discussion of the liabilities of the model of autism as a deficit see the introduction.

rotypical) children begin to show evidence of theory of mind by their fourth year, this argument goes, those with Autism Spectrum Disorder struggle to perform ordinary mindreading tasks. That capacity typically correlates with the ability to attribute false beliefs to other agents. To use the example from the foundational experiment in this line of thinking, if Sally did not see Anne move the marble to the red box, then you, observing this scene, ought to realize that she (unlike you) now has a mistaken belief about its location.[11] The close correlation between Autism Spectrum Disorder and the failure of such "false belief" tasks led Baron-Cohen and others to propose that such disorders represented a physiological impairment of theory of mind via damage to or underdevelopment of a particular part of the brain. By comparing the brain function of those who "pass" and "fail" tests like this one, modular nativists argue, we ought to be able to locate the region that houses this theory-of-mind mechanism. The methodology is foundational for the modular-nativist paradigm, although (as should be clear enough from the summary above) it frames disability in deeply troubling ways.[12]

It is noteworthy, then, that if Wordsworth's "Idiot Boy" frames poetic disability as a return to human origins, Scott's treatment of Davie more closely resembles the cognitive-scientific model of localized, functionally specific impairment. While Scott repeatedly invokes the discourse of idiocy, he also puts in question whether that term is really the best description for Davie. The narrator introduces Davie as possessing "neither idiocy nor insanity [. . .] but something resembling a compound of both" and as marked equally by "simplicity" and "extravagance" (40–41). This unaccountable nature seems to have entered the realm of folk wisdom too, as evidenced by the "hypothesis" of the "common people [. . .] that David Gellatley was no farther fool than was necessary to avoid hard labour" (58). Richardson has helpfully suggested that these skeptical or equivocal stances toward Davie register a growing suspicion that idiocy was not an adequate frame of reference and might not imply the general slowness of faculties that Enlightenment thinkers had postulated. Instead, Richardson argues, Romantic writers became increasingly sensitive to a model of an embodied and functionally differentiated mind, one with discrete and separable faculties that can be selectively under- or overdeveloped. One of the breakthroughs of the time was to recognize a range of disabilities as resulting not from a lack of development but from the *overdevelopment* of

---

11. For this "false belief task" experiment see Baron-Cohen, Leslie, and Frith, "Does the Autistic Child Have a 'Theory of Mind'?"

12. For a critique from disability studies see Jack, "'The Extreme Male Brain?'" For a critique of the way this approach has influenced cognitive approaches to literature see Savarese and Zunshine, "The Critic as Neurocosmopolite."

one particular faculty. Richardson links this idea of selective overdevelopment to the nascent "biological psychology" of early phrenologists which generates a small repertoire of "'partial' idiots" in Romantic literature.[13] With its focus on discrete, functionally differentiated "organs" within the brain, phrenology anticipated the accounts of functionally localized (or on some accounts "modular") brain function that continue to drive research on the brain in the cognitive sciences.

Phrenology is, to be sure, just as dubious an interpretive frame as Enlightenment anthropology or Baron-Cohen's concept of "mindblindness." Yet Richardson's reframing of Davie is compelling because it explains one alternative Scott saw to the Enlightenment discourse of idiocy and the model of poetry it implies. If Davie is actually not simply a "wild boy" or "idiot" but a selectively overdeveloped prodigy, then he is not simply another gloss on the primitive, lyric mind. Richardson treats Davie's gift for poetry as one of many possible talents Scott might have assigned him. He speculates that since Davie's brother was reportedly a great songwriter, "Davie's powers as well as his deficits may be congenital, a matter of familial inheritance" (167). But Davie, as well as his brother, could just as easily have been prodigious painters, or prodigious sportsmen, and would still have served as figures of an incipient model of the functionally differentiated mind. Per my argument Davie's poetic "overdevelopment" does not just reinforce the novel's interests in Scottish culture and traditional literature. It also launches a particular argument about poetry, one that significantly revises poetry's place in the Enlightenment developmental schema of "The Idiot Boy."

Davie's role as songster is a testament to poetry's overdetermined status in theories of ancient literature and culture and in studies of the mind. When, in *Biographia,* Coleridge wants to accuse Hartley's association theory of determinism, he accuses him of insulting the dignity of poetic activity. On such arguments, Coleridge explains:

> The inventor of the watch did not in reality invent it; he only looked on, while the blind causes, the only true artists, were unfolding themselves. [...] So must it have been with Mr. SOUTHEY and LORD BYRON, when the one *fancied* himself composing "RODERICK," and the other his "CHILDE HAROLD." (1.119–20)

---

13. Richardson, *British Romanticism* 164.

Coleridge's choice of poets is unsurprising: Southey was his friend, and he was currently soliciting favors from Byron.[14] But their writing processes are sacred enough to be juxtaposed with the watch and the watchmaker, an analogy of mechanical operation that had strong ties to natural theology. The so-called blind causes would assail divine activity as well as human activity, for which poetry is the metonym of choice.

Coleridge's aim here is to defend the unity of the mind against those who, like Hartley, would reduce it to its component parts. In particular, he rejected associationism's "mapping" of ideas and impressions onto particular nerves and fibers. Hazlitt seconded Coleridge's arguments and would later critique Gall and Spurzheim's phrenology the same way, arguing that the mind could not possibly be made up of local, functionally specific organs. Instead, Hazlitt asserted the unity of consciousness, arguing for a single sentient principle that could, at any time, have access to all of the mind's contents. At times he confessed that this approach was impressionistic, calling it his "dull, cloudy, English mysticism."[15] Like Coleridge, Hazlitt would in his literary criticism make poetry answerable to that single, undifferentiated faculty of mind he referred to simply as "consciousness."

Locke had been largely of Coleridge's opinion. In *An Essay Concerning Human Understanding* Locke grants that "sound may mechanically cause a certain motion of the animal Spirits, in the Brains of those Birds, whilst the Tune is actually playing; and that motion may be continued on to the Muscles of the Wings." His rationale was that such reflexes would enable immediate flight from danger and thus "tend to the Birds Preservation." But Locke can find no such explanatory basis for automation in singing, "which imitation can be of no use to the Bird's Preservation" (154–55). Not even poetry but also the birdsong to which it is compared in Romantic poetics was, for Locke, too willful an activity to be considered automatic. Thus even for Locke, nonpurposive song breaks free from the explanatory power of material psychology.

For Coleridge, this independence from mechanical causes is particularly important when the poetry in question is biblical poetry—the overdetermined variety of ancient poetry that surfaces again and again in histories of the poetic mind, from Lowth to Priestley and Anna Letitia Barbauld.[16] Coleridge, like Lowth, was strongly invested in biblical writers' status as full human agents as opposed to mere vessels for the inspired word. In his "Confessions of an

---

14. For a discussion of the fawning letters Coleridge wrote to Byron during the summer of 1815 see Earl Leslie Griggs, "Coleridge and Byron."

15. Hazlitt, *Selected Works* 1.63.

16. On Lowth see chapters 1 and 2. On Priestley's and Barbauld's treatment of Hebrew literature see chapter 3.

Inquiring Spirit," he specifically rejects such theories as detrimental to the character of the biblical poet King David: They imply that "this *sweet Psalmist of Israel* was himself a mere instrument as his harp, an *automaton* poet, mourner, and supplicant" (2.1136).[17] Coleridge—or his persona—will submit himself to the poet, a mere "instrument" to be played, such that "every several nerve of emotion, passion, thought, that thrids [sic] the *flesh-and-blood* of our common Humanity responds to the Touch" (1136). But the poet himself must be no such passive thing. Importantly, Coleridge pursues this argument about the integrity of human action by appealing not to scriptural authority but instead to a more self-evident fact about reading: that readers have bodies, and those bodies feel. Poetry is an example—in fact, *the* example—of free human action, and that freedom is crucial both for the historical efficacy of writing and the experience of reading. The issue at stake is not the authority of scripture but the value of poetry. Historical actors cannot be made into automata, especially if they are poets.

Davie Gellatley is not an "automaton poet." But his poetic practice seems associative or automatically prompted and runs afoul of Coleridge's association of poetry with rationality and freedom. In fact, if Davie is less like a wild boy than, as Richardson suggests, an "idiot savant" or a selectively overdeveloped prodigy, then his rote poetics would have invoked a long history of identifying the prodigious with the mechanical. It was Descartes's description of selective overdevelopments, after all, that underwrote the eighteenth-century discourse of automata. For Descartes, highly selective abilities were symptoms of mindlessness. If an animal outperforms a human at a specific task, Descartes argues, it is always to be observed that they will underperform humans in just about everything else. Since, Descartes argues, animals are essentially machines, they can dramatically outperform humans at particular, highly selective tasks but cannot display the general "dexterity" that characterizes the human:

> Hence, the fact that they do better than we do, does not prove that they are endowed with mind, for in this case they would have more reason than any of us, and would surpass us in all other things. It rather shows that they have no reason at all, and that it is nature which acts in them according to the disposition of their organs, just as a clock, which is only composed of wheels and weights is able to tell the hours and measure the time more correctly than we can do with all our wisdom."[18]

---

17. *Shorter Works and Fragments* 2.1111–71.
18. Descartes, *The Philosophical Works of Descartes* 1:117.

In this view Descartes differs sharply from Locke, who even when discussing animals frequently argued against mere automation. Unlike La Mettrie in the eighteenth century, the Romantic era's paradigm shift in the science of the mind did not produce a simple account of a clocklike "machine-man" whose bodily motions simply resulted from the "disposition" and reflexes of particular organs.

Yet Romantic science frequently took interest in the elements of embodied mental life that *did* seem to point to the organs that drove cognition. Those who, like Davie, raised the specter of the Cartesian prodigy or mechanical animal gave clues about the ways that the mind could be understood not just as an undifferentiated faculty of thought but also as a set of coordinated bodily organs. This change is at heart a difference in philosophical method—a difference in the way philosophers dealt with the evidence impairment provided, as a Cartesian model of the prodigy came back to the forefront of the conversation. And that difference of method is what I take to be the distinctive development between "The Idiot Boy" and *Waverley*.

This is why Scott's treatment of Davie is all the more provoking to the line of thinking with which Wordsworth plays in "The Idiot Boy." That poem makes the lyric a primal and first-person category against the third-person accumulation of narrative "incident." This return to cognitive and linguistic origins frequently effaced the social component of human mental development and resulted in the philosophical impasse that marked both Enlightenment anthropology's theories of solitary origin and Hume's skeptical epistemology. The emerging model of an embodied, functionally differentiated mind countervailed that early model of primitive cognition and looked instead to a functionally differentiated mind in which sociality is also a basic faculty. I locate this emerging model in Scott, specifically in *Waverley*'s argument about genre, to which I now turn.

SKEPTICAL, SENTIMENTAL, AND MODULAR LITERATURES

Discussions of Scott and genre are inevitably routed through discussions of the historical novel. When it comes to the cognitive claims entailed by particular genres, the historical novel points in the direction of sentimental history and Humean skepticism, a context that Duncan has helpfully unpacked. Duncan argues that Scott offers the fictional counterpart of Hume's skepticism by writing novels that trace "a Humean dialectical progression from metaphysical illusion through melancholy disenchantment to a sentimental and ironical reattachment to common life" (29). Sentimental history—a genre in which Hume himself excelled—makes readerly sentiment the vehicle of historical engagement. This paralleled the way that Hume's philosophy made the imagination the source of all knowledge, and made sentiment and custom take the place of hard metaphysical truths. In Scott's hands, sentimental history gives way to the overtly fictional novel, which Duncan argues "activate[s] skepticism rather than faith as the subjective cast of their reader's relation to history" (29). Paul Hamilton reads *Waverley* along similar lines. He identifies its arc as a "relinquishing of Kant's supposed advance on Humean philosophy" because "it reverts from the logical necessity of believing in valid representation to Hume's strictly psychological explanation of why we do so."[19]

Duncan, in particular, makes a strong correlation between Scott's rise to prominence and the revival of Hume's philosophy in the 1810s, which ended a decades-long reign by Reid and his students. In his explanation of Reid's sudden decline, Duncan attributes a good deal to the work of Thomas Brown, who, by providing a Humean reworking of Reid, weakened Reid's claims and paved the way for Hume's return. Notably, Brown wrongly equates Reid's faculties with Hume's feelings and suggests that the difference is merely one of emphasis: While the skeptic says that belief is *only* a feeling, Brown argues, the commonsense philosopher simply says that the force of that feeling is irresistible. For Duncan, this means that Brown "revives Hume's more subtle, dialectical stance" against Reid's stubborn insistence on directly apprehended realities (135). The problem with Brown's redaction, though, is that it effaces the terms of Reid's quarrel with Hume altogether. Reid's objection had been that the faculties by which we know the world are determined not by the imagination—the representational philosophy he termed the "way of ideas"—but by separate faculties, notably "conception."

Reid was for decades the most important name for that resistance to Humean skepticism. In the years following Reid's supposed decline, commonsense resistance to skepticism took a surprisingly materialist turn. Scottish converts to phrenology—notably the members of the Edinburgh Phrenological Society—recast Reid as an underappreciated materialist. Where Brown took great pains to bend Reid back toward the Humean system from which he had departed, the Edinburgh phrenologists made Reid the progenitor of a biologically minded, antiskeptical philosophy of mind that multiplied the mind's basic faculties. In many respects, phrenology earned its reputation as a pseudoscience. Yet in the hands of its Scottish redactors, in the Edinburgh circles that included George Combe, Andrew Combe, William A. F. Browne,

---

19. Hamilton, *Metaromanticism* 121.

Robert Edmund Grant, and Charles Darwin, phrenology mobilized a powerful argument about the relationship between mind and brain.[20] These circles, which had a massive influence on materialist philosophy of mind, and on Darwin's meditations on human mental development, produced a flawed but historically significant redaction of Reid's faculty psychology.[21] So, when Duncan acknowledges that "at its most sophisticated, Reid's argument anticipates neo-Darwinian or sociobiological explanations" of credulity, there is indeed a story to tell about the line that runs from Reid to the material mind (132).

In his "Preliminary Dissertation" to the *Transactions of the Phrenological Society*, George Combe is explicit about this intellectual debt, which he casts in conspicuously nationalist terms. He cites a review of Reid's *Inquiry* from the *Quarterly Review*, which had objected to Reid's claims for "common sense." In fact, the reviewer had pointed out that the existence of "simple and uncompounded faculties" was not "a point which no person had dared dispute," as Reid had proposed, but was actually quite controversial.[22] For Combe, the reviewer's "English" objection to Reid's premise was merely a matter of national difference. The *Quarterly* reviewer participates, Combe suggests, in a long tradition of English essayistic prose, one that descended from Addison to Johnson and that retained a native prejudice in favor of the Lockean "way of ideas." Locke admits that the mind is made up of component parts, the ideas received from sensation and reflection. Yet the empirical analysis of the mind that followed Locke tended to treat the mind as one thinking thing, as a single faculty of sensation that linked together the successive moments and objects of experience. Combe's materialist rejoinder is that the mind is, in fact, made up of many faculties, which run independently of one another. This alternative is, for Combe, peculiarly Scottish, since "the Scotch metaphysicians in general, adopt the opinion, from whatever source derived, that the mind manifests a plurality of faculties."[23] Combe thus repositions Reid as the proponent of a characteristically Scottish "faith" in independent faculties of mind against a looser, English faith in the mind's unity. This is a dubious characterization of Reid, to be sure, since he was often an outspoken defender of the unity of

---

20. In fact, there is a direct line of influence between Browne's retort to Charles Bell's *Anatomy and Philosophy of Expression*, delivered in Edinburgh in 1826, and Charles Darwin's *The Expression of the Emotions in Man and Animals* (1872). It was Browne, in fact, who proposed that Darwin become a member of the Plinian Society. On this exchange, see Desmond and Moore, *Darwin's Sacred Cause* 41.

21. See Darwin's M and N notebooks, known as the Notebooks on Man, Mind, and Materialism (*Metaphysics, Materialism, and the Evolution of Mind*).

22. Combe, *Transactions of the Phrenological Society* 29.

23. It is not clear where Hume falls in Combe's primarily polemical opposition of national metaphysical trends.

the mind. Yet Combe's reconstruction of Reid offered an important alternative to the version Brown had recently recuperated. That alternative was aligned not with a return to Hume but with the new Scottish materialism.[24] For those materialists, Reid and his commonsense successors "present an *analysis* of the human faculties" for which phrenology can identify "a corporeal organ, by means of which a particular faculty manifests itself."[25] Reid provided the theory—the list of mental capabilities—and it remained for the phrenologists to map those faculties onto the brain.

I propose that Scott also develops an analogous, Reidian resistance to skepticism in his own way. Duncan calls *Waverley* "an internal allegory of the emergence of the novel as the genre of modern life from premodern traditions of ballad, epic, allegory, and romance."[26] Accordingly, I argue, those premodern forms remain the locus of resistance to the sentimental, novelistic mode the novel otherwise aligns with modernity. These traditions, and the idea of "tradition" in general, emerge at the other end of Scott's process as a manufactured nostalgia. By the novel's end, they can signal only dissatisfaction with skeptical, sentimental modernity, rather than offering a solution to its problems. Scott's real innovation is to make "idiocy" serve as more than an object of nostalgia. If idiocy was typically associated with slowness of the Humean sensorium, Scott looks instead to the brute, subrational, even mechanical processes that, like Reid's innate faculties, work independently of the sentimental imagination.

In the early chapter titled "Castle Building," Scott makes sentimental narrative itself subject to this kind of reduction. In that chapter the young Edward Waverley is listening to a stultifying rehearsal of his family history. To explain how this dry detail occasionally gives way to interesting narratives—which to Waverley resemble sentimental histories—the narrator launches a conceit:

> Family tradition and genealogical history [. . .] is the very reverse of amber, which, itself a valuable substance, usually includes flies, straws, and other trifles, whereas these studies, being themselves very insignificant and trifling, do nevertheless serve to perpetuate a great deal of what is rare and valuable

---

24. Of course, Combe thinks that Reid does this somewhat inadvertently. In fact, he notes, Reid himself remains too committed to armchair philosophy, and an introspective method of investigation, to say much about practical matters. Reid's system is "merely intellectual rather than telling us anything practical about, say, particular people, in the eyes of "courts of law" (*Transactions* 51). Combe is surely thinking here of phrenology's most often caricatured aspect, the feeling of bumps on the skull, as well as its dubious ramifications for the legal system.

25. Ibid. 38

26. Duncan, *Scott's Shadow* 136.

in ancient manners, and to record many curious and minute facts which could have been preserved and conveyed through no other medium. (17)

In this analogy, sentimental narrative is a precious rarity, embedded in uninteresting dross the novel calls the "the oft-repeated tale of narrative old age." *Narrative* here serves in the older sense of the word, indicating Sir Everard's loquaciousness as he moves with "remorseless and protracted accuracy" through a "dry deduction of his line of ancestors."[27] It is this kind of sentimental narrative, when it offers a point of entry into otherwise dry detail, that defines the genre of history as practiced by Hume and that Duncan aligns with Scott's novelistic practice.[28] But the "reverse of amber" passage also suggests that such narratives depend on a prior, more tedious mode of accumulation and indicates Scott's interest in the relationship between sentimental narrative and more rote, automatic modes of cultural transmission.

At least at the outset of Waverley's disenchanting education, sentimentality still rules. Yet, as the novel demonstrates, and this passage makes explicit, rote forms of transmission are a necessary counterpart to those sentimental moments of greater interest. In other words, it is Hume's own sentimental mode that *Waverley* is deromanticizing. Moreover, the novel's disenchanting trajectory ultimately looks *toward* the ballad as a modernizing form rather than as the premodern vestige the sentimental novel leaves in its wake. In *Waverley,* traditional modes of transmission are most thoroughly associated not with family history and genealogy but with the ballad. In the narrator's gloss we can hear an echo of Lowth's comments on ancient verse, which Lowth emphasized as a technology of memory. Lowth casts sentiment as simply the most interesting of poetry's features, one that is present mainly to help sustain all of its *less* interesting functions. Sentiment "direct[s] the perception to the minutest circumstances, and of assisting the memory in the retention of them."[29] In short, there is an analogy here between family history—as a rote process of recitation, immersed in details—and Davie's immersion in the rote practices of traditional balladic literature.

Davie's unsentimental lyricism frequently manifests itself as a failure of communication or as an inattention to the social protocols expected of him.

---

27. Scott, *Waverley* 17. For this sense of "narrative," see Dryden's and Pope's uses cited in the Oxford English Dictionary. Both instances, like Scott's, make narrativity a trait of those advanced in years. In novels this had often been a class marker, as in the gothic servants of Walpole or Radcliffe, who frustrate main characters with their plodding, roundabout method of getting to the facts.

28. On Hume's histories and sentimental literature see especially Phillips, *Society and Sentiment*.

29. Lowth, *Lectures* 39.

Scott repeatedly depicts Davie as engrossed in song to the exclusion of all else. When Davie first approaches Waverley, for instance, he is totally engrossed in his minstrelsy and fails to notice Waverley until he is almost upon him. When Waverley asks if Bradwardine is home, Davie "replied,—and, like the witch of Thalaba, 'still his speech was song,'—

> The Knight's to the mountain
>   His bugle to wind;
> The Lady's to greenwood.
>   Her garland to bind.
> The bower of Burd Ellen
>   Has moss on the floor,
> That the step of Lord William
>   Be silent and sure.

"This," the narrator archly suggests, "conveyed no information" (41). Presumably sticking close to Waverley's point of view, the narrator here suggests that Davie's recitation is an automatically prompted tune. The comedy of the scene derives from Davie's response to a serious question with an apparently whimsical, associative response. Though Scott's footnote tells us that the song is original, it seems that Davie draws on two existing ballads, drawing proper names and a few keywords from "Burd Ellen and the Young Tamlane (Child 28) and "Lord William, or Lord Lundy" (254), which he adapts and remixes into the word-game or children's rhyme we read in the text.[30]

It may well be fruitful to speculate on the hidden meanings created by this juxtaposition of balladic sources. The reference to Southey's *Thalaba the Destroyer* pointedly suggests that Davie is speaking cryptically, like Southey's witch. Her "unintelligible song" has ample meaning, after all—just not to Thalaba.[31] Indeed, some readers identified Davie as speaking more than nonsense. Robert Chambers, for instance, wrote in 1825 that Davie only *seemed* dim-witted to the dim-witted folk annoyed by him; that is, to "Waverley, and such as, like him, did not comprehend the strange metaphorical meanings of [Davie's] replies and allusions."[32] Early on, an unsigned review of *Waverley* in the *British Critic* (August 1814) had built on Scott's own Shakespearean allusions, which align Davie with the figure of the "wise fool." After noting that

---

30. Burd Ellen is a disaffected mother who, when the young Tamlane asks her to rock her child, replies bitterly before Tamlane goes to sea. The first line locates her sitting "in her bower window." See James Francis Child, ed., *The English and Scottish Popular Ballads* 1.256.
31. Southey, *Thalaba the Destroyer* 2.90.
32. Chambers, *Illustrations of the Author of* Waverley 16.

"the similarity between himself and the fool in King Lear is peculiarly striking," the critic alerts the review's readers "to a circumstance in which they have doubtless anticipated us, the strong similarity between some turns in the character of Davy and those of Blanche of Devon: Particularly the warning given by both in wild and incoherent song."[33] This double comparison to *Lear* and Scott's own *Lady of the Lake* wrenches Davie into a fairly traditional understanding of Romantic poetics as naive yet prophetic utterance, or, as what Coleridge, speaking of the fool in *King Lear*, termed "inspired idiocy."[34]

Such equations are common in the most traditionally "Romantic" statements about poetry and idiocy. But those "strange metaphorical meanings" can also refer to the practices of Jacobite code, in which memorized song played a large part.[35] More generally, Langan reminds us, pure or decontextualized poetics "would approximate the 'gibberish' that Gaelic has become to those now under the sway of England and English," for which reason those readers who take Waverley's incomprehension at face value "do so at their peril."[36] Yet it is crucial in *Waverley*, both for its treatment of Scottish tradition and for the case it makes about the human mind, that Davie's own unintelligible song *need not* be an elliptical code or contain a deeper meaning. Intimations of Jacobitism aside, Waverley's encounters with Davie yield not a specific *éclaircissement* but only continued frustration with Davie's unintelligibility and with the apparent free association engaged in by this unlikely messenger. Davie's singing seems prompted only by chance associations of ideas and frequently conveys no information. It demands close engagement, but it cannot always be "read" and does not always seem to enclose a metaphorical or figural meaning.

While such a possibility sits uncomfortably within Wordsworthian theories of primitive sensuous utterance, or of poetry as fundamentally metaphorical, it is hardly foreign to a ballad matrix that runs from wordplay and nonsense choruses to the associative engagement of terms with specific historical content.[37] In recombining or remixing traditional source materials, a potentially meaningless set of signifiers could structure social environments around collective song or could instigate social upheaval or reconfiguration.

33. See John O. Hayden, *Scott: The Critical Heritage* 67–74, 70.
34. Coleridge, *The Literary Remains of Samuel Taylor Coleridge* 2.197.
35. For the use of the *Aeneid* and epic more generally in Jacobite code see Murray Pittock, "James Macpherson and Jacobite Code."
36. Langan, "The Poetry of Pure Memory" 75, 73.
37. The brute force of memory had always been crucial for oral poetics, but it became particularly important for Jacobite song that found its purpose in group settings rather than private reading, and also in that manner kept out of the way of the law. See Pittock, *Poetry and Jacobite Politics*.

Scott was deeply invested in the ballad's culture-building work: the way that communal, social song could build itself into a patrimony worth collecting in the massive *Minstrelsy of the Scottish Border*. Yet in *Waverley* he caricatures such production, emphasizing its difference from the communicative or expressive functions that characterized the speakers of Romantic lyrics.

Davie's trade is in a sort of brute, mechanical genre that nevertheless opens onto sociality. An emblem for this mechanical yet sociable strategy would be the tune that Waverley whistles in the chapter "Desolation." When Waverley arrives, Davie is entirely absorbed in his task. Then, on noticing Waverley, he fails to recognize him as anything but a foreign agent, and he becomes skittish. The tune—which lacks linguistic content and thus remains unrepresented in the novel—nevertheless acts as the occasion for recognition and the meeting of minds. A Humean might say that Davie associates the tune with Waverley and thus connects it to the idea he has of Waverley as a known, nonthreatening person. But much of the scene's affect comes from the way that recognizing Waverley pulls Davie out of his caricatured self-immersion and establishes what even the novel's sentimentality seems invested in as real contact between minds. Of course, Davie's subverting of communication presents an interesting parallel to "mind*blindness*," the coinage of Baron-Cohen that describes the supposed impairment of an innate, mindreading module. Vermeule suggests as much when she retroactively applies the term *mindblindness* to the "wild children" that stand as Davie's progenitors.[38]

Indeed, Scott does at times appear to describe Davie's disability as a failure to abide by social norms. When Waverley has just entered Scotland and encounters Davie for the first time, Davie is so engrossed in song that he does not notice Waverley. When he does, his greeting is marked by "lifting up his eyes," which the narrator reports "had hitherto been fixed in observing how his feet kept time to the tune" (41). Davie's self-immersion here, when read in light of the novel's insistence on his actual, physiological impairment, resonates with Vermeule's interest in reduced empathy and hindered understanding of the norms of social interaction. The minute attention to technical details—indeed of technique—is an occupational hazard of the poet. In the first decades of the nineteenth century, the best-known example of this type of caricature can be found in critiques of Wordsworth, especially Hazlitt's description of Wordsworth's poetry as egoistic, and Keats's subsequent iden-

---

38. Vermeule, *Why Do We Care?* It is not clear, of course, that Peter of Hanover, or any of the other eighteenth-century "wild children" or "idiots," bear diagnosis quite as easily as Vermeule suggests (i.e., that Peter is "not a wild child raised by bears" but "an autistic boy who suffered abuse in his family" [198]). Such an equation of idiocy with autism risks a verbal and a diagnostic slippage between "autism" in particular and "neurological deficits" in general.

tification of "the Wordsworthian or egotistical sublime."[39] Besides alluding to the sublime's long-standing association with solitude (in Burke's psychological aesthetics, the solitude of primitive man), the egotistical sublime draws on a critique of egoism that comes out of the sentimental tradition. Most influentially, Adam Smith, in *The Theory of Moral Sentiments,* described egoism or antisociality as a failure of proper social decorum. Just as we sympathize with others by projecting our own mental states onto them, Smith thought, we also imagine our way into the mind of a fictional, impartial observer, from which standpoint we can judge our own actions. Egoism, in Smith's sense, is a failure of this self-regulation by sympathy: a failure to gain a reflexive awareness of oneself by taking the perspective of another. Framed this way—the way Romantic criticism has often framed the matter—the egotistical poet is stuck in a kind of Humean skeptical dilemma or a primitive, sublime solitude. Davie's absorption in his technique might, perhaps, align that type of poetic self-absorption with a nascent physiology that differentiated task-oriented abilities like musicality from other activities like sociability. In this latter model, poetic involution would speak not of an originally solitary state but to the mind's own internal division of labor.

The result is a different form of poetic cognition than the one entailed by Wordsworth's "The Idiot Boy." It is possible, of course, to put lyrical impairment, as Wordsworth did, onto the track of stadial history. In the guise of Johnny Foy, the impaired poet marks the origin of a developmental narrative of consciousness and offers to bring his readers closer to that sensuous and figural mode of thought. On the other hand, it is possible to invoke lyrical impairment—and even theories of sociocultural development—without implying that cognition follows that same developmental narrative. Instead, as in *Waverley,* a selective ability for poetry might illuminate the fact that the mind is made of many parts.

BALLAD COLLECTORS AND SKULL COLLECTORS

If Wordsworthian idiocy is a reaction to Enlightenment anthropology and its focus on primitive cognition, then the movement from "The Idiot Boy" to *Waverley* marks a shift in the way that poetry and disability were brought together. I want to conclude this chapter by suggesting some ways that, despite Scott's distaste for the sciences of the mind, Davie spoke quite suggestively to

---

39. *Letters of John Keats* 2:387.

later literary criticism, as well as to the phrenological circles that formed in Edinburgh in the 1820s.

Scott himself offers a precedent for the diagnosis of literary characters, both in his own novels and in his writings on Shakespeare. In Scott's anonymous review of his own *Tales of My Landlord*, he looks back to his early treatment of Davie as the occasion for an ambitious literary-historical claim. He explains the role of literary characters like Davie—markedly impaired and kept in the houses of the nobility—by gesturing toward a still active yet threatened tradition of keeping household "fools." The review assures its readers that "there is ample testimony that a custom, referred to Shakespeare's time in England, had, and in remote provinces of Scotland, has still its counterpart, to this day" (437). Later, he speaks of the "wild wit" which these servants "often flung about them with the freedom of Shakespeare's licensed clowns" (438). On this reading, the Shakespearean fool was not just a court jester, licensed to speak freely, but was at least in many cases an outgrowth of a tradition for supporting the disabled. Strikingly, then, Scott's comments on Shakespeare medicalize the literary by diagnosing the Shakespearean fool.

On a number of occasions, Scott attempts to situate the fool in socioeconomic reality by looking to evidence of specific disabilities and the traditional Scottish customs that supported the care of those who could not care for themselves. Such informal customs, Scott goes on to explain, offer a substitute for official state support:

> There are (comparatively speaking) no poor's rates in the country parishes of Scotland, and of course no work-houses to immure either their worn out poor or the 'moping idiot and the madman gay,' whom Crabbe characterizes as the happiest inhabitants of these mansions, because insensible of their misfortunes.[40]

Scott locates Davie here as a member of a class of household "fools," who are kept out of benevolence and who "usually displayed toward their benefactors a sort of instinctive attachment" (438). Such a concern with traditional institutions of care has a precedent in Wordsworth's "The Old Cumberland Beggar," a poem in which he similarly opposed the more recent, systemized "HOUSE, misnamed of INDUSTRY," in favor of an earlier, practice, one embedded in a society based on reflexive sympathy.[41] We must take care to

---

40. Hayden, *Scott: The Critical Heritage* 438.
41. See "The Old Cumberland Beggar" in *Lyrical Ballads* 228–34. In fact, in his response to Wilson's complaints about "The Idiot Boy," Wordsworth gestures toward a similar tradition, though he looks not geographically toward Scotland but economically toward the poor. "Per-

understand the Shakespearean fool, Scott argues, in light of material contexts: the physiological conditions underlying intellectual disability and the social institutions that might provide for such individuals—especially when, as Scott alleged, those institutions of care were quickly disappearing.

By making Davie a gloss on Shakespeare's fool, Scott reframes literary history as an endeavor that might be continuous with the deep history of empirical realities, whether social, economic, or physiological. Moreover, Scott's oeuvre prompted many to engage in the same type of criticism. In the popular genre of "Scott originals" or "Waverley anecdotes," critics implicitly framed Scott's novels as documents of particular Scottish "types." The accounts of Davie Gellatley seem paradigmatic for this brand of criticism, since his poetic activities were those already being documented by early anthropologists of popular literature and music, and because discussions of his disability picked up on cognate discourses in similar fieldwork on the mind.[42]

The most notable was Chambers, who in his 1825 *Illustrations of the Author of* Waverley collects information on the supposed "originals" of a host of Scott's characters. Chambers had previously found success in detailing the lives of particular, ordinary individuals, some of whom had acquired a reputation but only some of whom had acquired fame. His multivolume *Traditions of Edinburgh* was local history in the strictest sense, and the fourth volume advertised "sketches of the most remarkable public and eccentric characters who flourished in Edinburgh during the last century." The "Illustrations" delved not only into popular, local knowledge about Scott's heroes—such as Robert Macgregor (the "original" of Rob Roy) and Lucy Ashton (the bride of Lammermoor)—but also into anecdotal and often conjectural details about the locals on whom Scott might have based his minor characters. After an overview of "the rustic idiots of Scotland"—who, he notes, are often known for a "cunning" and "sly humour" that often "baffle[s] sounder judgments"— Chambers turns to the purported original of Davie Gellatley as particularly notable (9).

---

sons in the lower classes of society," he writes, lack the kind of privileged disgust that Wilson expresses. "If an Idiot is born in a poor man's house, it must be taken car[e of] and cannot be boarded out, as it would be by gentlefolks, or sent [to a] public or private receptacle for such unfortunate beings." Wordsworth hedges, though, and suggests that this might not be a natural sympathy, but an acquired tolerance, since the poor, "seeing frequently among their neighbors such objects, easily [forget] what[ever] there is of natural disgust about them" (*The Letters of William and Dorothy Wordsworth* 356).

42. Shortly after reading *Waverley* in 1814, for example, Morritt of Rokeby mentioned to Scott that he took Davie to be "a transcript of William Rose's motley follower, commonly yclept Caliban." He was one of the first to read the novel, and with Erskine and Lockhart was one of the only to know firsthand, and from the very beginning, that Scott was the author (quoted in John Gibson Lockhart, *Memoirs of the Life of Sir Walter Scott, Bart* 2:545).

Chambers identifies Davie with the man known as "Daft Jock Gray of Gilmanscleugh," an individual who was then still living and whose identity with Davie Chambers asserts to be "past the possibility of doubt" (16). The identification soon became widespread, as Chambers's work became the source text for many of the cognate works produced throughout the nineteenth century, works that, like his *Illustrations,* served the double task of historical anecdote and literary criticism. In the twentieth century, that project was taken up by William Shillinglaw Crockett in a synthesis of information and anecdote titled *The Scott Originals* (1912). Of the various sources that had by then been suggested, Crockett prefers Chambers's case for Jock Gray and claims this identification to have been generally held "throughout the Border country" during Scott's lifetime (34). Jock Gray of Gilmanscleugh—so named for the farm on which he was raised, in the border village of Ettrick—bears striking similarities to Davie Gellatley, at least as Chambers tells the tale. "The face, mien, and gestures," he writes, "are exactly the same. Jock walks with all that swing of the body and arms, that abstracted air and sauntering pace" (14). Chambers recounts instances of Jock's prodigious memory, his ability to sing nearly any "national" song requested, and above all the disparity between his abilities as a minstrel and his lack of basic social decorum. In a cruel echo of Descartes's argument about selective dexterity, Chambers argues that "all Jock's qualifications," especially his "talents of music and mimicry [. . .] ingenious as they be, are nothing but indications of a weak mind" (15).

Yet the way Chambers discusses Jock's social aptitude also suggests that, like Scott, he locates a particular value in non-normative modes of social interaction. Chambers gives a lengthy description of Jock's other "remarkable gift" (which, he notes, "the author of Waverley has entirely rejected"), a gift for mimicry, imitation, or mirroring that straddles the line between innocent play and pointed satire. It is hard not to hear an echo of Robert Burns when Chambers notes that "like almost all rustic Scottish humorists," Jock "makes ministers and sacred things his chief and favourite objects" of satire (18). Jock's prodigious memory comes into play here, since his mimicry turns on his abilities to memorize large portions of sermons on first hearing and to imitate them humorously later in a way that "never fails to convulse his audience with laughter" (18). But it is also of a piece with Jock's general tendency to violate the norms of social decorum, as when he wanders about the church "up stairs and down stairs," rather than sitting attentively, or hits with a stick those who nod off during the service (20). The behaviors Chambers describes are playful. Yet, especially when they verge on the genre of kirk satire, they also suggest a more pointed form of critique. Chambers even depicts Jock as a kind of nonpartisan critic, since "Being himself of no particular sect, he feels not the least delicacy or compunction for any single class of divines—all are indiscriminately familiar to the powers of the universal Jock!" (18). In this respect Chambers's anecdotal supplement to Davie Gellatley's character is actually quite consonant with the novel, especially when we recall Scott's comparison of Davie to the free-talking "licensed fools" of Shakespeare. Like that moment in the *Tales of My Landlord* review, Chambers does not simply equate physiology with a literary mode; he also identifies atypical modes of social behavior—conceivably of many different varieties—with the high literary values of irony and satire.

Most interesting for my purposes is the connection Chambers notes between Jock Gray and James Hogg, known as the "Ettrick Shepherd."[43] Chambers alleges that "Jock, by means of his singing powers, was one of the first who circulated the rising fame of his countryman, the Ettrick Shepherd, many of whose early songs he committed to memory, and sung publicly over all the country round." He was particularly fond, according to Chambers, of Hogg's "Oh Shepherd, the weather is misty and changing" and "the well-known lyric of 'Love is like a dizziness,'" both of which performances seem to have become popular and to have become "the chief means of setting [Jock] up in the trade of a wandering minstrel" (17). Though both Hogg and Jock Gray were natives of Ettrick, the importance of the connection is not simply a matter of geography. It speaks of a broader connection between rural poetry and disability, especially for those poets whose reputations placed them midway between naive pastoral production and reflexive, anthropological projects of collection. In terms of Scottish Enlightenment theories of "barbarism" and stadial development, rural poet-collectors, from Burns to Hogg, came to occupy alternately the personae of "heaven-taught ploughman" or single-minded prodigy unable to perform in other domains. As Chambers puts it, "Where, for instance, was the perfection of musical genius ever found accompanied with a good understanding?" (15).

This drive to diagnose poetry as a kind of illness or constitutional failing occasionally emerges from a more traditional, nostalgic pastoralism's alignment of laboring-class poetics with natural and untutored genius. It can sometimes be detected in accounts of the type of the rural poet by (and about) Robert Burns, Hogg, or others. There is, for instance, Burns's own description of his childhood, when the personal traits he highlights are his "retentive memory, a stubborn sturdy something in my disposition, and an enthusias-

---

43. There is no evidence that Hogg knew of Jock Gray, and no apparent connection between Jock and Hogg's own narrative "John Gray O'Middleholm" (who, incidentally, is introduced as a man "of little wit, some cunning, and inexhaustible good nature"). See Hogg, *Winter Evening Tales, Collected among the Cottagers in the South of Scotland* 1.303.

tic idiot piety."⁴⁴ In Burns's case, this image of the poet is not so much the "heaven-taught plowman" as the dissolute and degraded figure Leask has linked to the period's interest in "diseases of the will." Working through James Currie's *Life of Burns,* Leask suggests that the commonsense philosopher's account of the poet constitutes a "psychopathology of genius."⁴⁵ Leask further argues that Currie "sought to exorcise a particularly Scottish pathology of mind that he associated with the philosophical associationism and mental *impotence* of Hume's metaphysics" (284). The deterministic, material model of the mind—which Leask identifies with Hume's "way of ideas"—is not simply a philosophical error but a condition to which individuals can revert if their will fails. And, of course, as Leask points out, Currie sees this condition as "endemic to Burns's vocation as a poet" (283). Unlike Scott and Chambers, who see cognitive disability as *mobilizing* poetry, Currie positions impairment as a useless category, one to which poets are particularly susceptible.

So, too, the celebrated "Ettrick Shepherd" was depicted in *Blackwood's* as a kind of rural savant. In an 1821 letter to Scott, Hogg complained of his treatment by John Wilson and his circle in the magazine's popular *Noctes Ambrosianae* series, where the Ettrick Shepherd was one of the recurring (mostly fictionalized) characters. Hogg refers to "the beastly usage of me by Blackwood, and some new cronies of his," who had reneged on their promise to cease using Hogg's name in the series once he had revoked his consent. "I am again misrepresented to the world," he protests: "I am neither a drunkard, nor an idiot, nor a monster of nature."⁴⁶ Here Hogg links poetry and "idiocy" in its pejorative sense, and, as in Currie's complaints about Burns, highlights the close association drunkenness and dissolution had with a more general pathology of mind, one that makes the poet seem less than human.⁴⁷ *Blackwood's* usage of Hogg is "beastly" both because the magazine is being inhumanely cruel and because the caricatured Ettrick Shepherd comes off (Hogg hints) as a strange phenomenon, a prodigious exception being documented like some rare species or "monster of nature."

The discourse of poetry as impairment, then, makes visible two different outcomes of poetic theory's origins in anthropology. From Enlightenment anthropology, which found in poetry a model of the primitive mind,

---

44. Burns, *The Works of Robert Burns* 4:21–22.
45. Nigel Leask, *Robert Burns and Pastoral* 283.
46. Hogg, *Works of the Ettrick Shepherd* xlix. See also Hogg's poem "Sandy Tod," about an encounter with a disabled boy while staying in Midlothian, which Karl Miller compares to "The Idiot Boy" ("Introduction" to Hogg's *Private Memoirs and Confessions of a Justified Sinner*).
47. Indeed, *idiot* in its nonspecific, pejorative sense is a frequent keyword in the *Noctes.* See Wilson, *Noctes.*

arose one common Romantic troping of poetry as the mind's native language: what Hazlitt called "the universal language which the heart holds with nature and itself."[48] But that could also easily take a different form, one that more pathologically associates poetry with geographical and cultural barbarism or with an unevenly developed set of faculties. The association with barbarism migrates from the anthropological project of documenting rural traditions to the psychological characterization of the poet-collectors themselves. It also indicates the path that studies of the embodied mind would take in the later nineteenth century.

By 1912 Crockett had documented Jock Gray, apparently the popularizer of Hogg in Hogg's own native Ettrick, with much the same attitude. Crockett's study of Davie Gellatley and Jock Gray hinges on a portrait of the latter by Smellie Watson. Crockett's reading is quite different. "A mere glance," he writes, "must deepen the conviction that it was Jock's veritable physiognomy which entered into the immortal portraiture of the fool of Waverley. Jock's is a rather handsome face," he admits, "but symptoms of the weak and stagnant brain are obvious" (37). Crockett draws here on a model of embodied mental life close to the one that I have been tracing in this chapter. His emphasis on Jock Gray as a visible specimen of impairment marks one endpoint of the logic portrayed in medically inflected writing about Burns and Hogg. Most important, it demonstrates a marked shift from Scott's and Chambers's lively and illustrative type of poet to the kind of "monster of nature" into which Hogg felt he, too, had been made.

Chambers's account of Jock Gray is influential on this physiological tradition. Tellingly, this portrait of Davie soon found common cause with the physiological theories about the human mind he encountered in the Edinburgh Phrenological Society. In fact, Chambers is known to posterity not for his Scott criticism but for his proto-evolutionary tract *Vestiges of the Natural History of Creation*. *Vestiges* is Chambers's magnum opus, a work of amateur or lay science (though it has also been called pseudoscience). It is an attempt to link astronomy with human development and thus bring the various branches of science together under one "uniformitarian" aegis. In 1861 Charles Darwin took issue with the Lamarckian residues in Chambers's theory but conceded that "it has done excellent service in calling in this country attention to the subject, in removing prejudice, and in thus preparing the ground for the reception of analogous views."[49]

---

48. Hazlitt, *Selected Writings* 2:165.

49. Darwin, *On the Origin of Species by Means of Natural Selection, or the Preservation of Favoured Races in the Struggle for Life* xvi. While *Vestiges* was first published in 1844, all references are to what Darwin called the "tenth and much improved edition" of 1853 (*On the Origin of Species* xv). See Chambers, *Vestiges*.

Among the Edinburgh phrenologists, Chambers would have heard ample evidence to connect lyric idiocy to the functionally differentiated mind. In *Transactions,* for instance, George Combe's examples include several that resonate with Davie, including "some cretins" who, though "endowed with weak minds, are born with a partic[ul]ar talent for copying paintings, for rhyming, or for music" (32). In fact, the paradigmatic example of these distinct mental faculties is a local, Scottish example of the tuneful idiot. Combe writes, "In Edinburgh, an idiot is seen upon the streets who whistles correctly several tunes, but cannot connect three abstract ideas; while we all know men of powerful intellects, who cannot perform three notes of the gamut" (30). Such selective abilities, which Combe presents as if they would be familiar to anyone, serve as a kind of commonsense evidence for an intuitive, protomodular account of the mind. "When these facts are seen and considered by men of plain sense," he writes, "they are impressed with the conviction that the human mind is endowed with a variety of powers," which vary in degree among individuals (30). This leads to the folk-faith that Combe had identified, against the English unity of the mind, as an item of Scottish common sense: "the belief, on the part of the public, in the existence of distinct faculties of the mind" (31). The impaired songster here is not just evidence for the philosopher of mind but also has a substantial influence on the popular consensus.

Like the most orthodox phrenological materialists, Chambers was convinced that all mental activity could be reduced to such automatic, physiologically instantiated faculties. At its boldest, this is a theory of the continuity of a material human mind with the animal forms from which it developed.[50] Impairment, for Chambers, remains a useful diagnostic tool. In the *Vestiges* he writes, "When the human brain is congenitally imperfect or diseased, or when it is in the state of infancy, we see in it an approach towards the character of the brains of some of the inferior animals" (297–98). Unlike Wordsworth's "Idiot Boy," *Vestiges* treats disability as a window into the automatic basis of human actions, which are usually obscured in higher-functioning individuals. Fascinatingly, Chambers takes the emerging discourse of the functionally differentiated mind (one where impairment serves as a diagnostic tool to isolate particular faculties) and twists it back to the track of stadial development. As a result, in his attempt to write together the histories of animal and human life, Chambers reinstates a developmental narrative into his theory of impairment. The instincts are primarily observable in children, Chambers writes, or (as he tellingly conflates) "in barbarism or idiocy." Impaired minds reveal the

---

50. In *Vestiges* Chambers writes, "The few gleams of reason, then, which we see in the lower animals, are precisely analogous to such a development of the fore-arm as we find in the paddle of the whale. Causality, comparison, and other of the nobler faculties, are in them[selves] *rudimental*" (298).

mechanism at work in human actions, but they do so by showing the origins of such abilities in prehuman forms. As Chambers chillingly puts it, with reference to G. J. Davey's observations at the Hanwell Lunatic Asylum, signs of "abnormal cerebration" in humans closely resemble "the specific healthy characteristics of animals lower in the scale of organization" (298). Impairment, that is, may be regression to an earlier developmental stage. Chambers's work shows how entangled the nascent evolutionary model of the human mind-brain became with stadial theory's developmental narrative of human origins. Chambers draws on and subsequently influences the discourse that produces the "idiot poet" as a particular symptom of the functionally differentiated mind. It is intriguing, and unsettling, to think that this direction in Chambers's thought—which ultimately influenced Charles Darwin—seems to have had its origins in his literary criticism, specifically in the image of idiocy on offer in Scott's first novel.

For Scott himself, Davie Gellatley is not just a prop in an argument about the functionally differentiated mind. He is also a figure with whom we are meant to sympathize and with whom we are to lament the demise of a previous age's more distributed model of the literary mind. Against the Enlightenment logic that affiliated poetry with the mind's developmental arc—with its primitive origins or its progressive, technologically mediated development—Scott offers a different account of poetry as cognition. It was one that depended upon its materials—that recruited them idiosyncratically, anachronistically, and with no necessary relationship to a given standard of sentiment, intellect, or sociability. And yet it was one that, as suggested both by Scott's theory of histories in amber and by Davie's playful non-answers in song, was crucial and constitutive for "the social." The reviewer who compared Davie to the *The Lady of the Lake*'s Blanche of Devon styles them both as sibylline, prophetic figures and so recruits Scott's images of poetic disability to the old idea of Percy's, of the minstrel as a privileged, bardic voice, performing an important cognitive skill for the community at large. But the song itself, that reviewer claims, is not just "wild" but also "incoherent."[51] By that account, privileged bardic status requires a removal from the social body and an antisocial immersion in the "wild," uncultured rudiments of thought—figured here as a precommunicative, private language. Although it is incoherent, it paradoxically makes society cohere.

This is an interpretive frame that *Waverley* often holds out as a possibility, especially as Scott makes the incoherent materials of poetic tradition come to support cultural memory. But the novel's tendency, I have suggested, is to

---

51. See Hayden, *Scott: The Critical Heritage* 67–74, 70.

categorically deny that Davie himself is actually a figure of antisociality in any meaningful sense. His modes of interacting with people are often unexpected and run athwart social convention and straightforward communication. But rather than frustrate the idea of social cohesion, Davie's eccentric modes of poetic sociability widen the scope of what sociability might look like and what musical and interpersonal forms they might take. Rather than gesture back toward an earlier phase of a universal, stadial development story, *Waverley* joins the project of reimagining poetic origins that James Macpherson had helped initiate in 1760. Scott, too, suggests that turning back to traditional poetry might be a way to defamiliarize what sociability means in the first place and to generate new alternatives.

AFTERWORD

Reading One's Own Mind

"Do you think of me as I think of you,
My friends, my friends"—She said it from the sea,
The English minstrel in her minstrelsy.[1]

BY ENDING with Walter Scott's *Waverley* in chapter 5, this book has made its way from the pre-Romantic moments of the ballad revival and Ossianic primitivism to the years typically aligned with second-generation Romanticism. In the age of Scott's novels—and beyond, as the above-quoted lines from Elizabeth Barrett Browning's "L. E. L.'s Last Question" (1839) demonstrate—poetry as "minstrelsy" continued to stand for a peculiarly charged type of inter-mental relation. If poetry was seen as capturing the inner workings of the human mind and producing fantasies of unmediated communication, that project was never fully divorced from its ties to social intelligence. By way of conclusion, I suggest one way that this tradition tracks forward into later Romanticism and what would become a classic account of "lyricized" poetry.[2]

A sensible way to end that story might be by returning to John Stuart Mill, who, despite his urge to define poetry as involuted soliloquy, was unable to fully untangle that model of poetry from popular song and social occasion.[3] And there might be good reasons to conclude with Mill: Against his own indications, *mindreading* might be as good a term as any for the kind of inter-mental relation he describes in that essay's imagined scene of interper-

---

1. Elizabeth Barrett Browning, "L. E. L.'s Last Question" (in Landon, *Selected Writings* 365–67) 1–3.
2. Virginia Jackson, *Dickinson's Misery* 7.
3. For this argument about Mill's "What Is Poetry?" see Prins and Jackson, *Lyric Theory* 3.

sonal observation, where reading a poem simulates "overhearing" someone else's inner monologue. In fact, that obsession with peering into other people's minds is one of Culler's main complaints about the post-Romantic concept of the lyric: that by reducing lyrics to the expressions of particular speakers or dramatic monologists, in particular narrative contexts, modern poetic theory has made poems look *too much* like stories and has let our interpretive protocols lean too heavily on strategies for decoding character and plot.[4] One way to read Mill's essay, then, would be as an effort to shift away from that type of social intelligence—that "passion for a story" about other people—toward a more refined exercise of introspective thought and feeling.[5]

An alternative destination, though, and the one I propose instead, is Letitia Elizabeth Landon, who weaves those two models of poetry back together. Landon's "The Improvisatrice" (1824) is a tale of failed courtship that hinges on the miscommunication between lovers; on the difficulties of knowing what another person is thinking; and on the anxieties that attend such socially intelligent guesswork. Styled as the first-person autobiography of a poet, the narrative is full of embedded poems that have supposedly been improvised by the protagonist in her alternating moments of dejection and elation. The "Advertisement" to the volume describes the poem's project as "an attempt to illustrate that species of inspiration common in Italy, where the mind is warmed from earliest childhood by all that is beautiful in Nature and glorious in Art."[6] That statement aligns the volume's mixed mode—its composite of first-person poetic autobiography and inset songs—with the almost anthropological project of describing a certain type of foreign-coded, or natural or spontaneous, folk practice.

As Angela Esterhammer and Erik Simpson have shown, "improvisation" was an important part of the model of literature that came out of traditional ballad literatures and ran against many of the assumptions of more canonical, literary models of Romantic authorship.[7] In that sense, the poem also holds in tension two different approaches to traditional poetry: as a repository of sensitive, cultivated feeling and as a set of stories about other people. As my epigraph from Elizabeth Barrett Browning's elegy for Landon suggests, Landon's "minstrelsy" is fundamentally connected to the type of inter-mental

---

4. Culler, *Theory of the Lyric* 115ff.

5. Mill, *Collected Works* 1.345. For this reading of the compartmentalization of "feeling" and "story" in Mill see the introduction.

6. Landon, "Advertisement" to *The Improvisatrice*.

7. Angela Esterhammer, *Romanticism and Improvisation, 1750–1850*; Erik Simpson, *Literary Minstrelsy*. On theories of improvisation in antiquarianism and popular literature see Esterhammer 59–77. On the "classical affiliations of modern Italian improvvisatori" see Esterhammer 62.

relationship "L. E. L." came to stand for. That elegy's opening lines, which relay what the title calls "L. E. L.'s Last Question," frames poetry itself as a particularly charged solicitation of relationship and acknowledgment. As Pinch has suggested, EBB's poem on L. E. L. speaks not just to the culture of celebrity but to a type of "second-person thinking" that, in Landon's hands, signals a broad, sustained "nineteenth-century interest in purely mental relations between persons."[8]

For the Improvisatrice, thinking about other people is foundational to and logically precedes thinking about oneself; the poet's means of accessing her own inner life is routed through her social orientation toward fictional characters. The Improvisatice's effusions might seem at first glance to be case studies in the model of poetry Mill would soon identify with the solitary, "overheard" speaker. Yet the poems generally replace lyric expression with balladic storytelling and place primary emphasis on an estranged, mediated mode of access to inner life. As the "Advertisement" explains, the Improvisatrice "is supposed to relate her own history; with which are intermixed the tales and episodes which various circumstances call forth." At each stage of the plot, from her initial self-description as a feeling artist and poet through her ill-fated love intrigues with Lorenzo, the Improvisatrice responds to moments of deep feeling not by turning inward but by imagining other people. The inset songs imagine and perform the character of Sappho; Ida, a spurned lover who tries to reclaim her beloved Julian's heart by serving him a love potion but is unaware the cup actually holds poison; and at least two poems ("The Hindoo Girl's Song" and "The Indian Bride") that try on voices from the tradition of literary Orientalism. This multiplication of poetic perspectives and forms is connected to what Kate Singer has called a poetics of "multiply mediated, affective, temporal experience." For Singer, *The Improvisatrice* shows how Landon reflexively plays with ideas of poetic presence and with "instantaneous, easily digested sentiment."[9] For my purposes here, what is most interesting is that modulation of poetic presence and alienation, of distance and proximity, lets Landon reimagine what it means to have a relationship with one's own mind. In his remarks on ancient poetry discussed in chapter 1, Lowth had suggested that the poet, and in fact the mind in general, thinks about other people using a basically figurative strategy: "From what he feels and perceives in himself, he conjectures concerning others; and apprehends and describes the manners, affections, conceptions of others from his own."[10]

---

8. On EBB's L. E. L. and the second-person scenes it imagines see Pinch, *Thinking about Other People in Nineteenth-Century British Writing* 97ff.
9. Singer, "Landon: In Sound and Noise" 2.
10. Lowth, *Lectures* 117.

Landon's *Improvisatrice* inverts that logic: We do not necessarily refer first to our own minds and then engage in labyrinthine metaphorical speculations in order to understand the minds of others. Rather, we observe other people, and imagine fictional characters, in order to access and process our own thoughts and feelings.

Landon's reversal of the relation between self-knowledge and social knowledge echoes a similar view on offer elsewhere in Romantic-era writing, notably in Baillie's *Plays on the Passions* and in Hazlitt's *Essay on the Principles of Human Action* (1805).[11] As chapter 1 noted, Hazlitt's philosophy of sensation was starkly first-person and introspective, to the point that he figures poetry as an internal, secret language of the heart. Yet, as I have argued elsewhere, in his early writings on moral philosophy he tried to reconcile that kind of inwardness with his fundamentally "benevolist" commitment to a social or prepersonal mind, one capable of altruistic motivations that come logically prior to any kind of self-interest. His surprising way of putting this was that volition itself is possible—people can be moved to act at all—only because of their ability to imaginatively sympathize with, and act on behalf of, fictional versions of their future selves.[12]

As Khalip has shown, Hazlitt's theory became aesthetic practice in the poetry of John Keats, with its commitment to the negatively capable imagination and the radically open sympathies of the "chameleon" poet.[13] Landon's proposition in *The Improvisatrice* is a bit different: The inset poems ask readers to engage simultaneously in two modes of reading or to toggle between them. On the one hand, each poem offers a sentimental narrative with its own cast of characters. On the other, all of those characters and their microplots need to be connected to, or seen through the eyes of, the Improvisatrice herself. Moreover, *The Improvisatrice* does not just pull readers toward the most obvious conclusion, where the inset poems should be decoded as expressions of the protagonist's own deep feeling. Rather, its overall tendencies are to estrange that protagonist (and her readers) from her own inner mental life and to render even that basic act of narrative sympathy for the Improvisatrice into a more complex, triangulated act of mapping fictional minds and the relations among them. In other words, *The Improvisatrice* trains readers to work

---

11. See Hazlitt, *Selected Writings* vol. 1. On Baillie's rerouting of self-knowledge see Richardson, "A Neural Theatre" 133–34.

12. See Hazlitt's *Essay on the Principles of Human Action*, in *Selected Writings*, Vol. 1. For my reading of Hazlitt's theory of mediated self-knowledge in light of "theory of mind" theory see Savarese, "Reading One's Own Mind."

13. See Khalip, *Anonymous Life* 25ff. For Keats's remarks on the chameleon poet see *Letters* 1.387.

in two different directions at once: to think of poems as stories, which should be routed back onto a central poetic presence or persona; and, in precisely the opposite way, to turn that poetic presence inside out—to reframe poetic inwardness as a distributed social network, as a set of relations to an array of nested fictional minds.

Read this way, *The Improvisatrice* signals that the aspect of poetry that Mill would repudiate as the "passion for a story" was not only alive and well but could even be recognized as deeply connected with the kinds of poetry that privileged inwardness and emotional expression. Landon's example also suggests that the early Romantic conversations this book has begun to map out—conversations about poetry as a window into the mind's specifically social powers—were still legible later in the period. One of Romanticism's most abiding interests, from Macpherson to Landon, was linking poetry to the mind's basic structures. As I believe this book has shown, one of the reasons that interest was so strong was that it did not just reinforce familiar models of cognition or of introspective feeling. On the contrary, it offered an opportunity to defamiliarize the mind and to experiment with new ways of weaving private and social cognition together.

BIBLIOGRAPHY

Abrams, M. H. *Natural Supernaturalism: Tradition and Revolution in Romantic Literature.* New York: Norton, 1971.

Addison, Joseph. *Selections from Addison's Papers.* Edited by Thomas Arnold. Oxford: Clarendon Press, 1886.

Adorno, Theodore. "Lyric Poetry and Society." *Telos* 20 (Summer 1974): 56–71.

Aikin, John. *An Essay on the Application of Natural History to Poetry.* Warrington: William Eyres, 1777.

———. *Essays on Song-Writing.* London: Joseph Johnson, 1772.

———. *A Sketch of the Animal Economy.* Warrington: William Eyres, 1781.

———. *Thoughts on Hospitals.* London: Joseph Johnson, 1771.

Aikin, John and Anna Letitia Aikin. *Miscellaneous Pieces in Prose.* London: Joseph Johnson, 1773.

Anderson, Miranda, George Rousseau, and Michael Wheeler, eds. *Distributed Cognition in Enlightenment and Romantic Culture.* Edinburgh: Edinburgh University Press, 2019.

Anonymous. "Remarks on the Principle of Credulity." *Monthly Magazine* 16 (1803): 504–5.

Armstrong, Isobel. "Anna Letitia Barbauld: A Unitarian Poetics?" In *Anna Letitia Barbauld: New Perspectives.* Edited by William McCarthy and Olivia Murphy 59–81. Lewisburg: Bucknell University Press, 2014.

Augoustinos, Martha, Iain Walker, and Ngaire Donaghue, eds. *Social Cognition: An Integrated Introduction.* London: Sage, 2014.

Baillie, Joanna. *Plays on the Passions.* Edited by Peter Duthie. Peterborough: Broadview Press, 2008.

Banfield, Ann. *Unspeakable Sentences: Narration and Representation in the Language of Fiction.* New York: Routledge, 1982.

Barbauld, Anna Letitia. *Lessons for Children of Three Years Old.* London: Joseph Johnson, 1778.

———. "Remarks on Mr. Gilbert Wakefield's Enquiry into the Expediency and Propriety of Public or Social Worship." In *Works of Anna Letitia Barbauld.* London: Longman, 1825.

———. *Selected Poetry and Prose.* Edited by William McCarthy and Elizabeth Kraft. Peterborough: Broadview Press, 2002.

———. *Works of Anna Letitia Barbauld.* London: Longman, 1825.

Baron-Cohen, Simon. "The Extreme Male Brain Theory of Autism." *Trends in Cognitive Science* 6, no. 6 (June 2002): 248–54.

———. *Mindblindness: An Essay on Autism and Theory of Mind.* Cambridge: MIT Press, 1995.

Baron-Cohen, Simon, Alan M. Leslie, and Uta Frith. "Does the Autistic Child Have a 'Theory of Mind'?" *Cognition* 21, no. 1 (October 1985): 37–46.

Bassiri, Nima. "The Brain and the Unconscious Soul in Eighteenth-Century Nervous Physiology: Robert Whytt's 'Sensorium Commune.'" *Journal of the History of Ideas* 74, no. 3 (July 2013): 425–48.

Bell, Charles. *The Anatomy and Philosophy of Expression as Connected with the Fine Arts.* London: John Murray, 1844.

Bennett, Jane. *Vibrant Matter: A Political Ecology of Things.* Durham: Duke University Press, 2010.

Bewell, Alan. *Natures in Translation: Romanticism and Colonial Natural History.* Baltimore: Johns Hopkins University Press, 2017.

———. *Wordsworth and the Enlightenment: Nature, Man, and Society in the Experimental Poetry.* New Haven: Yale University Press, 1989.

Blackwell, Thomas. *An Enquiry into the Life and Writings of Homer.* London, 1735.

Blair, Hugh. "Critical Dissertation on the Poems of Ossian, Son of Fingal." In Macpherson, *The Poems of Ossian and Related Works* 343–99.

Bogel, Frederic. *Literature and Insubstantiality in Later Eighteenth-Century England.* Princeton: Princeton University Press, 1984.

Boyd, Brian. *On the Origin of Stories.* Cambridge: Harvard University Press, 2009.

———. *Why Lyrics Last: Evolution, Cognition, and Shakespeare's Sonnets.* Cambridge: Harvard University Press, 2012.

Brathwaite, Helen. *Romanticism, Publishing, and Dissent: Joseph Johnson and the Cause of Liberty.* New York: Palgrave Macmillan, 2003.

Broadie, Alexander. "Introduction: What Was the Scottish Enlightenment?" In *The Scottish Enlightenment: An Anthology.* Edited by Alexander Broadie. Edinburgh: Canongate, 2010.

Bromwich, David. *Hazlitt: The Mind of a Critic.* New York: Oxford University Press, 1983.

Browning, Elizabeth Barrett. "L. E. L.'s Last Question," in Landon, *Selected Writings* 365–67.

Bugg, John. "How Radical Was Joseph Johnson and Why Does Radicalism Matter?" *Studies in Romanticism* 57, no. 2 (Summer 2018): 173–95.

Burd, Henry Alfred. *Joseph Ritson: Scholar at Arms.* Berkeley: University of California Press, 1967.

Burke, Edmund. *A Philosophical Enquiry into the Origin of Our Ideas of the Sublime and Beautiful.* Edited by Paul Guyer. New York: Oxford University Press, 2015.

———. *Reflections on the Revolution in France.* Edited by L. G. Mitchell. New York: Oxford University Press, 1999.

Burkett, Andrew, and James Brooke-Smith, eds. *Multi-Media Romanticisms*. Romantic Circles, November 2016. <https://romantic-circles.org/praxis/multi-media/praxis.2016.multi-media.intro.html>.

Burns, Robert. *The Works of Robert Burns*. Edited by James Hogg and William Motherwell. Glasgow: Archibald Fullarton, 1835.

Calè, Luisa, and Adriana Craciun. "The Disorder of Things." *Eighteenth-Century Studies* 45, no. 1 (Fall 2011): 1–13.

Casanova, José. *Public Religions in the Modern World*. Chicago: University of Chicago Press, 1994.

Cavell, Stanley. *In Quest of the Ordinary: Lines of Skepticism and Romanticism*. Chicago: University of Chicago Press, 1994.

Chambers, Robert. *Illustrations of the Author of* Waverley. 2nd ed. Edinburgh: John Anderson, 1825.

———. *Vestiges of the Natural History of Creation*. 10th ed. London: John Churchill, 1853.

Chandler, James. "The Languages of Sentiment." *Textual Practice* 22, no. 1 (2008): 21–39.

———. *Wordsworth's Second Nature: A Study of the Poetry and Politics*. Chicago: University of Chicago Press, 1984.

Cheyne, George. *An Essay of Health and Long Life*. London: George Strahan, 1724.

Child, James Francis, ed. *The English and Scottish Popular Ballads*. Cambridge: Cambridge University Press, 2015.

Chomsky, Noam. "A Review of B. F. Skinner's *Verbal Behavior*." *Language* 35, no. 1 (1959): 26–58.

Churchland, Patricia Smith. *Neurophilosophy: Toward a Unified Science of the Mind/Brain*. Cambridge: MIT Press, 1986.

Churchland, Paul. "Eliminative Materialism and the Propositional Attitudes." *Journal of Philosophy* 78 (1981): 67–90.

Clark, Andy. *Natural Born Cyborgs: Minds, Technologies, and the Future of Human Intelligence*. Oxford: Oxford University Press, 2004.

———. *Supersizing the Mind: Embodiment, Action, and Cognitive Extension*. Oxford: Oxford University Press, 2008.

Clark, Andy, and David Chalmers. "The Extended Mind." *Analysis* 58, no. 1 (January 1998): 7–19.

Cohn, Dorrit. *Transparent Minds: Narrative Modes for Presenting Consciousness in Fiction*. Princeton: Princeton University Press, 1978.

Coleridge, Samuel Taylor. *Biographia Literaria*. Edited by James Engell and W. Jackson Bate. Vol. 7 of *The Collected Works of Samuel Taylor Coleridge*. Princeton: Princeton University Press, 1983.

———. *Collected Letters of Samuel Taylor Coleridge*. Edited by E. L. Griggs. Oxford: Clarendon Press, 1956–71.

———. *Poetical Works I: Poems (Reading Text)*. Edited by J. C. C. Mays. Vol. 16 of *The Collected Works of Samuel Taylor Coleridge*. Princeton: Princeton University Press, 2001.

———. *The Literary Remains of Samuel Taylor Coleridge*. Edited by Henry Nelson Coleridge. London: William Pickering, 1836.

———. *Shorter Works and Fragments*. Edited by H. J. Jackson and J. R. de J. Jackson. Vol. 11 of *The Collected Works of Samuel Taylor Coleridge*. Princeton: Princeton University Press, 1995.

Combe, George. *Transactions of the Phrenological Society.* Edinburgh: John Anderson, 1824.

Coski, Christopher. "Emotion and Poetry in Condillac's Theory of Language and Mind." *The French Review* 80, no. 1 (October 2006): 157–70.

Cox, Jeffrey N. *Poetry and Politics in the Cockney School: Keats, Shelley, Hunt, and Their Circle.* Cambridge: Cambridge University Press, 1998.

Crockett, William Shillinglaw. *The Scott Originals: An Account of Notables and Worthies, the Originals of Characters in the Waverley Novels.* Edinburgh: T. N. Foulis, 1912.

Culler, Jonathan. *Theory of the Lyric.* Cambridge: Harvard University Press, 2015.

Cullhed, Anna. "Original Poetry: Robert Lowth and Eighteenth-Century Poetics." In *Sacred Conjectures: The Context and Legacy of Robert Lowth and Jean Astruc.* Edited by John Jarick 25–47. New York: T&T Clark, 2007.

Curley, Thomas M. *Samuel Johnson, the Ossian Fraud, and the Celtic Revival in Great Britain and Ireland.* New York: Cambridge University Press, 2009.

Currie, James. *Works of Robert Burns: with an Account of his Life, and a Criticism of his Writings.* Edinburgh: Creech, 1800.

Darwin, Charles. *The Expression of the Emotions in Man and Animals.* London: John Murray, 1872.

———. *Metaphysics, Materialism, and the Evolution of Mind: The Early Writings of Charles Darwin.* Edited by Paul H. Barrett. Chicago: University of Chicago Press, 1974.

———. *On the Origin of Species by Means of Natural Selection, or the Preservation of Favoured Races in the Struggle for Life.* 3d ed. London: John Murray, 1861.

De Bary, Philip. *Thomas Reid and Scepticism: His Reliabilist Response.* New York: Routledge, 2002.

DeLucia, JoEllen. *A Feminine Enlightenment: British Women Writers and the Philosophy of Progress, 1759–1820.* Edinburgh: Edinburgh University Press, 2015.

———. "'Far Other Times Are These': The Bluestockings in the Time of Ossian." *Tulsa Studies in Women's Literature* 27, no. 1 (Spring 2008): 39–62.

De Man, Paul. "Anthropomorphism and Trope in the Lyric." In *The Rhetoric of Romanticism* 239–62. New York: Columbia University Press, 1984.

Dennett, Daniel C. 1987. *The Intentional Stance.* Cambridge: MIT Press, 1989.

DeRose, Keith, "Reid's Anti-Sensationalism and His Realism." *Philosophical Review* 98, no. 3 (July 1989): 313–48.

Descartes, René. *The Philosophical Works of Descartes.* Translated by Elizabeth S. Haldane and G. R. T. Ross. Cambridge: Cambridge University Press, 1977.

Desmond, Adrian, and James Moore. *Darwin's Sacred Cause: How a Hatred of Slavery Shaped Darwin's Views on Human Evolution.* New York: Houghton Mifflin, 2009.

Duncan, Ian. *Scott's Shadow: The Novel in Romantic Edinburgh.* Princeton: Princeton University Press, 2007.

Dunn, John J. "Coleridge's Debt to Macpherson's Ossian." *Studies in Scottish Literature* 7, no. 1–2 (July–October 1969): 76–89.

Essick, Robert N. *William Blake and the Language of Adam.* Oxford: Clarendon Press, 1989.

Esterhammer, Angela. *Romanticism and Improvisation, 1750–1850.* Cambridge: Cambridge University Press, 2008.

Ferguson, Adam. *An Essay on the History of Civil Society.* 2nd ed. London: Millar and Cadell, 1768.

Ferguson, Frances. *Solitude and the Sublime: The Romantic Aesthetics of Individuation.* New York: Routledge, 1992.

Flesch, William. *Comeuppance: Costly Signaling, Altruistic Punishment, and Other Biological Components of Fiction*. Cambridge: Harvard University Press, 2007.

Fludernik, Monika. *Towards a "Natural" Narratology*. New York: Routledge, 1996.

Fodor, Jerry. *The Modularity of Mind*. Cambridge: MIT Press, 1983.

François, Anne-Lise. *Open Secrets: The Literature of Uncounted Experience*. Stanford: Stanford University Press, 2008.

Friedman, Albert B. *The Ballad Revival: Studies in the Influence of Popular on Sophisticated Poetry*. Chicago: University of Chicago Press, 1961.

Gaskill, Howard, ed. *The Reception of Ossian in Europe*. New York: Continuum, 2004.

Gerard, Alexander. *Plan of Education in the Marischal College and University of Aberdeen, with the Reasons of It. Drawn up by Order of the Faculty*. Aberdeen: James Chalmers, 1755.

Goldman, Alvin. *Simulating Minds: The Philosophy, Psychology, and Neuroscience of Mindreading*. New York: Oxford University Press, 2006.

Goldstein, Amanda Jo. "Irritable Figures: Herder's Poetic Empiricism." In *The Relevance of Romanticism: Essays on Romantic Philosophy*. Edited by Dalia Nassar. Oxford: Oxford University Press, 2014.

———. *Sweet Science: Romantic Materialism and the New Logics of Life*. Chicago: University of Chicago Press, 2017.

Goodman, Kevis. *Georgic Modernity and British Romanticism: Poetry and the Mediation of History*. Cambridge: Cambridge University Press, 2004.

———. "Reading Motion: Coleridge's 'Free Spirit' and Its Medical Background." *European Romantic Review* 26, no. 3 (2015): 349–56.

Gopnik, Alison, and Henry M. Wellman. "Why the Child's Theory of Mind Really Is a Theory." *Mind and Language* 7 (1992): 145–71.

Gordon, Robert M. "Folk Psychology as Simulation." *Mind & Language* 1, no. 2 (1986): 158–71.

Graham, Gordon. "Francis Hutcheson and Adam Ferguson on Sociability." *History of Philosophy Quarterly* 31, no. 4 (October, 2014): 317–29.

Griffiths, Devin. *The Age of Analogy: Literature and Science between the Darwins*. Baltimore: Johns Hopkins University Press, 2016.

Griggs, Earl Leslie. "Coleridge and Byron." *PMLA* 45, no. 4 (December 1930): 1085–97.

Groom, Nick. *The Making of Percy's Reliques*. Oxford: Clarendon Press, 1999.

Guillory, John. *Cultural Capital: The Problem of Literary Canon Formation*. Chicago: University of Chicago Press, 1993.

Halmi, Nicholas. *The Genealogy of the Romantic Symbol*. Oxford: Oxford University Press, 2008.

Hamilton, Paul. *Coleridge's Poetics*. Stanford: Stanford University Press, 1983.

———. *Metaromanticism: Aesthetics, Literature, Theory*. Chicago: University of Chicago Press, 2003.

Hartley, David. *Observations on Man, His Frame, His Duty, and His Expectations*. Vols. 1 and 2. London: Richardson, 1749.

Hartman, Geoffrey H. *The Unremarkable Wordsworth*. New York: Methuen, 1987.

———. *Wordsworth's Poetry, 1787–1814*. Cambridge: Harvard University Press, 1964.

Haugeland, John. "Mind, Embodied and Embedded." In *Mind and Cognition: 1993 International Symposium*. Edited by Yu-Houng H. Houng and J. Ho 233–67. Taipei: Academica Sinica, 1993.

Hayden, John O. *Scott: The Critical Heritage*. London: Routledge, 1970.

Hayles, N. Katherine. *How We Became Posthuman: Virtual Bodies in Cyberspace.* Chicago: University of Chicago Press, 2008.

———. *How We Think: Digital Media and Contemporary Technogenesis.* Chicago: University of Chicago Press, 2012.

Haywood, Ian. *The Making of History: A Study of the Literary Forgeries of James Macpherson and Thomas Chatterton in Relation to Eighteenth-Century Ideas of History and Fiction.* Madison: Fairleigh Dickinson University Press, 1986.

Hazlitt, William. *The Selected Writings of William Hazlitt.* 9 vols. Edited by Duncan Wu. London: Pickering and Chatto, 1998.

Heider, Fritz, and Marianne Simmel. "An Experimental Study of Apparent Behavior." *The American Journal of Psychology* 57, no. 2 (April 1944): 243–59.

Herder, Johann Gottfried. "Extract from a Correspondence on Ossian and the Songs of Ancient Peoples." In *German Aesthetic and Literary Criticism: Winckelmann, Lessing, Hamann, Herder, Schiller and Goethe.* Edited by H. B. Nisbet 154–61. Cambridge: Cambridge University Press, 1985.

———. "Fragment of a Treatise on the Ode." In *Selected Early Works, 1764–1767: Addresses, Essays, and Drafts; Fragments on Recent German Literature.* Edited by Ernest A. Menze and Karl Menges. Translated by Ernest A. Menze and Michael Palma. University Park: Pennsylvania State University Press, 1992.

———. *Herder: Philosophical Writings.* Edited and translated by Michael N. Forster. Cambridge: Cambridge University Press, 2002.

———. *Outlines of a Philosophy of the History of Man.* 2nd ed. Translated by T. Churchill. London: Joseph Johnson, 1803.

———. *The Spirit of Hebrew Poetry.* Translated by James Marsh. Burlington: Smith, 1833.

Heringman, Noah. *Romantic Rocks, Aesthetic Geology.* Ithaca: Cornell University Press, 2004.

———. *Sciences of Antiquity: Romantic Antiquarianism, Natural History, and Knowledge Work.* Oxford: Oxford University Press, 2013.

Herman, David. "Narrative Theory after the Second Cognitive Revolution." In Zunshine, *Introduction to Cognitive Cultural Studies* 155–75.

Hogan, Patrick Colm. "Literary Universals." In Zunshine, *Introduction to Cognitive Cultural Studies* 37–60.

Hogg, James. *Winter Evening Tales, Collected among the Cottagers in the South of Scotland.* Edinburgh: Oliver and Boyd, 1821.

———. *Works of the Ettrick Shepherd.* Edited by Thomas Thomson. London: Blackie and Son, 1874.

Hume, David, *A Treatise of Human Nature.* Edited by P. H. Nidditch. 2nd. ed. Oxford: Clarendon Press, 1978.

Hutcheson, Francis. *An Inquiry Concerning Beauty, Order, Harmony, Design.* Edited by Peter Kivy. The Hague: Nijhoff, 1973.

———. *Logic, Metaphysics, and the Natural Sociability of Mankind.* Edited and translated by James Moore and Michael Silverthorne. Indianapolis: Liberty Fund, 2006.

Hutchins, Edwin. *Cognition in the Wild.* Cambridge: MIT Press, 1995.

Jack, Jordynn. "'The Extreme Male Brain?' Incrementum and the Rhetorical Gendering of Autism." *Disability Studies Quarterly* 31, no. 3 (2011).

Jackson, Noel. *Science and Sensation in Romantic Poetry.* Cambridge: Cambridge University Press, 2008.

Jackson, Virginia. *Dickinson's Misery: A Theory of Lyric Reading*. Princeton: Princeton University Press, 2005.

Jacobus, Mary. *Tradition and Experiment in Wordsworth's Lyrical Ballads (1798)*. Oxford: Clarendon Press, 1976.

———. "Wordsworth and the Language of the Dream." *ELH* 46, no. 4 (Winter 1979): 618–64.

Jager, Colin. *The Book of God: Secularization and Design in the Romantic Era*. Philadelphia: University of Pennsylvania Press, 2007.

———. "Can We Talk about Consciousness Again?" In *Romantic Frictions*. Edited by Theresa Kelley. *Romantic Circles*, September 2011. <https://romantic-circles.org/praxis/frictions/HTML/praxis.2011.jager.html>.

James, Felicity, and Ian Inkster, eds. *Religious Dissent and the Aikin-Barbauld Circle, 1740–1860*. Cambridge: Cambridge University Press, 2012.

Janowitz, Anne. "Amiable and Radical Sociability; Anna Barbauld's 'Free Familiar Conversation.'" In *Romantic Sociability: Social Networks and Literary Culture in Britain, 1770–1840*. Edited by Gillian Russell and Clara Tuite 62–81. Cambridge: Cambridge University Press, 2006.

Jarvis, Simon. *Wordsworth's Philosophic Song*. Cambridge: Cambridge University Press, 2007.

Keats, John. *Letters of John Keats*. Edited by Hyder Edward Rollins. Cambridge: Harvard University Press, 1958.

Khalip, Jacques. *Anonymous Life: Romanticism and Dispossession*. Stanford: Stanford University Press, 2008.

Kivy, Peter. *The Seventh Sense*. Oxford: Oxford University Press, 1976.

Klancher, Jon. *Transfiguring the Arts and Sciences: Knowledge and Cultural Institutions in the Romantic Age*. Cambridge: Cambridge University Press, 2013.

Kraft, Elizabeth. "Hearing Eighteenth-Century Occasional Poetry by and about Women: Swift and Barbauld." *ABO: Interactive Journal for Women in the Arts, 1640–1830* 1, no. 1 (2011).

Kramnick, Jonathan. *Actions and Objects from Hobbes to Richardson*. Stanford: Stanford University Press, 2010.

———. "Against Literary Darwinism." *Critical Inquiry* 37, no. 2 (Winter 2011): 315–47.

Lacoue-Labarthe, Philippe, and Jean-Luc Nancy. *The Literary Absolute: The Theory of Literature in German Romanticism*. Albany: State University of New York Press, 1988.

La Mettrie, Julien Offray de. *Machine Man and Other Writings*. Translated by Ann Thomson. Cambridge: Cambridge University Press, 1996.

Landon, Letitia Elizabeth. *The Improvisatrice: And Other Poems*. London: Hurst, Robinson, 1824.

———. *Selected Writings*. Edited by Jerome McGann and Daniel Riess. Peterborough: Broadview, 1997.

Landreth, Sara. "Breaking the Laws of Motion: Pneumatology and *Belles Lettres* in Eighteenth-Century Britain." *New Literary History* 43, no. 2 (Spring 2012): 281–308.

Lane, Harlan. *The Wild Boy of Aveyron*. Cambridge: Harvard University Press, 1976.

Langan, Celeste. "The Poetry of Pure Memory: Teaching Scott's Novels in the Context of Romanticism." In *Approaches to Teaching Scott's Waverley Novels*. Edited by Ian Duncan and Evan Gottlieb. New York: Modern Language Association of America, 2009.

Latour, Bruno. *Reassembling the Social: An Introduction to Actor-Network-Theory*. Oxford: Oxford University Press, 2005.

Leask, Nigel. *Robert Burns and Pastoral: Poetry and Improvement in Late Eighteenth-Century Scotland*. Oxford: Oxford University Press, 2010.

Lehrer, Keith. "Conception without Representation, Justification without Inference: Reid's Theory." *Nous* 23, no. 2 (April 1989): 145–54.

Levin, Susan. *Dorothy Wordsworth and Romanticism*. Jefferson, NC: McFarland, 2009.

Levinson, Marjorie. "A Motion and a Spirit: Romancing Spinoza." *Studies in Romanticism* 46, no. 4 (2007): 367–408.

Lewis, Jayne. *Air's Appearance: Literary Atmosphere in British Fiction, 1660–1794*. Chicago: University of Chicago Press, 2012.

Liu, Alan. "A Forming Hand: Creativity and Destruction from Romanticism to Emergence Theory." Rutgers Center for Cultural Analysis, March 2, 2006.

Locke, John. *An Essay Concerning Human Understanding*. Edited by Peter H. Nidditch. Oxford: Clarendon Press, 1979.

Lockhart, John Gibson. *Memoirs of the Life of Sir Walter Scott, Bart*. Philadelphia: Carey, Lea, and Blanchard, 1887.

Lowth, Robert. *Lectures on the Sacred Poetry of the Hebrew*. Translated by George Gregory. London: Joseph Johnson, 1787.

Macpherson, James. *Introduction to the History of Great Britain and Ireland*. London: Becket and de Hondt, 1771.

———. *The Poems of Ossian and Related Works*. Edited by Howard Gaskill. Edinburgh: Edinburgh University Press, 1996.

Madden, Edward H. "Was Reid a Natural Realist?" *Philosophy and Phenomenological Research* 47, no. 2 (December 1986): 255–76.

Magnuson, Paul. *Coleridge and Wordsworth: A Lyrical Dialogue*. Princeton: Princeton University Press, 1988.

Mallet, Paul Henri. *Northern Antiquities: or, a Description of the Manners, Customs, Religion and Laws of the Ancient Danes, and Other Northern Nations*. Translated by Thomas Percy. London: T. Carnon, 1770.

Mandell, Laura. "Prayer, Feeling, Action: Anna Barbauld and the Public Worship Controversy." *Studies in Eighteenth-Century Culture* 38 (2009): 117–42.

McCarthy, William. *Anna Letitia Barbauld: Voice of the Enlightenment*. Baltimore: Johns Hopkins University Press, 2008.

McDowell, Paula. *The Invention of the Oral: Print Commerce and Fugitive Voices in Eighteenth-Century Britain*. Chicago: University of Chicago Press, 2017.

McGann, Jerome J. *The Poetics of Sensibility: A Revolution in Literary Style*. Oxford: Clarendon Press, 1996.

McKeon, Michael. "The Origins of Interdisciplinary Studies." *Eighteenth-Century Studies* 28, no. 1 (1994): 17–28.

McKusick, James. *Coleridge's Philosophy of Language*. New Haven: Yale University Press, 1986.

McLane, Maureen N. *Balladeering, Minstrelsy, and the Making of British Romantic Poetry*. Cambridge: Cambridge University Press, 2008.

———. *Romanticism and the Human Sciences: Poetry, Population, and the Discourse of the Species*. New York: Cambridge University Press, 2006.

McLane, Maureen N., and Laura Slatkin. "British Romantic Homer: Oral Tradition. 'Primitive Poetry' and the Emergence of Comparative Poetics in Britain, 1760–1830." *ELH* 78, no. 3 (2011): 687–714.

Mee, Jon. *Dangerous Enthusiasm: William Blake and the Culture of Radicalism in the 1790s.* Oxford: Clarendon Press, 1994.

Miall, David S. "Wordsworth's 'First-Born Affinities': Intimations of Embodied Cognition." *Poetics Today* 32, no. 4 (Winter 2011): 693–715.

Mill, John Stuart. *Collected Works of John Stuart Mill.* Vol. 1. *Autobiography and Literary Essays.* Edited by J. M. Robson. Toronto: University of Toronto Press, 1963.

Miller, Karl. "Introduction" to *Private Memoirs and Confessions of a Justified Sinner* by James Hogg. New York: Penguin Books, 2006.

Milnes, Tim. "Beyond Excess: Romanticism, Surplus, and Trust." *College Literature* 42, no. 4 (Fall 2015): 683–98.

———. *The Truth about Romanticism: Pragmatism and Idealism in Keats, Shelley, Coleridge.* Cambridge: Cambridge University Press, 2010.

———. *William Wordsworth—The Prelude.* London: Palgrave, 2009.

Morton, Timothy. "Joseph Ritson, Percy Shelley and the Making of Romantic Vegetarianism." *Romanticism* 12, no. 1 (April 2006): 52–61.

Mulholland, James. "James Macpherson's Ossian Poems, Oral Traditions, and the Invention of Voice." *Oral Tradition* 24, no. 2 (2009): 393–414.

———. *Sounding Imperial: Poetic Voice and the Politics of Empire, 1720–1830.* Baltimore: Johns Hopkins University Press, 2013.

Natarajan, Uttara. "Introduction: Hazlitt's *Essay on the Principles of Human Action—1805–2005.*" In *Metaphysical Hazlitt: Bicentenary Essays.* Edited by Uttara Natarajan, Tom Paulin, and Duncan Wu 1–14. New York: Routledge, 2005.

Newman, Steve. *Ballad Collecting, Lyric, and the Canon: The Call of the Popular from the Restoration to the New Criticism.* Philadelphia: University of Pennsylvania Press, 2007.

Niles, John D. *Homo Narrans: The Poetics and Anthropology of Oral Literature.* Philadelphia: University of Pennsylvania Press, 1999.

Norton, D. F. *David Hume: Common-Sense Moralist, Sceptical Metaphysician.* Princeton: Princeton University Press, 1982.

Noyes, John K. *Herder: Aesthetics against Imperialism.* Toronto: University of Toronto Press, 2015.

Olender, Maurice. *The Languages of Paradise: Race, Religion, and Philology in the Nineteenth Century.* Cambridge: Harvard University Press, 1992.

Ong, Walter J. *Orality and Literacy.* New York: Routledge, 2013.

Paley, Morton. *Apocalypse and Millennium in English Romantic Poetry.* Oxford: Clarendon Press, 1999.

Paley, William. *Natural Theology.* London: Faulder, 1802.

Palmer, Alan. *Fictional Minds.* Lincoln: University of Nebraska Press, 2004.

———. *Social Minds in the Novel.* Columbus: The Ohio State University Press, 2010.

Percy, Thomas. *Four Essays, as Improved and Enlarged in the Second Edition of* The Reliques of Ancient English Poetry. London: Dodsley, 1767.

———. *Reliques of Ancient English Poetry.* London: Dodsley, 1765.

Pfau, Thomas. *Romantic Moods: Paranoia, Trauma, and Melancholy.* Baltimore: Johns Hopkins University Press, 2005.

———. *Wordsworth's Profession.* Stanford: Stanford University Press, 1997.

Phillips, Mark Salber. *Society and Sentiment: Genres of Historical Writing in Britain, 1740–1820*. Princeton: Princeton University Press, 2000.

Pinch, Adela. *Strange Fits of Passion: Epistemologies of Emotion from Hume to Austen*. Stanford: Stanford University Press, 1996.

———. *Thinking about Other People in Nineteenth-Century British Writing*. Cambridge: Cambridge University Press, 2010.

Pittock, Murray. "James Macpherson and Jacobite Code." In *Gaelic to Romantic: Ossianic Translations*. Edited by Fiona J. Stafford and Howard Gaskill. Amsterdam: Rodopi, 1998.

———. *Poetry and Jacobite Politics in Eighteenth-Century Literature and Thought*. Cambridge: Cambridge University Press, 1994.

Poovey, Mary. *A History of the Modern Fact: Problems of Knowledge in the Sciences of Wealth and Society*. Chicago: University of Chicago Press, 1998.

Porter, Dahlia. *Science, Form, and the Problem of Induction in British Romanticism*. Cambridge: Cambridge University Press, 2018.

Potkay, Adam. *The Story of Joy: From the Bible to Late Romanticism*. Cambridge: Cambridge University Press, 2007.

Premack, David, and Guy Woodruff. "Does the Chimpanzee Have a Theory of Mind?" *Behavioural and Brain Sciences* 1, no. 4 (December 1978): 515–26.

Price, Fiona. *Revolutions in Taste, 1773–1818: Women Writers and the Aesthetics of Romanticism*. New York: Routledge, 2016.

Prickett, Stephen. *Modernity and the Reinvention of Tradition: Backing into the Future*. Cambridge: Cambridge University Press, 2009.

———. *Words and the Word: Language, Poetics, and Biblical Interpretation*. Cambridge: Cambridge University Press, 1988.

Priestley, Joseph. *Course of Lectures on the Theory of Language and Universal Grammar*. Warrington: W. Eyres, 1762.

———. *An Examination of Dr. Reid's Inquiry into the Human Mind on the Principles of Common Sense, Dr. Beattie's Essay on the Nature and Immutability of Truth, and Dr. Oswald's Appeal to Common Sense in Behalf of Religion*. London: Joseph Johnson, 1774.

Priestman, Martin. *The Poetry of Erasmus Darwin: Enlightened Spaces, Romantic Times*. Aldershot: Ashgate, 2014.

Prins, Yopie, and Virginia Jackson, eds. *The Lyric Theory Reader*. Baltimore: Johns Hopkins University Press, 2014.

Raber, Karen. *Animal Bodies, Renaissance Culture*. Philadelphia: University of Pennsylvania Press, 2013.

Ready, Kathryn. "'And Make Thine Own Apollo Doubly Thine': John Aikin as Literary Physician and the Intersection of Medicine, Morality and Politics." In *Religious Dissent and the Aikin-Barbauld Circle, 1740–1860*. Edited by Felicity James and Ian Inkster 70–93. Cambridge: Cambridge University Press, 2011.

Redfield, Marc. "Wordsworth's Dream of Extinction." *Qui Parle* 21, no. 2 (Spring/Summer 2013): 61–68.

Regan, John. "Ambiguous Progress and Its Poetic Correlatives: Percy's *Reliques* and Stadial History." *ELH* 81, no. 2 (Summer 2014): 615–34.

Reid, Thomas. *Essay on the Intellectual Powers of Man*. Edited by Derek R. Brookes and Knud Haakonssen. University Park: Pennsylvania State University Press, 1996.

———. *An Inquiry into the Human Mind on the Principles of Common Sense.* Edited by Derek R. Brookes. University Park: Pennsylvania State University Press, 1997.

Richardson, Alan. *British Romanticism and the Science of the Mind.* Cambridge: Cambridge University Press, 2001.

———. "Facial Expression Theory from Romanticism to the Present." In Zunshine, *Introduction to Cognitive Cultural Studies* 65–83.

———. *The Neural Sublime: Cognitive Theories and Romantic Texts.* Baltimore: Johns Hopkins University Press, 2010.

———. "A Neural Theatre: Joanna Baillie's 'Plays on the Passions.'" In *Joanna Baillie, Romantic Dramatist: Critical Essays.* Edited by Matthew Crochinus. New York: Routledge, 2004.

Richetti, John J. "Performance in Eighteenth-Century English Verse." In *A Companion to British Literature*, Vol. 3: *Long Eighteenth-Century Literature 1660–1830*. Edited by Robert DeMaria, Heesock Chang, and Samantha Zacher 189–206. Oxford: Wiley, 2014.

Ritson, Joseph. *Ancient Songs, from the Time of King Henry the Third to the Revolution.* London: Joseph Johnson, 1790.

———. *An Essay on Abstinence from Animal Food, as a Moral Duty.* London: Richard Phillips, 1802.

Rousseau, Jean-Jacques. *Essay on the Origin of Languages and Writings Related to Music.* Edited and translated by John T. Scott. Hanover: University Press of New England, 1998.

Rowland, Anna Weirda. *Romanticism and Childhood: The Infantilization of British Literary Culture.* Cambridge: Cambridge University Press, 2012.

Ryan, Vanessa. "The Physiological Sublime: Burke's Critique of Reason." *Journal of the History of Ideas* 62, no. 2 (April 2001): 265–79.

Sachs, Jonathan. *The Poetics of Decline in British Romanticism.* Cambridge: Cambridge University Press, 2018.

Saunders, Thomas Bailey. *The Life and Letters of James Macpherson.* New York: Macmillan, 1894.

Savarese, John. "Cognitive Scaffolding, *Aids to Reflection.*" In, *Distributed Cognition in Enlightenment and Romantic Culture.* Edited by Anderson, Rousseau, and Wheeler 139–55.

———. "Reading One's Own Mind: Hazlitt, Cognition, Fiction." *European Romantic Review* 24, no. 4 (2013): 437–52.

———. "Wordsworth between Minds." In, *Multi-Media Romanticisms*. Edited by Burkett and Brooke-Smith. <https://romantic-circles.org/praxis/multi-media/praxis.2016.multi-media.savarese.html>.

Savarese, Ralph James, and Lisa Zunshine. "The Critic as Neurocosmopolite; Or, What Cognitive Approaches to Literature Can Learn from Disability Studies." *Narrative* 22, no. 1 (January 2014): 17–44.

Schmidt, Royal J. "Cultural Nationalism in Herder." *Journal of the History of Ideas* 17, no. 3 (1956): 407–17.

Schofield, Robert E. *The Enlightened Joseph Priestley: A Study of His Life and Work from 1773 to 1804.* University Park: Pennsylvania State University Press, 2004.

Scott, Walter. *Waverley.* Edited by Peter Garside. Edinburgh: Edinburgh University Press, 2007.

Sellars, Wilfred. "Empiricism and the Philosophy of the Mind." In *The Foundations of Science and the Concepts of Psychology and Psychoanalysis.* Edited by Herbert Feigl and Michael Scriven 253–329. Minneapolis: University of Minnesota Press, 1956.

Sha, Richard C. *Imagination and Science in Romanticism.* Baltimore: Johns Hopkins University Press, 2018.

Sheehan, Jonathan. *The Enlightenment Bible: Translation, Scholarship, Culture.* Princeton: Princeton University Press, 2005.

Shelley, Percy Bysshe. *Shelley's Poetry and Prose.* Edited by Donald H. Reiman and Neil Fraistat. 2nd. ed. New York: Norton, 2002.

Simpson, Erik. *Literary Minstrelsy 1770–1830: Minstrels and Improvisers in British, Irish, and American Literature.* Basingstoke: Palgrave, 2008.

Singer, Kate. "Landon: In Sound and Noise." In *Multi-Media Romanticisms.* Edited by Burkett and Brooke-Smith. <https://romantic-circles.org/praxis/multi-media/praxis.2016.multi-media.singer.html>.

Skrbina, David. *Panpsychism in the West.* Cambridge: MIT Press, 2005.

Smith, Adam. *The Theory of Moral Sentiments.* Edited by D. D. Raphael and A. L. Macfie. Oxford: Clarendon Press, 1976.

Southey, Robert. *Thalaba the Destroyer.* 2nd. ed. London: Longman, 1809.

Spolsky, Ellen. *Gaps in Nature: Literary Interpretation and the Modular Mind.* Albany: State University of New York Press, 1993.

Stafford, Fiona J. *The Sublime Savage: A Study of James Macpherson and the Poems of Ossian.* Edinburgh: Edinburgh University Press, 1988.

Stanley, Joshua. "Wordsworth and 'the Most Unhappy Man of Men': Sentimentalism and Representation." *European Romantic Review* 26, no. 2 (2015): 185–204.

Starr, G. Gabrielle. *Feeling Beauty: The Neuroscience of Aesthetic Experience.* Cambridge: MIT Press, 2015.

Stewart, Dugald. "Account of the Life and Writings of Adam Smith, LLD." In *Glasgow Edition of the Works and Correspondence of Adam Smith.* Vol. 3. Edited by W. P. D. Wightman, J. C. Bryce, and I. S. Ross 263–351. Oxford: Clarendon Press, 1980.

Stewart, Susan. *Crimes of Writing: Problems in the Containment of Representation.* New York: Oxford University Press, 1991.

Sutherland, Kathryn. "The Native Poet: The Influence of Percy's Minstrel from Beattie to Wordsworth." *Review of English Studies* 33, no. 132 (November 1982): 414–33.

Taylor, Charles. *Human Agency and Philosophy: Philosophical Papers I.* Cambridge: Cambridge University Press, 1996.

Thorpe, Clarence DeWitt. "Addison and Hutcheson on the Imagination." *ELH* 2, no. 3 (November 1935): 215–34.

Tollefsen, Deborah Perron. *Groups as Agents.* Cambridge: Polity Press, 2015.

Tooby, John, and Irven DeVore. "The Reconstruction of Hominid Behavioral Evolution through Strategic Modeling." In *Evolution of Human Behavior: Primate Models.* Edited by Warren G. Kinzey 183–238. Albany: SUNY Press, 1987.

Tribble, Evelyn. *Cognition in the Globe: Memory and Attention in Shakespeare's Theatre.* New York: Palgrave, 2011.

Trumpener, Katie. *Bardic Nationalism: The Romantic Novel and the British Empire.* Princeton: Princeton University Press, 1997.

Tsur, Rueven. *Toward a Theory of Cognitive Poetics.* New York: North-Holland, 1992.

Turner, Bryan S. *Regulating Bodies: Essays in Medical Sociology.* New York: Routledge, 2002.

Turner, Mark. *The Literary Mind: The Origins of Thought and Language.* New York: Oxford University Press, 1996.

Valenza, Robin. *Literature, Language, and the Rise of the Intellectual Disciplines in Britain, 1680–1820.* Cambridge: Cambridge University Press, 2009.

Vallins, David. *Coleridge and the Psychology of Romanticism: Feeling and Thought.* Basingstoke: Palgrave, 2002.

Vermeule, Blakey. *The Party of Humanity: Writing Moral Psychology in Eighteenth-Century Britain.* Baltimore: Johns Hopkins University Press, 2000.

———. *Why Do We Care about Literary Characters?* Baltimore: Johns Hopkins University Press, 2009.

Vickers, Neil, *Coleridge and the Doctors, 1795–1806.* New York: Oxford University Press, 2004.

———. "Review of *British Romanticism and the Science of the Mind* by Alan Richardson." *Studies in Romanticism* 43, no. 1 (Spring 2004): 146–50.

Voitle, Robert B. "Shaftesbury's Moral Sense." *Studies in Philology* 52, no.1 (January 1955): 17–38.

Wakefield, Gilbert. *An Enquiry into the Expediency and Propriety of Public or Social Worship.* London, 1792.

Wang, Orrin N. C. "Ghost Theory." *Studies in Romanticism* 46, no. 2 (Summer/Fall 2007): 203–25.

Wellman, Janina. *The Form of Becoming: Embryology and the Epistemology of Rhythm, 1760–1830.* Cambridge: MIT Press, 2017.

Wheeler, Michael. *Reconstructing the Cognitive World: The Next Step.* Cambridge: MIT Press, 2005.

Wheeler, Michael, and Andy Clark. "Culture, Embodiment and Genes: Unravelling the Triple Helix." *Philosophical Transactions of the Royal Society B: Biological Sciences* 363, no. 1509: 3563–75.

White, Daniel E. *Early Romanticism and Religious Dissent.* Cambridge: Cambridge University Press, 2007.

Whitney, Lois. "English Primitivistic Theories of Epic Origins." *Modern Philology* 21, no. 4 (May 1924): 337–78.

Whytt, Robert. *An Essay on the Vital and Other Involuntary Motions of Animals.* Edinburgh: Hamilton, Balfour, and Neill, 1751.

Wilson, John. *Noctes Ambrosianae.* New York: Redfield, 1854.

Wood, David, Jerome S. Bruner, and Gail Ross. "The Role of Tutoring in Problem Solving." *Journal of Child Psychology and Psychiatry* 17 (1976): 89–100.

Wood, Paul B. *The Aberdeen Enlightenment: The Arts Curriculum in the Eighteenth Century* Aberdeen: Aberdeen University Press, 1993.

Woof, Robert, ed. *William Wordsworth: The Critical Heritage.* New York: Routledge: 2001.

Wordsworth, Dorothy. *The Grasmere Journals.* Edited by Pamela Woof. Oxford: Clarendon Press, 1991.

Wordsworth, William. *The Five-Book Prelude.* Edited by Duncan Wu. Oxford: Blackwell, 1997.

———. *Lyrical Ballads and Other Poems, 1797–1800.* Edited by James Butler and Karen Green. Ithaca: Cornell University Press, 1993.

———. *The Major Works.* Edited by Stephen Gill. Oxford: Oxford University Press, 2000.

———. *Poems in Two Volumes, and Other Poems, 1800–1807.* Edited by Jared R. Curtis. Ithaca: Cornell University Press, 1983.

———. *The Prelude: 1799, 1805, 1850*. Edited by M. H. Abrams, Stephen Gill, and Jonathan Wordsworth. New York: Norton, 1979.

Wordsworth, William, and Dorothy Wordsworth. *The Letters of William and Dorothy Wordsworth, the Early Years 1878–1805*. 2nd ed. Edited by Ernest de Selincourt. Oxford: Clarendon Press, 1967.

Yardley, Lucy. *Material Discourses of Health and Illness*. New York: Routledge, 2013.

Yousef, Nancy. *Isolated Cases: The Anxieties of Autonomy in Enlightenment Philosophy and Romantic Literature*. Ithaca: Cornell University Press, 2004.

———. *Romantic Intimacy*. Stanford: Stanford University Press, 2013.

Zunshine, Lisa, ed. *Introduction to Cognitive Cultural Studies*. Baltimore: Johns Hopkins University Press, 2010.

———. "Rhetoric, Cognition, and Ideology in A. L. Barbauld's *Hymns in Prose for Children* (1781)." *Poetics Today* 23, no. 1 (Spring 2002): 123–39.

———. *Why We Read Fiction*. Columbus: The Ohio State University Press, 2006.

INDEX

actor-network theory, 117n40

Addison, Joseph, 3, 13, 25–28, 37, 40, 59, 148

address. *See* apostrophe

affect. *See* emotion

Aikin, John, 14, 73, 74n9, 77–80, 82–83; *Essay on the Application of Natural History to Poetry*, 77–78; *Essays on Song-Writing*, 90, 92–94, 98; *A Sketch of the Animal Economy*, 78–79; *Thoughts on Hospitals*, 77, 79–80, 82

Aikin, Lucy, 78, 95n67

airs, 51, 73, 75–76, 78–80, 82, 92n58

allegory, 65, 131–32, 149

analogy, 12, 29, 35n49, 49, 77n21, 80, 82, 104, 115–16, 123, 131–3, 144, 150, 160, 161n50

anatomy, 33, 47–48, 63–64, 78–79, 141–43, 148–49

ancient Greek poetry. *See* Greek poetry

ancient poetry. *See* antiquarianism

animals, 38–39, 63–64, 78, 117–18, 120–22, 127, 144–46, 148n20, 161–62

animism, 14, 44, 50, 52–54, 57, 65–66, 71–75, 80, 94, 118, 121–22, 128–29

antiquarianism, 3–5, 13–15, 18, 20–22, 25–32, 34–40, 42–43, 47, 49–50, 58–59, 64, 67, 70, 78n24, 94, 98, 111, 166n7

apostrophe, 31, 64, 72–73, 75, 77, 80, 94, 110, 113

approbation, 27–28, 59, 82

ascribing mental states. *See* mental state ascription

associationism, 31, 72, 79–85, 89, 97, 99–101, 128–30, 133, 143–45, 151–53, 159. *See also* Hartley, David

asylums, 162

atmosphere. *See* airs

atomism, 39

Austen, Jane, 122

automata, 143–46

automaticity, 62–63, 114, 143–46, 150–51, 161. *See also* irritability

autonomy, 3, 6, 22, 73–75

Baillie, Joanna, 77, 168

ballad revival. *See* ballads

ballads, 1, 3, 11–13, 15, 25–27, 34–40, 59, 69–70, 92–93, 95n67, 105, 111, 116, 135–38, 149–53, 165–67

Barbauld, Anna Letitia, 4, 14, 40, 70, 71–101, 103–5, 110n18, 127, 130, 144; *Eighteen Hundred and Eleven*, 80n29; *Hymns in Prose for Children*, 14, 95–101; *Lessons for Children*, 96; "On Monastic Institutions," 74–75, 89–90, 93, 104, 110n18, 127; "On Prejudice," 86–88, 90, 96–97, 99–101, 104, 130; "The Origin of Song-Writing," 93–94; "Remarks on Mr. Gilbert Wakefield's Enquiry," 71–73, 75–76; "Seláma, an Imitation of Ossian," 94–95; "A Summer Evening's Meditation," 80–81; "Thoughts on the Devotional Taste," 73–74, 80–81, 87–88; "The Warrington Academy," 77; "What Is Education," 86

bards and bardic poetry, 28, 35–38, 40–42, 45, 49n22, 61, 66, 70, 126, 162

belief, 8, 44, 50, 53, 56–60, 85–89, 97–98, 104–6, 124, 137, 142, 147–48, 161

Bell, Charles, 148n20

benevolence, 4, 18, 24n25, 38–39, 72, 74–76, 81–83, 85, 155, 168

benevolism. *See* benevolence

biblical historicism, 29–32, 42, 91–92, 144–45. *See also* Lowth, Robert

Blackwell, Thomas, 13, 25, 27–29, 31, 47, 49, 64, 91

Blair, Hugh, 13, 25, 28–29, 45–47, 49–50, 53, 55, 59, 61, 65, 68, 71, 75, 93n60, 95

Blake, William, 19n5, 37n56, 39n62, 43

Boerhaave, Herman, 62

Bonaparte, Napoleon, 45, 109, 124

Boyle, Robert, 63

brain, 2, 7, 10–13, 15, 33, 47, 56, 62–65, 78–80, 100, 141–44, 148–49, 160–62

brain lesions, 10–11, 142

Brown, Thomas, 147, 149

Browne, William A. F., 147, 148n20

Browning, Elizabeth Barrett, 165–67

"Burd Ellen and the Young Tamlane" (Anon.), 151

Burke, Edmund: *Philosophical Enquiry into the Origin of Our Ideas of the Sublime and Beautiful*, 3, 7, 80, 93, 154; *Reflections on the Revolution in France*, 86–88; "second nature" and tradition, 113, 118. *See also* second nature

Burney, Charles, 111

Burns, Robert, 23, 120, 123, 157–60

Byron, George Gordon, Lord, 143–44

Chambers, Robert, 151, 156–63; *Illustrations of the Author of* Waverley, 151, 156–58; *Vestiges of the Natural History of Creation*, 160–62

Chatterton, Thomas, 120, 123

Cheyne, George, 39

childhood, 6, 10, 19n5, 21, 32–33, 35, 51, 56–59, 74–75, 78, 86–88, 90, 95–97, 99–101, 128–30, 139, 141–42, 151, 158, 161. *See also* development

classicism, 20–21, 38, 43, 51–52, 67, 92–94, 98, 152n35, 166n7; *See also* Blackwell, Thomas; Greek poetry; Homer

cognitive aesthetics, 4, 7

cognitive approaches to literature and culture, 2–4, 7–12, 60n49, 68–69

cognitive cultural studies, 7

cognitive historicism, 12–13, 60n49

cognitive linguistics, 7–8, 58n45

cognitive narratology, 4–5, 8–12, 55, 69, 153

cognitive niche construction, 89

cognitive poetics, 4, 7, 68

cognitive rhetoric, 100

cognitive scaffolding, 13–15, 18–19, 33–36, 38–39, 76, 86, 88–90, 92, 95–101, 103–5, 109–19, 123, 129–30. *See also* distributed cognition; pedagogy

Coleridge, Samuel Taylor, 3, 50, 67n62, 82, 105, 108–15, 121, 127–29, 137, 139; *Biographia Literaria*, 111–14, 131n68, 132–33, 139n7, 143–44; "Confessions of an Inquiring Spirit," 144–45; "Frost at Midnight," 127; letter to Josiah Wedgewood, 109–10, 117, 125, 127–28; on Shakespeare, 152; "Religious Musings" 109; "Rime of the Ancient Mariner," 53, 108

Collins, William, 45, 50

Combe, Andrew, 147

Combe, George, 147–49, 161

common sense, 9, 14, 23n21, 41, 44, 46, 48, 54–59, 81, 84–88, 138, 147–49, 159, 161. *See also* Reid, Thomas

conception (Reid's theory of), 56, 84–85, 147. *See also* common sense; Reid, Thomas

Condillac, Étienne Bonnot de, 22, 139
conjectural history, 1, 14, 23–25, 28, 30, 35n52, 39–40, 50, 59, 68, 70, 72, 76, 90–95, 118, 125, 129
conjecture, 4, 13, 23, 29–32, 39, 59, 72, 78, 80, 122, 129, 140, 167. *See also* conjectural history; speculation
Crockett, William Shillinglaw, 157, 160
curiosity, 23, 87
Currie, James, 159

Darwin, Charles, 38, 58n46, 148, 160, 162
Darwin, Erasmus, 30, 38, 77
David, 73, 75, 145
dejection, 120, 166
Descartes, René, 48, 145–46, 157
development (Enlightenment theories of), 6, 13–14, 17–19, 22–25, 27–28, 35–38, 59, 70–72, 74–76, 81–82, 89–101, 104, 111–12, 116–17, 125, 135–36, 143, 158–59; and evolutionary theory, 160–63; uniformitarian commitments of, 20–21, 24–26, 28, 49–50, 59, 67–68, 160, 163. *See also* childhood; conjectural history; recapitulation; stadial theory
disability, 11n24, 15, 103–5, 109–11, 116–18, 120–22, 135–36, 138–43, 146, 149–63. *See also* head injury; theory of mind
disciplinarity, 18–22, 44, 69–70, 77–78, 114; and "predisciplinarity," 18, 77–78
disembodiment, 2, 41–43, 48, 51–52, 60–63, 167. *See also* ghosts; spirit
Dissent, 14, 30–31, 70, 72–75, 77–81, 83, 90
Dissenting academies, 77–78
distributed cognition, 8n15, 12–16, 18–19, 33–39, 89, 103–8, 115, 117–18. *See also* cognitive scaffolding; embedded mind; enactivism; extended mind; group minds; socially distributed cognition
Dryden, John, 150n27
dualism, 47–48, 52

Edinburgh Phrenological Society, 138, 147–49, 155, 161
egoism (epistemological), 2–3, 18, 22–23, 27–28, 31–32, 55–56, 71–73, 75, 118, 153–54, 167

embedded mind, 36, 40, 43, 76–83, 86, 88–90, 104, 109–10, 121. *See also* cognitive niche construction; cognitive scaffolding
emblem, 131–32
embodied mind, 2, 14, 30–31, 33, 38–39, 43–44, 47–48, 51–52, 56, 60–65, 72, 76–83, 85–86, 103, 114, 117, 119, 121–23, 127–28, 135–38, 141–44, 147–49, 155, 160–61. *See also* brain; nerves
emergence, 80–81, 89, 107
emotion, 1, 4–6, 10n22, 21–23, 26–32, 36, 38–40, 45, 49, 51–54, 56–57, 60, 63, 69, 71–73, 75, 80, 82–83, 87, 94, 105, 115, 118, 120, 128–29, 136, 139–40, 145, 148n20, 153, 166–69. *See also* sentimentalism; social feeling; sympathy
empiricist poetics. *See* poetics of sensation
enactivism, 106–7, 129
epic poetry, 22n14, 27–28, 45, 60, 69, 92, 149, 152n35. *See also* Blackwell, Thomas; Homer; Macpherson, James
evolutionary psychology, 8–9, 69, 100
evolutionary theory, 25, 38, 69, 89n52, 147–48, 160–62
experimentalism. *See* experiments
experiments, 3–4, 13–15, 19–25, 28, 40, 43–44, 50, 60, 63, 65, 80, 86, 93–94, 98, 103–5, 108, 111n22, 117, 129, 141–42, 169
extended mind, 15, 103–7, 110, 114, 119, 128–33. *See also* externalism
externalism (theory of mental content), 4, 18, 33–34, 38, 72, 84–85; "active externalism," 103–5. *See also* extended mind

facial expression, 12n27, 32–33, 58, 136, 148n20
faculty psychology, 6–7, 56–58, 84–85, 148–49, 161–62
Ferguson, Adam, 24–26, 28–29, 33, 36, 39, 50, 75, 76n16, 78, 86, 90–92, 93n60
figurative language, 13, 17, 22, 27–33, 54, 64–65, 91, 116–17, 131–32, 140–41, 166–67. *See also* metaphor; personification
folk literature. *See* ballads
folk psychology, 9, 14, 41, 43–44, 57–59, 69
forgery, 4, 14, 41–42, 45–47, 50, 59, 95
functional differentiation. *See* faculty psychology

Gall, Franz Joseph, 144

Galvani, Luigi, 63
genius, 21, 35–38, 50, 158–59
Gerard, Alexander, 47–49, 60, 62, 64
ghosts, 41–42, 51–52, 54, 59–60, 62, 64, 94. *See also* spirit
Godwin, William, 30n35
Goethe, Johann Wolfgang von, 39n62, 43, 45
Grant, Robert Edmund, 148
Gray, Jock, 157–58, 160
Gray, Thomas, 45, 125
Greek poetry, 21–22, 28, 30, 98
Gregory, George, 30–31
group minds, 8n15, 34n48, 109–10, 115–18; and theories of nation and nationalism, 34–37, 42–43, 111–13, 115, 124–25

Haller, Albrecht von, 62–63, 79
Hartley, David, 30–31, 72, 79–84, 86–89, 99–101, 128, 143–44
Hays, Mary, 74
Hazlitt, William, 15, 20, 25, 42, 108, 153; *Essay on the Principles of Human Action*, 20, 21n13, 143, 168; "On Poetry in General," 21, 160, 168; "Why the Arts Are Not Progressive," 20–21
head injury, 79, 121–23
Hebrew poetry, 21, 29–32, 42, 49, 50–51, 67–68, 72–73, 75, 91–92, 95, 98–99, 144–45
Heidegger, Martin, 88
Herder, Johann Gottfried, 13, 22, 28–29, 32–34, 38, 41–42, 46, 48–49, 58n46, 90, 105; *Extract from a Correspondence on Ossian*, 32n41, 41–43; "Fragment of a Treatise on the Ode," 22; "On the Cognition and Sensation of the Human Soul," 32–33; *Outlines of a Philosophy of the History of Man*, 32n41, 33, 105; *The Spirit of Hebrew Poetry*, 49; *Treatise on the Origin of Language*, 28, 32, 90
historicism, 35n49, 69. *See also* biblical historicism; cognitive historicism
history of the disciplines. *See* disciplinarity
Hobbes, Thomas, 37
Hogg, James, 158–60
Home, John, 45

Homer, 21, 22n14, 27–28, 67. *See also* Blackwell, Thomas
hospitals, 78–79, 82
human nature, 5n7, 6, 17–18, 20–21, 23–25, 29–30, 32–33, 35, 38, 43, 49–50, 59, 83, 85, 113. *See also* origins, human; second nature
Hume, David, 23–24, 26, 31, 45, 55–58, 137, 146–47, 148n23, 149–50, 153–54, 159
Hutcheson, Francis, 23, 24n25, 26, 31n37, 72, 80n29, 81–83, 90, 95n69
Hutchinson, Mary, 124
Hutchinson, Sara, 123

idiocy, Enlightenment and Romantic concept of, 116–18, 136–43, 145–46, 149, 151–63
imagination, 18, 22, 26–27, 32, 46, 50, 56, 73, 93n60, 94, 99, 106–7, 116, 127, 128–33, 136–37, 147–49, 154, 159, 167–68
imitation, 14, 76, 93–94, 98, 144, 157. *See also* mimicry
Improvisatrice, The (Landon), 15, 166–69
infancy. *See* childhood
innatism, 4, 7, 11, 13, 16, 18, 29, 34, 38, 41, 44, 57–58, 69–70, 72, 75–76, 81–83, 85, 87–88, 95–97, 100–101, 117, 129, 141, 149, 153; art instinct, 27, 70; language instinct, 29. *See also* moral sense theory; natural sociability theory
intention, 8–9, 43–44, 61, 63–65, 84, 94, 117
interdisciplinarity. *See* disciplinarity
introspection, 2, 4, 15, 19–21, 48–50, 64, 70, 73, 110, 120, 149n24, 166–69. *See also* self-observation
irritability, 33n45, 62–63

Jacobitism, 42n5, 138, 152
Johnson, Joseph, 30
Johnson, Samuel, 41n3, 45–46, 88n49, 148

Kant, Immanuel, 53, 56–57, 137, 147
Keats, John, 15, 153–54, 168
King Lear (Shakespeare), 152

L'Ouverture, Toussaint, 15, 108, 124–26, 128
La Mettrie, Julein Offray de, 33n46, 146

Index

Landon, Letitia Elizabeth, 15, 165–69
literary Darwinism, 8–9, 69
literary universals, 3, 7, 11, 13, 21, 25, 28, 59, 66–68, 70, 98–99
Locke, John, 26n28, 48, 100, 106, 109, 116, 139, 144, 146, 148
Lockhart, John Gibson, 156n42
"Lord William, or Lord Lundy" (Anon.), 151
Lowth, Robert, 13, 29–33, 49, 53, 59, 64, 66n57, 67–68, 71–73, 75, 90–91, 95, 98, 117–18, 135, 144, 150, 167
Lucretius, 39n62, 43
lyric, 3, 5, 15, 19–20, 21, 55, 69–70, 92–93, 128, 137, 139–40, 153, 161, 165–66; "lyricization" of poetry, 5, 68, 128, 165; and narrative, 6, 8, 15, 64, 69–70, 116–17, 139–40, 167; and song, 15, 92–93, 135, 137

Macpherson, James, 14, 16, 28, 40–70, 72, 93–95, 98, 105, 163, 165, 169; *Fingal*, 45, 60; *Fragments of Ancient Poetry*, 14, 28, 40–41, 45, 50–51, 54–55, 60–65, 67–70; *Introduction to the History of Great Britain and Ireland*, 49, 51–52, 62
Mallet, Paul Henri, 49, 59
Malthus, Thomas, 38
materialism, 9n19, 14, 15, 20, 39n62, 43–44, 47, 51–54, 60–63, 65–70, 78–79, 135, 138, 147–49, 161
mediated self-knowledge, 21n13, 57–58, 64, 168–69. *See also* self-observation
medicine and medical writing, 38–39, 76–79, 82, 110–11, 122–23, 155, 159–60
memory, 15, 35, 51, 88–90, 97, 99, 103–4, 109–11, 113, 115–16, 118–19, 121, 125–30, 135–37, 140, 149–50, 152, 157–58, 162
memory loss, 103–4, 109–10, 115, 118–19, 125–28, 140
mental state ascription, 8–11, 31–32, 43–44, 56–58, 61–65, 71, 141–42, 167–68
metaphor, 13, 17, 27–32, 49, 64–65, 81, 109, 116–17, 122–23, 140–41, 151–52, 168
Mill, John Stuart, 5–7, 11, 15, 68, 70, 165–67, 169
mimicry, 10, 99, 157
mindreading. *See* attributing mental states; theory of mind

minstrels and minstrelsy, 15, 34–40, 115, 135–38, 149–53, 158, 162, 165–66. *See also* ballads
mnemonics. *See* memory
modularity, 7, 10–11, 135, 141–44, 147–49, 153–54
Monboddo, James Burnett, Lord, 139
moral sense theory, 23, 26, 31, 72, 75n15, 80n29, 81–83, 90, 95n69
More, Henry, 62

narrative, interest in, 6, 8–11, 39–40, 55, 68–69, 94, 149–50, 166–67, 169
natural history, 1, 18, 22–24, 26, 75, 77–78, 90, 125n56, 160–62. *See also* conjectural history; development; Ferguson, Adam
natural sociability theory, 3–4, 11–14, 17–18, 22–26, 34, 38–40, 55–57, 70, 71–75, 81–83, 94, 97, 100–101, 117–18, 146
natural theology, 47, 80–83, 115, 133, 144. *See also* Paley, William
nature, 14, 21, 23–25, 27, 29–33, 35, 38–39, 49–50, 53–54, 71, 73, 75, 80, 105–6, 108, 113, 115, 118–28, 132–33, 145, 149, 160, 166. *See also* human nature
neo-Lucretianism. *See* Lucretius
nerves, 2, 33, 47, 56, 63, 78–80, 84, 144, 145
neuroplasticity, 33
Noctes Ambrosianae (Wilson), 159
novels, 4, 8n16, 11, 15, 61, 66, 69, 135–38, 146–47, 149–51, 162–63; historical novel, 137–38, 146–47

"Ode on the Popular Superstitions of the Highlands of Scotland" (Collins), 45, 50
odes, 21–22, 32n41, 45, 50, 93, 125
Ogilvie, William, 46
"one life" argument, 109–10, 127
orality, 5, 11–12, 25–29, 32n41, 35n49, 41–42, 54n35, 61, 64, 66, 69, 76, 91, 94–101, 111–12, 118–19, 135–36, 152
ordinary language, 58, 108–15, 119, 121, 123
origins, human, 1, 3–4, 6, 13, 17–25, 27, 31, 38, 41, 44, 47–49, 55, 59, 67–68, 71–72, 75, 92–93, 115–19, 139–42, 146. *See also* childhood; development; infancy

origins of language, 1, 17–19, 21–22, 27–29, 31–33, 38, 64–65, 90–94, 116–17, 140–41
origins of literature, 1, 6, 13, 17–18, 21–22, 28–32, 72, 90–94, 116–17, 140–41, 143
Ossian. *See* Macpherson, James
Ossianism, 28, 40, 42, 43n11, 94–95

Paley, William, 80n29. *See also* natural theology
Palgrave Academy, 77
palingenesia, 51–52
panpsychism, 52–53, 65
pantheism, 52, 62–63, 106, 109, 127
parallelism, 67–68, 98
passions. *See* emotion; poetics of sensation
pathetic fallacy, 53–54, 65. *See also* animism; apostrophe; projectivism
pedagogy, 76–78, 86–88, 90, 95–101, 104
Percy, Thomas, 13, 34–40, 90, 115, 162; *Essay on the Ancient English Minstrels*, 35–36; *Reliques of Ancient English Poetry*, 35–36
personification, 31–32, 53, 71–73, 75, 120–21. *See also* animism
Persuasion (Austen), 122
phrenology, 138, 143–44, 147–49, 155, 160–61
physiognomy, 160
physiological psychology. *See* embodied mind
Plato, 106
Plinian Society, 148n20
poetic inwardness, 1–7, 19–20, 22, 26–28, 30–31, 35–36, 39–40, 48–49, 53–54, 70–72, 165, 168–69. *See also* introspection; poetics of sensation
poetics of sensation, 1–2, 4, 13, 2–22, 26–29, 39–40, 47, 49, 52, 55, 61, 66, 91. *See also* Blackwell, Thomas; Homer; poetic inwardness; primitivism
politics (Romantic-era), 2, 6–7, 17–18, 26n30, 30–31, 34–38, 42–43, 53, 73–75, 76n16, 82–83, 86–88, 113n28, 123–25, 138, 152, 155n41
Pope, Alexander, 23, 150n27
popular poetry. *See* ballads; minstrelsy
poverty of the stimulus, 10, 56–58. *See also* innatism; modularity

pragmatism, 85n41
predisciplinarity. *See* disciplinarity
Priestley, Joseph, 4, 30–31, 52, 77, 80, 83–85, 87, 90–93, 96, 98, 117, 144; *Course of Lectures on the Theory of Language and Universal Grammar*, 90–92, 98; *Disquisitions Relating to Matter and Spirit*, 52; *An Examination of Dr. Reid's Inquiry*, 85
primitivism, 6, 14, 17–18, 27–29, 31, 38, 44, 49–50, 52–55, 59, 61, 64–68, 71–72, 75, 90–94, 96, 116–18, 125, 135–37, 140–41, 143, 146, 152, 154, 158–60, 165
"Progress of Poetry, The" (Gray), 125
projectivism, 9, 31–32, 52–56, 65–66, 71–73, 75, 118, 121, 154, 167
prose poetry, 67–68, 94–99
prosody, 22, 25, 67–68, 91, 95–99, 113, 119
Providentialism, 81–82, 124, 127
public worship controversy, 73–75, 96
Pythagoras, 51–52

Quarrel of the Ancients and the Moderns, 20–21, 92n56

Radcliffe, Ann, 150n27
radical antiquarianism, 36–37, 40, 51–52; and cockney classicism, 43–44
recapitulation, 22n17, 95–97, 99, 113, 116–17, 121, 141, 161–62. *See also* development
Reid, Thomas, 4, 14, 44, 46–48, 50n24, 52, 55–60, 64–65, 81, 84–88, 137–38, 147–49
relationality, 2, 13, 22, 37, 39, 76, 80, 83, 86
reliabilism, 85
Ritson, Joseph, 13, 34–40, 115; *Ancient Songs*, 36–40; *An Essay on Abstinence from Animal Food*, 38–39
Rokeby, Morritt of, 156n42
Rousseau, Jean-Jacques, 22, 26n28, 28, 90
Ruskin, John, 53

Sappho, 167
Scott, Walter, 4, 15, 40, 117n38, 135–63, 165; *The Bride of Lammermoor*, 156; *The Lady of the Lake*, 152, 162; *Minstrelsy of the Scottish Border*, 153; *Rob Roy*, 156; *Tales of My Landlord*, 155, 158; *Waverley*, 15, 135–43, 145–58, 160, 162–63, 165

second nature, 113, 128, 133. *See also* Burke, Edmund

self-observation, 15, 20, 21n13, 48, 50, 57–58, 108, 129, 154, 168–69. *See also* introspection; mediated self-knowledge

Sensibility (literary movement), 43, 46

sensibility (philosophy of mind), 32n41, 62–64, 72, 80, 121

sentimental fiction, 137–38, 149–50, 168

sentimental history, 50–51, 137, 146–47, 149–50

sentimentalism, 10, 18, 25, 29, 36, 40, 47, 49–50, 62, 80–82, 87, 97–101, 139, 146–47, 153, 167. *See also* moral sense theory; social feeling; sympathy

Shaftesbury, third Earl of, 23, 26

Shakespeare, William, 88–89, 151–52, 155–56, 158

Shelley, Percy Bysshe, 17–18, 27, 39n62, 43

skepticism, 2–3, 53, 55–58, 73, 85, 88, 121, 122n49, 137–38, 146–49, 153–54. *See also* projectivism

Smith, Adam, 10, 23, 31, 50, 78, 154

social feeling, 8, 10, 17–18, 25, 27–28, 31–33, 39, 55, 56, 73–75, 80–83, 97–101, 116. *See also* moral sense theory; natural sociability theory; sympathy

social intelligence, 4–5, 8–10, 13, 29, 43–44, 54–57, 61, 65–66, 68–69, 71–72, 94–95, 100–101, 108, 116–18, 128–30, 139, 150–51, 153–54, 165–69. *See also* attributing mental states; social feeling; theory of mind

social passions. *See* social feeling

socially distributed cognition, 13–14, 16, 35–36, 39–40, 109–11, 115–18, 121–22. *See also* group minds

solipsism. *See* egoism; projectivism; skepticism

solitude. *See* egoism

Southey, Robert, 143–44, 151

speculation, 24, 30–31, 50, 82, 143, 151, 168. *See also* conjecture

Spinoza, Baruch, 52, 106n9

spirit, 3, 18n2, 36, 41–43, 47, 51–52, 54, 59, 62, 64, 78–79, 82, 106n9, 107, 113n28, 114–15, 127–31, 133, 144–45. *See also* ghosts

Spurzheim, Johann, 144

stadial theory, 27, 49–50, 68, 111, 154, 158, 161–63. *See also* development

stage directions, 61, 64–65, 70

Sterne, Laurence, 62

Stewart, Dugald, 14, 23–24, 50

sublime, 3, 7, 47, 55, 80–81, 87, 93, 126, 154. *See also* Burke, Edmund

symbol (literary), 131–32

symbols and symbolic processing, 103, 128

sympathy, 6, 8, 10, 17–18, 31–32, 38–39, 56, 73, 114, 116, 124, 136, 139, 153–55, 162, 168. *See also* social feeling

taste, 3, 21, 25–26, 59, 73–74, 80–81, 87, 136

Taylor, William, 95n67

teleology, 81–82, 101. *See also* natural theology; Providentialism

Thalaba the Destroyer (Southey), 151

theopathy, 74n12, 80–81, 99–101

theory of mind, 4–5, 9–11, 15–16, 18, 31, 34, 57–58, 69, 141–42, 153–54, 165, 167–69; and disability, 10–11, 11n24, 15, 141–42, 153–54; modular nativist theory of, 10–11, 58, 141–42, 153; and the novel, 4–5, 9–11; rationality theory of, 10, 57–58; simulationist theory of, 10, 31

Tucker, Abraham, 62

Unitarianism, 109–10, 127. *See also* one life argument

unity of the mind, 32, 48, 84, 144, 148–49, 161

Vallon, Annette, 124

vehicular hypothesis, 62

verbal parallelism. *See* parallelism

vitalism, 43, 47, 52–53, 62–64, 79, 123, 127

volition, 9n20, 21n13, 62–63, 130, 143–45, 159, 168

Wakefield, Gilbert, 73–75, 96

Walpole, Horace, 150n27

Warrington Academy, 77–78, 90, 95

Watson, Smellie, 160

Wedgewood, Josiah, 109

Whytt, Robert, 62–5, 79

will. *See* volition

Wilson, John, 139, 155n41, 159

Wollstonecaft, Mary, 30n35

Wordsworth, Dorothy, 105, 121–23
Wordsworth, William, 4, 6, 12, 14–15, 40, 42, 53, 66, 68; 103–33, 152–53; "The Brothers," 118–19; "Expostulation and Reply," 115; "Goody Blake and Harry Gill," 117; "The Idiot Boy," 15, 116–18, 123, 125, 136, 138–43, 146, 154, 161; "The King of Sweden," 124; "Lines Composed a Few Miles above Tintern Abbey," 130; "Lines Written in Early Spring," 53, 120; *Lyrical Ballads*, 15, 106, 108, 111–19; "The Old Cumberland Beggar," 118, 120, 155–56; "Old Man Travelling," 121–22, 127; preface to *Lyrical Ballads*, 6, 66, 68, 74, 111–16, 118–19, 123, 127–28, 140; *The Prelude*, 15, 103, 106–8, 110–11, 119, 125–33; *The Recluse*, 105–6; "Resolution and Independence," 120–23; "Simon Lee," 116; "The Tables Turned," 108, 115, 122, 128; "To Toussaint L'Ouverture," 15, 108, 124, 126, 128; "The world is too much with us," 53

COGNITIVE APPROACHES TO CULTURE
Frederick Luis Aldama, Patrick Colm Hogan, Lalita Pandit Hogan, and Sue J. Kim, Series Editors

This series takes up cutting edge research in a broad range of cognitive sciences insofar as this research bears on and illuminates cultural phenomena such as literature, film, drama, music, dance, visual art, digital media, and comics, among others. For the purpose of the series, "cognitive science" is construed broadly to encompass work derived from cognitive and social psychology, neuroscience, cognitive and generative linguistics, affective science, and related areas in anthropology, philosophy, computer science, and elsewhere. Though open to all forms of cognitive analysis, the series is particularly interested in works that explore the social and political consequences of cognitive cultural study.

Romanticism's Other Minds: Poetry, Cognition, and the Science of Sociability
JOHN SAVARESE

Eternalized Fragments: Reclaiming Aesthetics in Contemporary World Fiction
W. MICHELLE WANG

Capturing Mariposas: Reading Cultural Schema in Gay Chicano Literature
DOUG P. BUSH

Necessary Nonsense: Aesthetics, History, Neurology, Psychology
IRVING MASSEY

Shaming into Brown: Somatic Transactions of Race in Latina/o Literature
STEPHANIE FETTA

Resilient Memories: Amerindian Cognitive Schemas in Latin American Art
ARIJ OUWENEEL

Permissible Narratives: The Promise of Latino/a Literature
CHRISTOPHER GONZÁLEZ

Literatures of Liberation: Non-European Universalisms and Democratic Progress
MUKTI LAKHI MANGHARAM

Affective Ecologies: Empathy, Emotion, and Environmental Narrative
ALEXA WEIK VON MOSSNER

A Passion for Specificity: Confronting Inner Experience in Literature and Science
MARCO CARACCIOLO AND RUSSELL T. HURLBURT

www.ingramcontent.com/pod-product-compliance
Lightning Source LLC
Chambersburg PA
CBHW030111010526
44116CB00005B/204